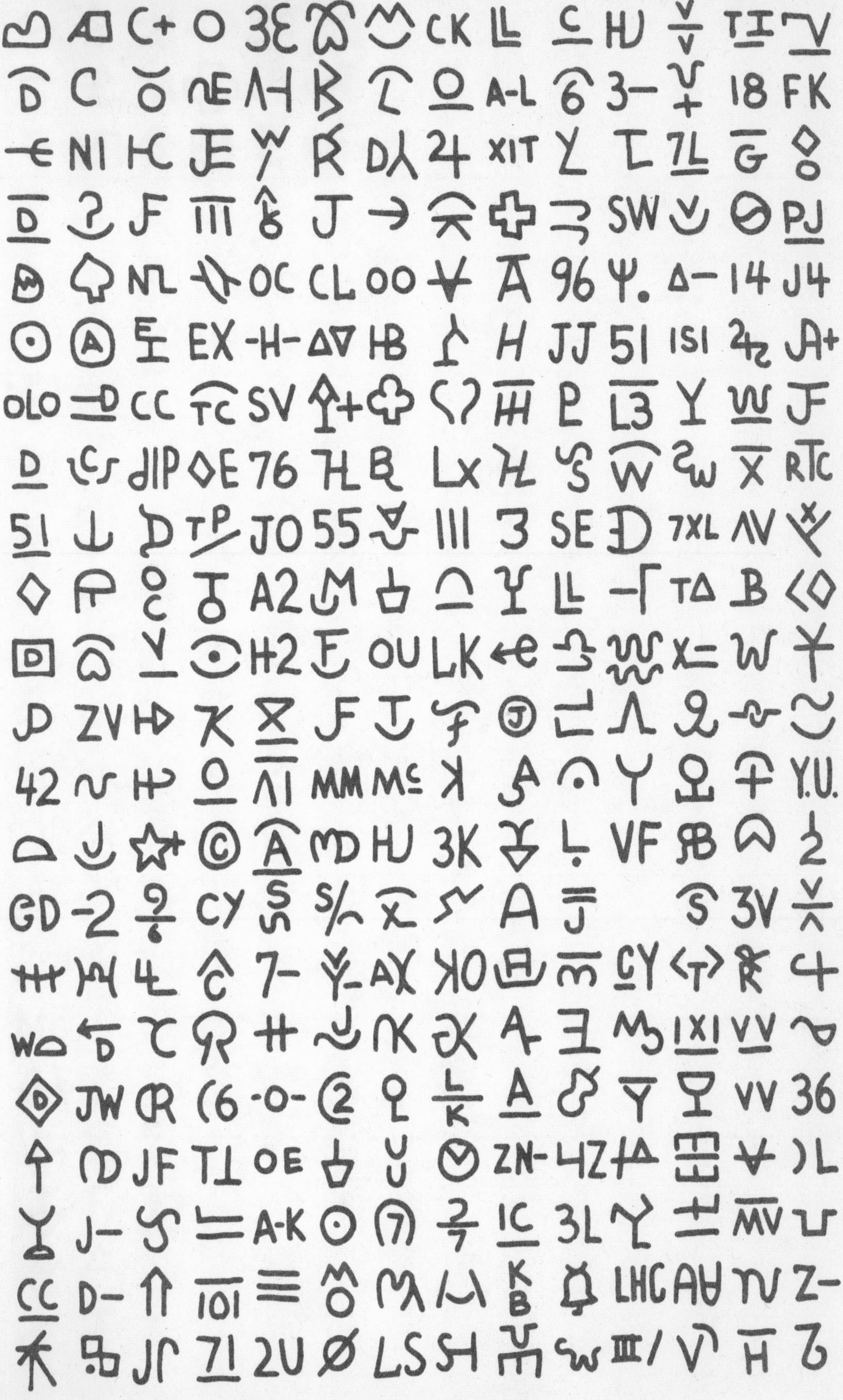

Roundup of
BEEF
COOKERY

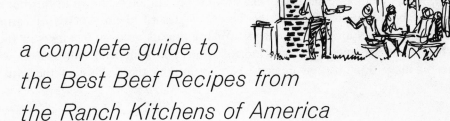

*a complete guide to
the Best Beef Recipes from
the Ranch Kitchens of America*

edited by
DEMETRIA TAYLOR

*and prepared
in collaboration with the*
American National CowBelles

STERLING PUBLISHING CO., Inc.   New York

THE BRANDING IRON

To brand—to mark with a fiery-hot iron—is a very ancient custom, used over 4000 years ago. Branded animals were first introduced into America in 1424 by Hernando Cortes, via a band of horses which he brought with him to the New World to facilitate his search for gold. Those first horses were branded by what the modern cowboy would call Circle A, Crazy X and Holy Cross.

While branding did not begin in the West, it was practiced there with the most art and enthusiasm. Old-time ranchers wanted all of their possessions to bear their personal marks. Even today, a cattleman's brand usually means something. It might refer to a geographical location, to equipment, initials or a sentimental memory. Will Rogers, for example, had a brand called the "Dog Iron," which reminded him of happy hours he had spent loafing in front of a cozy fireplace.

There are stamp brands, running brands and trail brands; each of these kinds can be rocking, lazy, flying, connected or a bar. The decorative characters shown in this book are examples of brands used today in the United States to identify herds of cattle roaming the ranges. They are representative of many brands used by members of the American National Cattlemen's Association, of which the American National Cow-Belles is an auxiliary organization dedicated to promoting the welfare of the cattle industry.

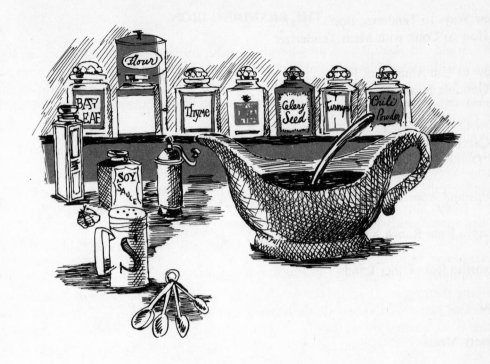

CONTENTS

INTRODUCTION

When you want the best, go straight to the top. And who would know more about the best beef recipes than the wives of cattlemen? We are indebted to them for the majority of the recipes in this book, and to the commercial authorities whom we consulted for the latest information and instruction on the use of foil in beef cookery, the approved methods of using meat tenderizer and the best ways to barbecue beef. These experts also gave us helpful hints about buying beef and storing it in the refrigerator or freezer. We are passing them on to you.

A menu suggestion with every recipe will serve as a springboard for your own ideas, as we bow to family preferences. With more than 400 tested recipes at your command you could serve beef nearly every day of the year without fear of menu monotony!

Here are recipes that follow the tide of family budgets from high to low, recipes for holidays, company dinners and special occasions of all kinds. You will revel in recipes from other lands, with all ingredients available at your market, and discover the tastiness of thrifty beef cuts when they are cooked properly and seasoned delightfully. We will help you to use your barbecue equipment as never before, so that you surprise everyone with new and different ways to barbecue beef, and we will show you how to serve leftover beef in such a way that the family will think it's a brand new dish.

The efficient cross-referenced index should also be helpful, enabling you to find the recipe you want quickly.

HOW TO BUY BEEF AND VEAL

Government Inspection

Two things should guide you in buying beef, the federal inspection stamp and the grade marking. The federal inspection stamp is round and purple and looks like this:

All meat sold in interstate commerce must pass inspection by trained federal inspectors. The stamp is your guarantee that the meat has met specified government standards for safety and wholesomeness. The purple vegetable dye used for stamping is not harmful and need not be cut away. Besides telling you that the meat has passed U.S. inspection, it gives the official number of the meat-packing establishment.

Grading

The grade marking is your second guide. Beef is graded by a federal specialist with a stamp which runs along the length of the carcass like a purple ribbon.

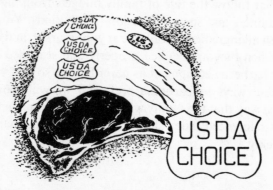

As a home shopper, you are concerned primarily with two grades of beef, choice and good, which are sold generally in retail markets. Following are the five top federal grades:

Prime: The finest grade. Supply is limited and it is seldom available in retail stores. Most frequently found in top-quality hotels and restaurants.

Choice: The most popular grade. Lean and well marbled.

Good: Leaner than choice grade.

Standard: Quite lean. Not widely available.

Commercial: Very lean, with little or no marbling.

Beef graded by an individual meat packer has a particular quality brand, which is another buying guide for you.

How Much to Buy

Boneless meat . . . . ¼ lb. per serving
Bone-in meat . . . . ½ lb. per serving
Bony meat. . . . . ¾ to 1 lb. per serving
    Plan on 2 or 3 servings for hearty appetites.

HOW TO STORE BEEF IN THE REFRIGERATOR

Pre-packaged smoked or cured beef and beef sausage may be stored in their original wrappings.

Remove paper from fresh meat, and cover it loosely with wax paper, aluminum foil or transparent plastic film. If it is pre-packaged, loosen wrappings to allow circulation of air.

Store in the meat container or in the coldest section of the refrigerator.

Refrigerator Storage Timetable for Beef and Veal
Refrigerator temperature 36° to 40°

TYPE OF MEAT	STORAGE TIME FOR MAXIMUM QUALITY
Beef	
Standing rib roast	5 to 8 days
Steaks	3 to 5 days
Pot roasts	5 to 6 days
Stew meat	2 days
Ground	2 days
Liver (sliced)	2 days
Heart	2 days
Veal	
Roasts	5 to 6 days
Chops	4 days
Liver (sliced)	2 days
Sweetbreads (cooked)	2 days

All kinds of cooked beef and veal should be stored for 4 days for maximum quality.

HOW TO STORE MEAT IN THE FREEZER

Temperature

Meat must be kept frozen at 0° or lower. It is not wise to refreeze thawed meat because of the loss of juices during thawing and the possibility of its deteriorating between the time of thawing and refreezing.

Wrapping

Be sure all meat is wrapped properly before storing. Packaged meats purchased frozen should be kept frozen and placed in the freezer in their original packages. Transparent wrappers on meats sold from self-service cases give sufficient freezer-storage protection for periods of one to 2 weeks only. If you wish to store the meat for a longer time, cover the cellophane with regular freezer wrapping paper.

Freezer Storage Timetable

Freezer temperature 0° or colder

MEAT IN FREEZER WRAPPING	LIMIT OF TIME FOR MAXIMUM QUALITY
Beef (steaks, roast)	6 to 8 months
Veal	3 to 4 months
Variety cuts of beef and veal	3 to 4 months
Ground beef	3 to 4 months
Cooked beef	3 to 4 months

HOW TO COOK BEEF AND VEAL

It is most important that you use a low cooking temperature. This keeps the juice and flavor in the meat, making it more tender and palatable, while it cuts down shrinkage and prevents burnt fat drippings.

Dry heat: Oven-roasting; oven-broiling; pan-broiling; pan-frying.

Moist heat: Braising and pot-roasting; water-cooking.

Is Your Meat Done?

Roasts: Use a roast meat thermometer (see below).

Broiled: Cut a small slit in the meat and note the color and degree of "doneness" inside.

Braised and water-cooked: Pierce the meat with a sharp-tined fork to test for tenderness.

The Roast Meat Thermometer

For a true test of whether your roast is done, use a roast meat thermometer. Insert the point of the thermometer into the center of the thickest part of the meat without touching the bone. As the meat roasts, the thermometer indicates its internal temperature. Before removing the roast check to be sure that the thermometer has not been displaced. *Note:* Do not use for broiling, braising or water-cooking.

Roasting

Place roast fat side up on a rack in an open, low-sided pan. Do not add water. Do not cover. Insert a roast meat thermometer. Roast in a slow oven (325°). *Note:* Do not sear.

Roasting Timetable for Fresh Beef and Veal

Meats roasted from refrigerator temperature in an open pan in slow oven (325°):

BEEF	WEIGHT	APPROXIMATE ROASTING TIME	INTERNAL TEMPERATURE
Rib roast, standing, bone-in.	4 lbs.	1¾ hrs.	140° (rare)
Time based on short cut,		2¼ hrs.	160° (medium)
6 in. from the tip of the rib		3 hrs.	170° (well-done)
to the chine bone (back-	6 lbs.	3¼ hrs.	140° (rare)
bone). If cut longer than		3¾ hrs.	160° (medium)
6 in., roast will take less		4¼ hrs.	170° (well-done)
time.	8 lbs.	3½ hrs.	140° (rare)
		4½ hrs.	160° (medium)
		5 hrs.	170° (well-done)
	10 lbs.	4½ hrs.	140° (rare)
		5 hrs.	150° (medium)

BEEF	WEIGHT	APPROXIMATE ROASTING TIME	INTERNAL TEMPERATURE
	13 lbs.	5 hrs.	140° (rare)
		5½ hrs.	150° (medium)
	16 lbs.	4¾ hrs.	130° (rare)
		5¼ hrs.	140° (medium)
	20 lbs.	4½ hrs.	130° (rare)
		5 hrs.	140° (medium)
Rib roast, boned and rolled. Time based on roast 4½ to 5 in. wide for 4-lb. roast, 5½ to 6½ in. wide for 6-lb. roast. Thinner roasts of same weight will require less cooking time.	4 lbs.	2¾ hrs.	140° (rare)
		3¼ hrs.	160° (medium)
		3½ hrs.	170° (well-done)
	6 lbs.	3½ hrs.	140° (rare)
		4¼ hrs.	160° (medium)
		4¾ hrs.	170° (well-done)
Rump roast, bone-in. (See also Braising—Pot Roast.)	4 lbs.	2½ hrs.	140° (rare)
		3 hrs.	160° (medium)
		3¼ hrs.	170° (well-done)
Sirloin tip roast. (See also Braising—Pot Roast.)	4 lbs.	2¼ hrs.	140° (rare)
		2¾ hrs.	160° (medium)
		3¼ hrs.	170° (well-done)
VEAL			
Leg, bone-in	5 lbs. (piece)	3½ hrs.	180°
	8 lbs. (piece)	4½ hrs.	180°
Leg, boned	20 lbs.	8 hrs.	180°
Loin	5 lbs.	2¾ hrs.	180°
	8 lbs.	3½ hrs.	180°
Shoulder, bone-in	5 lbs.	3½ hrs.	180°
	8 lbs.	4 hrs.	180°
Shoulder, boned and rolled. (See also Braising.)	4 lbs.	3½ hrs.	180°
	8 lbs.	4½ hrs.	180°

Braising

Season meat, dip in flour if desired, then brown in a small amount of hot fat or oil. Add a little liquid, such as water, milk, tomato juice or bouillon. Cover and cook slowly on top of range or in a moderate oven (350°). Cook until fork-tender.

"Pot roasting" is a popular term applied to braising large cuts. The braising method is called "stewing" when enough liquid is used to cover the meat.

Braising Timetable

Meats braised from refrigerator temperature

BEEF	WEIGHT	APPROXIMATE COOKING TIME (AFTER BROWNING)
Pot roast, rump, sirloin tip, heel or round, or eye of round	3 lbs.	3 hrs.
	5 lbs.	3 ½ hrs.
Pot roast or steak		
(1 to 2 in. thick)	2 to 4 lbs.	2 ½ hrs.
(½ in. thick)	1 to 1 ½ lbs.	20 to 30 min.
Flank steak, rolled, with stuffing	1 ½ to 2 lbs.	2 hrs.
Short ribs (2×2×4 in.)		2 hrs.
Stewing beef, neck plate, shank, chuck (1 ¾-in. cubes)		2 hrs.
Oxtails		3 hrs.
Liver (½-in. slices)		½ hr.
Heart	3 to 3 ½ lbs.	2 ½ hrs.
VEAL		
Shoulder roast, boned and rolled	3 to 5 lbs.	2 hrs.
Loin or rib chops (½ to ¾ in. thick)		¾ hr.
Cutlets, frenched (¼ to ½ in. thick)		½ hr.
Steak and cutlets		¾ hr.
Breast		2 ½ hrs.
Heart	¾ to 1 lb.	1 ¾ hrs.

Water-Cooking

Cover meat with water and simmer (don't boil) until fork-tender. "Boiling" is the popular term used for cooking the meats listed below. Tests prove that these meats are more tender if cooked at a simmering rather than a boiling temperature.

Water-Cooking Timetable

BEEF	WEIGHT	APPROXIMATE COOKING TIME
Brisket, corned	2 ½ to 6 lbs.	3 to 4 hrs.
Brisket or plate, fresh	2 ½ to 6 lbs.	3 to 4 hrs.
"Boiling beef," neck, plate, chuck (1 ¾-in. pieces)		2 hrs.
Crosscut shanks (2 in. thick)		2 ½ hrs.
Tongue, fresh or smoked (remove skin after cooking)		1 hr. per lb.
Oxtails	2 lbs.	4 hrs.
Sweetbreads (remove membrane after cooking)		25 min.
Heart	3 to 3 ½ lbs.	4 hrs.

VEAL	WEIGHT	APPROXIMATE COOKING TIME
Knuckle	1 ½ to 2 lbs.	2 hrs.
Heart	¾ to 1 lb.	2 ¼ hrs.
Tongue (remove skin after cooking)	1 ¼ to 1 ½ lbs.	2 ½ hrs.
Sweetbreads (remove membrane after cooking)		15 to 20 min.

Broiling

In the oven: Preheat broiler. Read directions that came with your range for special mechanical adjustments which give best broiling results. Have steaks and chops cut one to 2 inches thick. If less than one inch thick, they should be pan-broiled. Slash edges of fat of steak or chops in several places to prevent curling. Place the meat on the broiling rack so that the surface of the meat is about 3 inches from the source of heat. See broiling timetable (below) for the approximate time each side should be broiled. Turn once. Season before serving.

In a pan: Thinner slices of broiling beef may be broiled in a heavy skillet. Rub skillet very lightly with fat or oil. Brown the meat on one side, then turn and brown on other side. Reduce heat. Turn meat as needed to cook and brown evenly. Use no cover or water. Season before serving. *Note:* Veal chops, steaks and cutlets should not be broiled. (See braising schedule.)

Broiling Timetable

	THICKNESS	APPROXIMATE MINUTES PER SIDE
Beefsteaks, rib, club, tenderloin, T-bone, porterhouse, sirloin, and strip steak	1 in.	5 (rare) 6 (medium) 7 (well-done)
	1 ½ in.	8 (rare) 10 (medium) 11 (well-done)
	2 in.	15 (rare) 17 (medium) 19 (well-done)
Hamburger patties	1 in.	5 (medium)
Liver slices, calf, young beef (brush with melted butter or margarine)	½ in.	6 (well-done)

Pan-Frying

"Pan-frying" is a term applied to cooking meats in a small amount of fat or oil in a skillet.

For small beefsteaks, cube steaks or thin slices of round or chuck steak, pan-fry slowly for about 5 minutes on each side.

To pan-fry liver (veal), dip slices in seasoned flour. Pan-fry slowly for about 10 minutes on each side.

Pressure Cooking

"Pressure cooking" is cooking in steam at a temperature higher than boiling. This shortens the cooking time and softens or dissolves connective tissue. Meats must be browned either before or after pressure cooking. Meats suitable for braising or water-cooking are best for pressure cooking.

Cooking Frozen Beef

Cook frozen beef without thawing ahead, but increase the cooking time to allow for thawing during the cooking process. There are two exceptions, however: solid packaged ground meat and cubed meat which should be shaped or browned should be thawed in the refrigerator before cooking. Cook packaged, branded frozen meat according to directions on the package.

Frozen meat may be thawed in the refrigerator and cooked according to the methods and cooking schedules for unfrozen meat. The time for thawing varies according to refrigerator temperature and the size of the meat. Suggested thawing schedule:

1-in. steaks .	24 hrs.
3-in. roasts	48 hrs.

Roasting Frozen Meat

Roast according to the method for unfrozen meat. Insert roast meat thermometer midway through cooking period. Increase cooking schedule one to 2 hours, depending on thickness of roast.

Oven-Broiling Frozen Meat

Place frozen steaks and chops 4 inches from heat source. Broil 1 ½ to 2 times the required time for unfrozen meat.

Pan-Broiling Frozen Meat

Place frozen steaks and chops in warm (not hot) skillet with a tablespoon of fat or oil. Heat slowly and turn until meat is thawed, then continue to cook as for unfrozen meat.

Braising, Frying and Water-Cooking Frozen Meat

Cook according to the method for unfrozen meat. Increase the cooking time according to the thickness of the meat.

NEW WAYS TO TENDERIZE BEEF

For years cooks have known the possibilities of tenderizing beef by marinating it in flavorful liquids, and many new recipes call for this process alone. Recently, however, food markets from coast to coast began to feature a new product which tenderizes meat in such a way that it is possible to broil round steak or beef chuck and to cook pot roast in an oven like rib roast.

The refined papain (from the tropical papaya melon) used in making the tenderizer separates the connective tissues of meat. This allows meat tissues to expand and results in faster cooking, reduced shrinkage, retention of juices and greater tenderness.

A teaspoon of tenderizer mixed with each pound of ground meat before cooking means bigger, juicier burgers and meat loaves. When stew meat is cut in small pieces and then tenderized, it requires only about 45 minutes cooking time. A pot roast which is cut into portion-size chunks and tenderized before it is cooked takes less than an hour to braise.

How to Cook with Meat Tenderizer

To prepare steaks (round, chuck, flank, etc.) and other small cuts:

1. Sprinkle meat tenderizer evenly on all sides (as you would salt), allowing about ½ teaspoon per pound. Do not add salt.

2. Pierce all surfaces with fork at intervals of 1 inch. This allows the tenderizer to penetrate and seal in the juices. Let stand at room temperature for 30 to 40 minutes for cuts up to 1 inch thick, 1 hour for thicker cuts. Or, if you prefer, cover loosely and refrigerate overnight.

3. Pan- or oven-broil to taste in preheated skillet, grill (rubbed with suet) or broiler. Turn only once. Serve rare, medium or well-done, as you prefer.

To prepare roasts (chuck, blade, rump, round, etc.):

1. Sprinkle all surfaces (side, top and bottom) of meat as you would salt (about ½ teaspoon per pound). Do not add salt.

2. Pierce meat all over with kitchen fork at intervals of one inch. Plunge the fork in deep. This lets the tenderizer penetrate the meat and prevents loss of juices. Cover loosely with wax paper and leave overnight in the refrigerator (18 to 24 hours) or, if you prefer, let stand at room temperature for 1 hour before cooking.

3. Place roast on rack in shallow pan. Start in preheated oven set at 325°. Roast in oven until done without a cover, and don't add water. Follow the timetable on page 14.

4. Since the use of meat tenderizer cuts cooking time by about one-fourth, be careful not to overcook.

5. Follow manufacturer's instructions.

HOW TO USE ALUMINUM FOIL

It's hard to remember what we did before the days of aluminum foil. Nowadays we use it in so many different ways. In meat cooking it saves time and trouble in the kitchen and at the barbecue grill (page 161).

The following recipes point up some of the newest techniques for using heavy-duty or broiler foil in meat cooking, as the foil gondola for roasts, "do-ahead" dinners and foil packets.

Gondola Roasts and Gravy Making
(using 14-inch broiling foil)

Roasting is easier and cleaner in an open foil gondola, which catches all the juice for more flavorful gravy and leaves the pan clean.

How to make the gondola: Tear off a sheet of broiling foil twice the length of the meat. Fold the long edges of foil up to form sides. Then draw the end corners together with the foil pulled inward to the meat. Fold the corners double to seal securely and to make handles by which the gondola may be lifted. Place on shallow baking pan or cooky sheet to roast. After roasting, juices may be poured off from the gondola to decant the fat and to measure accurately for gravy making.

GONDOLA ROAST BEEF—with Yorkshire pudding

The roast may be a standing rib roast or a boned and rolled roast. Season all surfaces with salt and pepper. Place meat in foil gondola, made according to directions above, in a shallow roasting pan. Insert meat thermometer into thickest part of roast without touching bone. Roast at 350°, allowing 18 minutes per pound for *rare* (internal temperature 140°), 20 minutes per pound for *medium* (internal temperature 160°), or 22 minutes per pound for *well-done* (internal temperature 170°). Before carving, allow the roast to become firm for at least 10 minutes after it comes out of the oven. During this time, pour drippings from gondola into measuring cup. Reserve ¼ cup of drippings for Yorkshire pudding (see below for recipe) if desired.

YORKSHIRE PUDDING IN FOIL   4 to 6 Servings

Prepare batter for Yorkshire pudding about 15 minutes before meat is done. Make a shallow foil pan from an 11-inch length of broiling foil by turning up 2 inches on all 4 sides. Fold over corners to seal securely. To make batter: beat together 1 cup sifted all-purpose flour, ½ teaspoon salt, 2 eggs and 1 cup milk for about 1 minute with a rotary beater. Place foil pan on cooky sheet. Pour ¼ cup of hot drippings into foil pan. Pour Yorkshire batter over the hot drippings. Turn oven up to hot (400°), place pudding in oven and bake for 25 minutes. Serve immediately.

SUGGESTED MENU: If Yorkshire pudding is omitted, wrap baking potatoes in foil and bake in the oven with the roast. Serve with buttered green peas and a mixed salad. For dessert, fruit pie.

BROILED HAMBURGER DINNER   4 to 6 Servings

This dinner is cooked completely in the broiler in less than 15 minutes. Place the vegetable (any canned favorite) on foil in the bottom of the broiler pan. Put grid in place; preheat. Place hamburgers and potatoes on the grid; broil. Drippings from meat add additional flavor to vegetables below.

Green Beans

Line lower part of broiler pan with broiling foil. Drain 2 No. 303 cans (1-lb. ea.) of cut green beans. Spread on foil on bottom of pan. Replace grid or rack; preheat broiler compartment to 550° (5 to 8 minutes).

Hamburger Steaks

1 ½ lbs. lean ground beef   1 teaspoon Ac'cent
1 teaspoon salt   ¼ cup finely-chopped onion
½ cup water

Combine all ingredients; shape into 4 to 6 patties at least 1 to 1½ inches thick. Place on preheated broiler. Broil 3 minutes on one side and 5 to 8 minutes on the other.

Broiled Potato Slices

Pare potatoes; slice lengthwise ½ inch thick. Brush with oil; sprinkle with salt and pepper. Place on broiler pan. Broil for 5 minutes on one side and 5 to 8 minutes on the other, or until tender when pierced with a fork.

"DO-AHEAD" MEAT LOAF WITH BISCUIT TOPPING 6 Servings

1½ lbs. lean ground beef
1 cup chopped parsley
1 large chopped onion
1 to 1½ teaspoons salt
¾ teaspoon Ac'cent
¼ teaspoon pepper

1½ teaspoons Worcestershire sauce
½ cup fine bread crumbs
1 cup water or tomato juice
1 egg
1 package prepared refrigerated biscuits

Combine all ingredients except biscuits; mix well. Shape meat mixture to form a loaf. Make a foil gondola by tearing off a length of heavy-duty foil almost twice the length of meat; place meat lengthwise on foil. Press sides of foil up along sides of meat loaf. Bring foil up at ends, pressing center inward, and leaving two corners standing out like wings. Bring corners together and fold over twice to form a firm seal. This makes handles at each end by which gondola may be lifted. Gondola should not press against meat; cup it away so that heat can reach exposed surface easily.

Place gondola in shallow pan or on baking sheet. Bake in moderate oven (325°) for 30 minutes. Remove from oven; cool. Leave loaf in gondola, cover with broiling foil, and place in refrigerator.

Remove meat loaf from refrigerator half an hour before serving. Remove foil cover and place gondola on shallow pan or baking sheet. Bake in moderate oven (325°) for 20 minutes, then remove from oven. Open package of refrigerated biscuits. Separate each biscuit; roll between palms of hands to finger length. Arrange shaped biscuits over top of meat loaf. Return meat with biscuit topping to hot oven (425°) for 10 minutes or until biscuits are golden brown. Pour off and measure drippings to make gravy, if desired (page 195).

Suggested Menu: Glazed carrots, green beans with mushrooms and a tossed salad with the meat loaf. For dessert, raspberry jam turnovers with cream cheese.

HAMBURGER PACKET DINNER 1 Serving

1 slice cheese
¼ lb. ground beef patty, flattened
1 slice onion
1 small potato, sliced or quartered
1 carrot, cut in sticks (or any favorite vegetable)

½ teaspoon salt
½ teaspoon Ac'cent
2 tablespoons ketchup
1 14-in. square broiling foil

Place the cheese, beef, onion, potato and carrot (or other vegetable) in center of foil. Sprinkle with salt and Ac'cent. Spread meat with ketchup. Fold double the opposite edges of foil and the ends to make a loose but firm packet. Repeat to make number of servings required. Place packets on cooky sheet and bake in hot oven (400°) for 45 minutes.

Suggested Menu: Begin with cream of asparagus soup. Serve a tossed salad with the hamburger packets. For dessert, custard bread pudding.

HOBO BEEF SUPPER

2 lbs. lean ground beef
* salt and pepper
4 potatoes, cut in strips
6 carrots, split and quartered
4 onions, cut in thick slices
3 stalks celery, cut in 4-in. pieces

½ cup ketchup
2 tablespoons Worcestershire sauce
2 tablespoons butter or margarine
1 teaspoon prepared mustard
   juice of 1 lemon
½ cup vinegar

Season ground beef to taste with salt and pepper; shape into 6 or 8 thick cakes. Place each cake in center of square of heavy aluminum foil. Divide prepared vegetables between the squares so that each portion is more or less equal. Pull foil up to form a cup. Combine remaining ingredients in saucepan, and bring to a rapid boil. Spoon about 1 tablespoon of hot sauce into each cup, then twist the cup edges together tightly. Place foil packets in shallow baking dish or pan. Bake in moderate oven (350°) for 1 hour. Reheat remaining sauce and serve with meat.

SUGGESTED MENU: Serve with tossed salad, hot rolls and assorted relishes and pickles. Vanilla ice cream with fresh or frozen strawberries and cookies for dessert.

FROSTED MEAT LOAF

6 to 8 Servings

1½ lbs. lean ground beef
1 cup chopped parsley
1 large chopped onion
1½ teaspoons salt
¾ teaspoon Ac'cent
1½ teaspoons Worcestershire sauce

¼ teaspoon pepper
½ cup fine bread or cracker crumbs
1 cup water or tomato juice
1 egg
3 cups mashed potatoes

Combine all ingredients except mashed potatoes; mix well. Shape meat mixture to form a loaf. Make a foil gondola for baking by tearing off a length of heavy-duty foil almost twice the length of the meat; place meat lengthwise on foil. Press sides of foil up along sides of meat loaf. Bring foil up at ends, pressing center inward. This leaves 2 corners standing out like wings. Bring corners together and fold over twice to make a firm seal and form handles. Foil should not touch sides of meat so that heat can reach exposed surface easily.

Place gondola in shallow pan or on baking sheet. Bake in moderate oven (325°) for 45 to 60 minutes.

When meat loaf is baked, pour off drippings from one end of gondola to make gravy (page 195). Frost hot meat loaf with fluffy mashed potatoes. Place under broiler for a few minutes to brown lightly.

SUGGESTED MENU: Baked acorn squash, buttered green peas and lettuce wedges with Russian dressing with the meat loaf. For dessert, chocolate tapioca cream parfait.

---

* Whenever salt and pepper, flour and other such ingredients are listed in unspecified quantity, use them according to your own taste.

HOW TO CARVE

Let the man of the house do it! Encourage him to learn this art and acquire skill in its practice. But keep the tools sacrosanct—don't use the knives he uses for carving to cut twine or open packages. In fact, don't use them at all!

Here are some helpful hints for you as a hostess, along with some "do's" and "dont's" for the carver.*

Carving Beef and Veal

The Right Tools: A carving knife must have a blade of high-quality steel that takes and holds a keen edge. Good knives need only occasional sharpening. Two carving sets are essential: *a standard set* for large roasts, consisting of a knife with an 8- or 9-inch blade, and a fork with a guard and a sharpening steel; *a steak set* for small roasts and steaks, consisting of a knife with a 6- or 7-inch blade and a matching fork with or without a guard.

Other useful tools are the *"carver's helper,"* which has two widely-spaced tines to steady the roast for carving, and the *roast meat slicer,* with an 11-inch flexible blade especially adapted for carving thin slices.

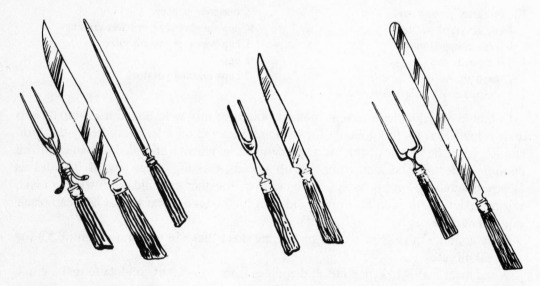

Although a good blade needs only occasional sharpening, it should be steeled before each use.

1. Hold the steel in the left hand, thumb on top of the handle, with the point upward.
2. Place the heel of the knife blade against the far side of the tip of the steel (see diagram *a*). The steel and the blade should meet at an angle of about 25°.

---

*This section comes from "Meat Carving Made Easy," published by the National Live Stock and Meat Board, 407 S. Dearborn Street, Chicago, Illinois.

a

3. Bring the knife blade down across the steel toward the left hand with a quick swinging motion. The entire edge of the blade should pass lightly over the steel (see diagram *b*).

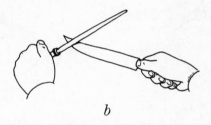

b

4. Bring the knife into first position again but with the blade against the near side of the steel (see diagram *c*). Repeat the same motion, passing the blade over the steel.

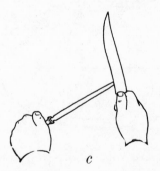

c

5. Repeat, alternating from side to side. A dozen strokes will make the edge true.

The Right Way to Carve

Standing rib roast: Have short ribs removed at market. Use for another meal (see index for recipes). If desired, the meat retailer will also separate the backbone from the ribs.

1. After roasting, cut backbone from ribs. Remove before putting roast on platter.

2. Place roast on platter with smaller cut surface uppermost and rib side to left of carver with rib ends toward him.

3. Insert fork, guard up, between 2 top ribs. From the far outside edge slice across grain of meat from right to left, or toward ribs (see diagram *d*). Use a long, smooth, even stroke; don't "saw." Make each slice from ⅛ to ⅜ inch thick. Cut close along rib with tip of knife, releasing the slice (see diagram *e*).

d

e

4. Lift slice on knife blade, supporting it with fork, to side of platter or onto separate platter (see diagram *f*).

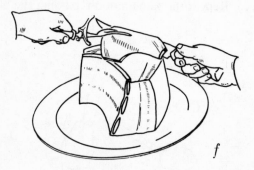
f

5. Cut enough slices to serve everyone before transferring them to dinner plates.

Rolled roast: Place roast with larger cut surface on platter.

1. Push fork with guard up, or the "carver's helper" into left side of roast, about 2 inches from top.

2. Slice across grain toward fork, from right to left (see diagram *g*).

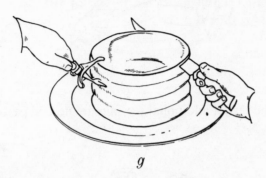

g

3. After each slice is carved, lift it to the side of the platter or to another hot platter.

4. As you reach each cord, sever it with knife tip, loosen it with fork and let it fall to platter.

5. A rolled roast that is long and narrow must be placed horizontally on the platter, but you should still slice it across the cut end, or "face."

Porterhouse, T-bone and pin-bone sirloin steaks:

1. A steak is always carved with the grain.

2. Place the steak on a platter or board with fat side away from the carver.

3. Insert fork at left.

4. Cut close around bone with point of knife (see diagram *h*). Lift bone out.

h

5. Cut across full width of steak in 1-inch slices (see diagram *i*).

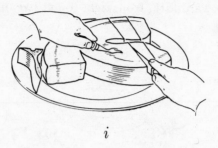

i

6. Serve the flank end last, if additional servings are needed (see diagram *j*).

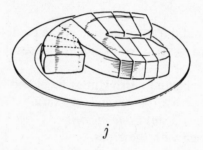

j

Chuck blade:
1. Place on platter with bone away from carver.
2. Insert fork at left.
3. Separate a section by running the knife between two muscles, then close to the bone (see diagram *k*).

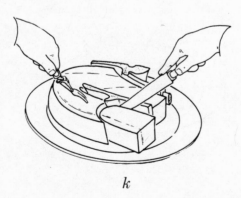

k

4. Turn the separated section so that grain of meat is parallel with platter (see diagram *l*).

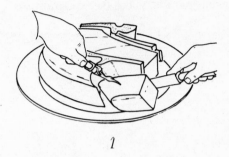

l

5. Hold section with fork; slice across grain (see diagram *m*).

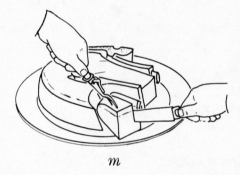

m

6. Separate remaining sections; note direction of fibers and slice across the grain.
Corned beef and beef brisket:
1. Place with round side away from carver.
2. Trim off excess fat.
3. Cut thin slices from 3 sides at an angle and in rotation, in order to slice across the grain (see diagram *n*).

n

Beef tongue:
1. Place with round edge toward carver.
2. Slice off excess tissue and cartilage from large end.
3. Continue making even, parallel slices (see diagram *o*).

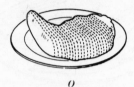

o

Loin of veal: Ask meat retailer to loosen backbone by sawing across ribs, parallel to backbone. Remove backbone before bringing to table.
1. Place with rib side facing carver.
2. Insert fork in top.
3. Start at the right; slice so that there will be one slice with bone and one slice without.

"Do's" and "Don't's" for the Carver

Do
1. Stand up to carve if it's easier.
2. Find where the bones are located.
3. Cut across the grain except for steaks.
4. Before carving, plan servings so that choice portions will be distributed equally.
Don't
1. Use a dull knife.
2. Change the angle of the blade while making a slice.
3. Cut second helpings before they are needed.

Hints for the Hostess

1. A large roast will carve more easily after it stands for 20 to 30 minutes.
2. Limit garnishes to a minimum.
3. Provide a second platter to receive the slices as they are cut.
4. Place glasses and dishes where they will not be in the carver's way.

SOUPS AND APPETIZERS

SOUPS AND APPETIZERS

Beef can take its rightful place in any course on the menu, from soup to dessert. All kinds of delightful soups are included in this section: the range varies from the clearest bouillon to the heartiest meat and vegetable mixtures.* You will also find a number of piquant spreads which can be served as appetizers.

If you are wondering about beef as a dessert, remember mince pies and suet puddings! You'll find recipes for both in this book.

BEEF AND VEGETABLE CHOWDER   6 Servings

½ lb. ground boneless chuck
1 garlic clove, minced
1 tablespoon fat or salad oil
4 medium carrots, quartered
6 small onions, halved
4 cups boiling water
1 No. 2½ can (3½ cups) tomatoes

2 cups celery, diced
1 small cabbage, cut in 6 pieces
3 teaspoons salt
1¼ teaspoons pepper
2 teaspoons beef extract or 2 bouillon cubes
1 bay leaf
½ cup uncooked rice

Sauté chuck and garlic in fat or oil in deep kettle or Dutch oven, stirring until brown. Add remaining ingredients. Cover, and simmer for 30 minutes, or until vegetables are tender.

"MEAL-IN-ONE" SOUP   Makes 1 gallon

½ lb. stewing beef
1 lb. beef bones
2 teaspoons salt
2 medium-size onions, chopped
1 bay leaf
1 cup celery and leaves, chopped

½ teaspoon pepper
½ cup uncooked rice
1 medium potato, diced
3 medium carrots, diced
¼ cup parsley, minced
1 No. 303 can (1 lb.) tomatoes

Cover meat and bones with cold water. Add salt, onions, bay leaf, celery and pepper. Simmer for 2 to 3 hours. Add rice, potato and carrots and continue cooking for about an hour. Remove bones. Add parsley and tomatoes. Measure liquid, and add enough water to make 1 gallon of soup. Continue cooking for 15 to 20 minutes. Adjust seasoning if necessary.

---

*See other soup recipes on page 54 and page 90.

TIP-TOP BEEF AND VEGETABLE SOUP
8 to 10 Servings

3 to 4 lbs. soup bone or beef shank
2 tablespoons bacon fat
2 qts. cold water
1 teaspoon salt
1 small onion, chopped
1 No. 303 can (1 lb.) tomatoes
6 sprigs parsley

¼ head young cabbage, shredded
5 to 6 carrots, sliced
2 cups fresh green beans, cut in thirds
1 cup potato, diced
½ cup celery, chopped
¼ cup uncooked rice or barley

Brown meat or bones in hot bacon fat. Cover with cold water; bring to a boil slowly. Add salt and onion. Simmer for 2 hours. Add vegetables and rice or barley. Simmer 1 hour longer.

MULLIGATAWNY (SOUP)
8 Servings

1 cup uncooked rice
2 qts. beef broth
2 cups leftover beef, cut into ½-in. cubes

2 cups leftover vegetables (corn, peas, string beans, etc.)

Cook rice for 1 hour in broth, add vegetables and cubed beef. Cook for 10 minutes. Season to taste.

POTATO SOUP WITH BEEF BALLS
6 Servings

8 medium potatoes, quartered
2 large onions, sliced
2 cups celery, diced
1 tablespoon salt
¼ teaspoon pepper
1 ½ qts. beef stock

1 lb. lean ground beef
1 egg
3 tablespoons milk
½ teaspoon salt
½ teaspoon curry powder
¼ cup fine bread crumbs

Cook potatoes, onions and celery with salt and pepper in beef stock until done. Combine remaining ingredients; shape into balls the size of a walnut. Drop from teaspoons into boiling soup mixture. Cook for 5 minutes.

BOUILLON IMPERIAL
6 Servings

2 lbs. lean beef (shank or neck)
6 cups water
1 qt. cooked tomatoes
4 carrots, finely chopped
6 stalks celery and leaves, finely chopped
1 small onion, thinly sliced
1 small green pepper, minced

3 whole cloves
½ teaspoon whole peppercorns
¼ cup tarragon vinegar
Salt and pepper
Chopped parsley or thin slices of lemon (optional)

Cut meat into small pieces and add water; simmer 2½ to 3 hours. Add all remaining ingredients except vinegar, salt and pepper. Simmer for another ½ hour. Strain through a thick piece of cheesecloth. Add vinegar; season to taste with salt and pepper. Reheat. If desired, garnish each cup of bouillon with chopped parsley or a thin slice of lemon.

PERLONY KRUP (RUSSIAN SOUP)

8 Servings

1 cup barley
2 qts. beef stock
¼ cup dried mushrooms, soaked

2 egg yolks
1 cup sour cream

Cook barley in beef stock until tender. Cut mushrooms in small pieces and add. Mix egg yolks and sour cream and add just before serving. Season if necessary.

BEEF-OLIVE BALLS

Roll stuffed olives in well-seasoned ground beef. Broil. Serve on cocktail picks.

LIVER WITH WATER CHESTNUTS

4 to 6 Servings

1 lb. calf's liver, sliced ½ in. thick
1 No. 2 can water chestnuts

1 lb. sliced bacon

Cut liver slices in 1-inch squares. Slice water chestnuts. Cut strips of bacon in 2½- or 3-inch pieces. Place square of liver on slice of chestnut. Wrap in strip of bacon and fasten with skewer or wooden pick. Broil.

CHOPPED LIVER CANAPE SPREAD

Makes about 2 cups

½ lb. calf's liver
butter or margarine (more than 2 tablespoons)
1 large onion, minced

2 hard-cooked eggs, chopped
seasoning to taste (dry mustard, salt, pepper and paprika)

Fry liver in part of butter or margarine (1 tablespoon), taking care not to overcook. Chop fine by hand in wooden bowl. Fry onion in more butter or margarine (one tablespoon); rechop with liver. Add eggs. Mix in seasonings. Work in additional butter or margarine to get a good spreading consistency. Serve with crisp crackers.

SMOKED TONGUE SPREAD

Makes about 5 cups

4 cups cooked smoked tongue, ground
1 small onion, minced
1 cup mayonnaise

2 tablespoons prepared mustard
1½ tablespoons horse-radish
salt and pepper to taste

Combine all ingredients. Mix well. Spread on crisp crackers. This may also be used as a dip.

BEEF APPETIZER PASTRIES
40 Servings

pastry dough made with 4 cups flour or
2 pkgs. pie-crust mix
2 tablespoons butter or margarine
½ garlic clove
½ lb. cooked veal, ground
½ teaspoon salt
⅛ teaspoon pepper
¼ cup thick white sauce or condensed cream of
celery soup
¼ cup black olives, chopped

Make your favorite pastry dough or prepare pie-crust mix according to directions. Chill in refrigerator for 1 hour. Melt butter or margarine in heavy frying pan. Add garlic; sauté over moderate heat for 5 minutes. Remove piece of garlic; add meat, salt and pepper. Cook over moderate heat for 10 minutes. Add white sauce or cream of celery soup. Remove from heat. Add olives. Roll dough 1/16 inch thick; cut into 40 two-inch squares. Place a little of the meat mixture on each square; roll up diagonally. Bake in hot oven (450°) for 15 minutes, or until golden brown. These can be made in advance and stored in refrigerator until you are ready to use them.

SWEDISH LIVER LOAF
75 Servings

1 lb. beef liver
¼ cup minced onion
½ lb. ground pork sausage
2 eggs
2 cups light cream
¼ teaspoon pepper
1 teaspoon salt
1 teaspoon sugar
¼ teaspoon nutmeg
¼ teaspoon allspice
2 cups flour

Parboil liver for 5 minutes; put through food chopper, using fine knife. Add all ingredients in order given; mix thoroughly after each addition. Pack in well-greased loaf pan and cover. Set in pan of water and bake in moderate oven (350°) for 2 hours. Remove cover often during the first hour. When cold, cut into cubes. Stick with cocktail picks, dip into Thousand Island dressing or any favorite sauce and eat as an appetizer.

BEEF-STUFFED MUSHROOM APPETIZERS
25 Servings

1 ½ lbs. medium-size mushrooms
1 lb. lean ground beef
¼ cup mayonnaise
1 tablespoon prepared mustard
½ teaspoon sugar
1 tablespoon minced onion
1 tablespoon chopped parsley
2 teaspoons salt

Remove stems from mushrooms. Wash caps in salt water; set aside. Broil mushroom caps, rounded side down, for 3 minutes. Combine remaining ingredients. Shape into balls which fit mushroom caps. Place balls in mushroom caps. Broil about 2 inches from heat for about 5 to 8 minutes. Serve piping hot.

BURNING BUSH

Makes 2 balls, ¾ cup each

1 jar (2 ½ oz.) dried beef
1 pkg. (8 oz.) cream cheese
1 teaspoon prepared horse-radish

1 teaspoon cut chives
2 tablespoons capers
　dash Worcestershire sauce

Chop dried beef fine. Divide cream cheese into 2 parts. Combine one half with horse-radish and chives; mold into a ball and roll in chopped dried beef. Add capers and Worcestershire sauce to remaining half. Form into a ball and roll in dried beef. Serve with crackers.

APPETIZER BEEF BALLS

Makes 40 to 50 balls

¼ cup finely-minced onion
¼ cup butter or margarine
1 lb. lean ground beef
½ cup soft bread crumbs
1 ½ teaspoons salt

⅛ teaspoon ground pepper
1 egg
$1/_3$ cup milk
⅛ teaspoon ground allspice

Brown onion lightly in butter or margarine and remove from pan. Combine all remaining ingredients. Shape into tiny balls and brown in same skillet, turning the balls lightly to brown on all sides. Continue to cook slowly for about 20 minutes or until balls are brown.

RECIPES FROM RANCH KITCHENS

RECIPES FROM RANCH KITCHENS

Half the fun of cooking is in exchanging recipes with neighbors and friends, whether you do it over the back fence, through the mail or by contributing to a cookbook.

Treasured recipes from personal files have been collected in this section—favorite recipes that have been prepared in ranch kitchens for many years. Now, we hope, they will be concocted afresh in suburban and apartment kitchens, where you will share in our ranch way of life.

You will become familiar with many thrifty cuts which are no less flavorful and nutritious than the popular steaks and roasts: brisket, short ribs, blade, arm, flank, rump, sirloin tip, round, and so on.

Surveys and statistics prove what every meat retailer and housewife knows—that ground beef takes first place in popularity. Its versatility knows almost no bounds and eliminates any possibility of monotony in serving it. Made into loaves or patties, added to casserole dishes, combined with spaghetti, macaroni or noodles, it has recipe uses galore.

In tribute to this all-American family favorite we give you new and delightful ground beef recipes as well as intriguing recipes for other thrifty cuts.

BRAISED SHORT RIBS JARDINIERE   4 to 5 Servings

2 tablespoons fat or salad oil	1 cup water
3 lbs. beef short ribs, cut into individual portions	5 medium potatoes, halved
	5 small onions
3 teaspoons salt	2 parsnips, halved
¼ teaspoon pepper	2 carrots, halved

Heat fat or oil in heavy skillet. Brown short ribs in hot fat or oil. Sprinkle with salt and pepper. Add water, cover, and cook slowly for 1 hour, or bake in moderate oven (350°). Add vegetables and cover. Cook until vegetables and ribs are fork-tender, or about 30 minutes more.

SUGGESTED MENU: Add lettuce wedges with French dressing. For dessert, stewed rhubarb and soft sugar cookies.

SAN CLEMENTE SHORT RIBS

4 Servings

4 lbs. short ribs of beef
1 can (8 oz.) tomato sauce
1 cup water
1 tablespoon sugar
1 tablespoon horse-radish
1 bay leaf

1 teaspoon dry mustard
1 teaspoon vinegar
¼ teaspoon pepper
1 teaspoon salt
2 onions, chopped
1 tablespoon Worcestershire sauce

Have ribs cut into portion-size pieces. Place in pan large enough to spread in single layer. Combine remaining ingredients and heat for 5 minutes; cool. Pour over meat. Allow meat to marinate for several hours, turning once or twice. Place meat and marinade in Dutch oven, cover and simmer for 2 hours, or until very tender. Baste with marinade several times during cooking.

Suggested Menu: Succotash and salad of sliced beets and celery go well with the short ribs. For dessert, baked custard with fruit sauce.

FAMILY-STYLE SHORT RIBS

6 Servings

3 lbs. beef short ribs
2 tablespoons fat or salad oil
1 teaspoon salt
⅛ teaspoon pepper
1½ cups water

2 bouillon cubes
2 tablespoons vinegar
1 teaspoon Worcestershire sauce
2 medium-size onions, in ¼-in. slices

Brown short ribs on all sides in fat or oil; pour off drippings. Season with salt and pepper. Add water, bouillon cubes, vinegar, Worcestershire sauce and onions. Cover tightly and cook slowly for 2 hours, or until meat is tender. Pour out cooking liquid and measure. It may be necessary to add a little water in order to have 1½ cups. Thicken liquid for gravy (page 195).

Suggested Menu: Whipped potatoes, buttered green beans and tomato aspic salad with the short ribs. For dessert, Lady Baltimore layer cake.

FAVORITE ROLLED RIBS

6 Servings

2 to 3 lbs. short ribs of beef
  salt and pepper
½ cup onion, chopped
¼ cup celery, diced

¼ cup green pepper, minced
1 garlic clove, minced
2 tablespoons parsley, minced
1 cup dry red table wine (optional)

Have ribs cut longer than usual. Remove all bone with a sharp knife. Sprinkle meat with salt and pepper on both sides. Mix together remaining ingredients and spread on boned side of meat; roll up and tie with soft string. Place in roasting pan or heavy baking pan. Roast in hot oven (400°) for about 40 minutes, or until meat is well browned. Reduce heat to moderate (325°). Continue roasting until meat is tender, or about 2 hours. If desired, dry red table wine may be added to pan during last hour of roasting. Thicken pan liquid for gravy (page 195); serve with meat.

Suggested Menu: Scalloped potatoes, stewed tomatoes and coleslaw to accompany the meat. Deep-dish peach pie for dessert.

BEEF SHORT RIBS IN RAISIN SAUCE

6 to 8 Servings

3 lbs. beef short ribs
3 tablespoons fat or salad oil
  salt and pepper
1 onion, quartered
½ cup brown sugar, firmly packed
1 teaspoon dry mustard
1 tablespoon flour

2 tablespoons vinegar
2 tablespoons lemon juice
1 teaspoon lemon peel, grated
1 bay leaf
1½ cups water
½ cup seedless raisins

Cut ribs into portion-size pieces; brown in fat or oil. Pour off drippings; season ribs with salt and pepper. Add onion. Combine remaining ingredients and bring to boil. Pour over short ribs. Cover closely and cook slowly for about 2 hours, or until meat is tender. Thicken sauce for gravy if desired (page 195).

SUGGESTED MENU: Serve parslied potatoes and buttered green beans with the ribs. Add a salad of sliced tomatoes and onion rings. For dessert, crumb-topped peach pie.

BARBECUED SHORT RIBS

4 to 5 Servings

3 lbs. beef short ribs (cut in portion-size pieces)
1 onion, chopped
2 tablespoons fat or salad oil
¼ cup vinegar
2 tablespoons sugar

1 cup ketchup
½ cup water
3 tablespoons Worcestershire sauce
1 teaspoon prepared mustard
½ cup celery, sliced
2 teaspoons salt

Brown short ribs with onion in hot fat or oil. Combine remaining ingredients and add to ribs. Cover and cook slowly for 1½ to 2 hours, or until tender.

SUGGESTED MENU: Creamy mashed potatoes, parslied cauliflower and chopped spinach with the ribs. Add a crisp salad. For dessert, purple plum deep-dish pie.

SPICED SHANK OF BEEF

6 Servings

3 lbs. beef shank
¼ cup vinegar
2 teaspoons salt
2 tablespoons sugar
½ teaspoon cinnamon
½ teaspoon cloves

¼ teaspoon pepper
1 bay leaf
1 teaspoon Worcestershire sauce
1 onion, sliced
3 tablespoons fat or salad oil

Cut shank in portion-size pieces. Put into deep bowl. Combine vinegar, salt, sugar, cinnamon, cloves, pepper, bay leaf and Worcestershire sauce and bring to boil. Cook for 5 minutes, cool and pour over meat. Let stand for 4 hours, turning meat occasionally. Remove meat, saving spiced marinade. Brown meat and onion in fat or oil. Add marinade and enough hot water to cover meat. Cover and simmer for 2 hours, or until meat is tender. Thicken gravy (page 195).

SUGGESTED MENU: Buttered noodles, sliced carrots and okra with lemon butter with the beef. Add a tossed salad. For dessert, fresh pears, bel paese cheese.

SMOTHERED BEEF CUBES   4 Servings

2 lbs. beef (shank or neck)
  seasoned flour
2 onions, chopped
2 to 3 tablespoons fat or salad oil
½ cup sour cream

½ cup water
2 tablespoons cheese, grated
1 teaspoon salt
⅛ teaspoon pepper

Bone beef; cut in 1-inch cubes. Roll in seasoned flour. Brown beef cubes and chopped onions in hot fat or oil in heavy skillet or Dutch oven. Combine remaining ingredients; pour over beef. Cover and simmer for 2 hours. Add a little more water during cooking if necessary. Serve hot with pan gravy (page 195).

SUGGESTED MENU: With the smothered beef cubes serve fluffy mashed potatoes and buttered zucchini squash. For dessert, fruit gelatin.

IDAHO BEEF AND BEAN STEW   4 to 6 Servings

1 lb. dried lima beans
2 lbs. beef (shank or neck)
  salt and pepper

¼ teaspoon celery salt
1 small onion, chopped

Soak beans overnight. Drain; place in heavy kettle. Bone beef; cut in 2-inch cubes. Add to beans. Season with salt, pepper, celery salt and onion; add enough water to cover. Simmer over low heat for 2½ hours, or until done.

SUGGESTED MENU: Serve braised celery and buttered green beans with the stew. For dessert, lemon pudding-cake.

FLANK STEAK CHILI   5 to 6 Servings

1 flank steak (1½ to 2 lbs.)
1 teaspoon salt
  dash pepper
  flour
2 tablespoons fat or salad oil

1 medium-size onion, sliced
1 No. 303 can (1 lb.) tomatoes
1 green pepper, sliced
2 teaspoons chili powder
¼ cup cold water

Use meat tenderizer (page 19). Season with salt and pepper, if desired. Sprinkle with flour. Brown both sides in hot fat or oil in skillet. Top with onion, tomatoes and green pepper; cover. Bake in moderate oven (350°) for 2 hours. Mix chili powder with cold water. Stir into gravy around steak; spoon gravy over meat.

SUGGESTED MENU: Hashed-brown potatoes, buttered green beans and lettuce wedges with French dressing complete the main course. For dessert, apple dumplings.

STUFFED FLANK STEAK WITH CARAWAY SEEDS   6 Servings

2 lbs. flank steak, cut thin
  salt and pepper
  onion salt
  celery salt

1 pkg. bread stuffing
  fat or salad oil
2 cups water
1 teaspoon caraway seeds (or more to taste)

Tenderize steak (page 19); season with salt, pepper, onion salt and celery salt.

Prepare stuffing as directed on package. Spread on steak. Roll up steak like a jelly roll, in the direction of the grain of the meat. Fasten edges together with wooden picks and lace firmly with white string. Brown on all sides in fat or salad oil. Add water and caraway seeds. Cover tightly and simmer for 2 hours or until tender. (Add more water from time to time if necessary.) Remove roll to platter. Strain gravy, and thicken if desired (page 195). Serve over slices of steak.

SUGGESTED MENU: With the steak serve cream-style corn and buttered lima beans. Serve apple and raisin coleslaw as the salad. For dessert, orange and banana ambrosia.

STUFFED FLANK STEAK BURGUNDY   6 to 8 Servings

1 flank steak (2 lbs.)	salt and pepper
4 cups soft bread crumbs	¼ cup water
½ cup bacon fat, melted	seasoned flour
1 small onion, minced	1 cup Burgundy wine
1 teaspoon poultry seasoning	1 can condensed cream of mushroom soup

Tenderize steak (page 19). Prepare stuffing by mixing bread crumbs, part of your melted bacon fat ($^1/_3$ cup), onion, poultry seasoning, salt, pepper and water. Spread stuffing evenly over steak. Roll up steak with stuffing inside (roll from one wide edge to the other). Tuck ends in, fasten with wooden picks and tie with white string. Cut roll in two pieces; dust each with seasoned flour. Heat remaining bacon fat in large, heavy skillet and brown steak rolls. Add wine, cover and simmer for 1 ½ hours or until meat is tender, turning roll occasionally. Remove picks, slice steak rolls and place on hot platter. Add mushroom soup to drippings in pan; blend well; bring to a boil; put in warm gravy bowl; serve with steak rolls.

SUGGESTED MENU: With the steak serve whipped potatoes, Lyonnaise carrots, baby lima beans. Add water cress salad. For dessert, baked pears and cookies.

LONDON BROIL   6 Servings

1 top-quality flank steak (2 to 2 ½ lbs.)	1 can (3 oz.) broiled sliced mushrooms, undrained
1 can (10 ½ oz.) beef gravy	

Have meat dealer score steak lightly, crisscross fashion, on both sides. Place flank steak 3 inches from heat on broiler rack in preheated broiler. Broil for 4 to 5 minutes on each side. Slice diagonally in thin slices across grain of the meat. Add mushrooms with their liquid to gravy. Heat gravy and pour some of it over the beef slices; serve remainder separately.

SUGGESTED MENU: Baked potatoes, shoe-string beets and a tossed salad with the steak. For dessert, hot mince pie and hard sauce.

LONDON BROIL WITH BUTTER-WINE SAUCE   6 Servings

1 top-quality flank steak (about 2½ lbs.)
⅓ cup butter or margarine

3 tablespoons dry red table wine
3 cups cooked rice

Preheat broiler. Place tenderized (page 19) flank steak on rack with surface about 3 inches below source of heat. Broil for 3 minutes on each side. Meanwhile, melt butter or margarine in large frying pan, add wine and heat until bubbling. Cut flank steak on the diagonal into thin slices. Drop slices into frying pan and cook for one minute. Remove to hot platter. Surround with border of rice. Pour remaining wine sauce in frying pan over rice and steak. Serve at once.

SUGGESTED MENU: Mashed butternut squash and green peas with tiny onions go well with the London broil. Add water cress with blue cheese dressing. For dessert, blueberry pie.

STUFFED FLANK STEAK   6 to 8 Servings

2 tablespoons butter or margarine
1 medium-size onion, chopped
1 egg, well beaten
3 tablespoons warm water
½ teaspoon salt
  dash pepper

½ teaspoon poultry seasoning
3 cups bread crumbs
1 flank steak (about 2 lbs.)
2 tablespoons fat or salad oil
½ cup boiling water

Melt butter or margarine in skillet. Add onion. Cook until golden brown; set aside. Combine egg, warm water, salt, pepper, poultry seasoning, bread crumbs, and add to the onion. Mix well, and spread over steak. Starting from the long side, roll meat up like jelly roll; tie securely with twine. Set oven for moderate (325°).

Heat fat or oil over high flame in large skillet that has heat-resistant handle. Brown rolled meat on all sides. Sprinkle with additional salt and pepper, if desired. Add ½ cup boiling water, cover skillet and bake for 1½ hours, or until meat is tender. Remove strings; cut in crosswise slices.

SUGGESTED MENU: Baked yams, eggplant Creole and a green salad complete the main course. For dessert, pumpkin custard.

FLANK TENDERETTE   6 Servings

1 flank steak (2 to 2½ lbs.)
½ lb. cooked sausage
1½ cups mashed potato

½ teaspoon poultry seasoning
  salad oil

Tenderize flank steak (page 19); spread with about 2 cups of savory stuffing made with cooked country sausage, mashed potato and poultry seasoning. Roll up like jelly roll. Tie or skewer securely. Oven-roast on V-shaped rack in shallow pan or broil on a portable spit or oven rotisserie. Do not add water or cover during roasting. Allow 40 to 50 minutes at 425°. The tenderette should have a rich brown coat and a pink heart. Baste with a little salad oil during cooking.

SUGGESTED MENU: Start with consommé garnished with shredded sharp cheddar cheese. Serve the roast with horse-radish, a casserole of spoon bread, green beans and a tossed salad. Have lemon or raspberry tarts for dessert.

MUSHROOM-STUFFED FLANK STEAK (PATIO BROIL)   6 Servings

2 to 2 ½ lbs. flank steak, 1 in. thick
    2 cans (4 oz. ea.) sliced mushrooms
    2 tablespoons crumbled blue cheese

2 tablespoons butter or margarine
    salt and pepper
1 garlic clove

Have a pocket cut in steak at the market. Combine mushrooms, cheese and butter or margarine. Spread mushroom mixture inside pocket; close with skewers. Use meat tenderizer (page 19); sprinkle with salt and pepper. Rub surface with garlic. Broil steak for about 5 minutes on each side. Remove to platter. Cut diagonally across grain.

SUGGESTED MENU: Creamed potatoes, buttered green peas and summer squash with the steak. For dessert, berries and cream.

CORN-STUFFED FLANK STEAK   6 Servings

1 flank steak (about 2 ½ lbs.)
2 tablespoons flour
1 teaspoon salt
¼ teaspoon pepper

1 teaspoon Ac'cent
    corn stuffing
2 tablespoons fat or salad oil
2 cups tomato juice

Score steak on both sides with knife or 3-blade chopper. Combine flour, salt, pepper and Ac'cent. Pound ½ flour mixture into each side of steak with edge of saucer. Spread stuffing on steak; roll up like jelly roll. Tie with string. Brown roll in hot fat. Transfer to baking pan; pour tomato juice over roll. Bake in moderate oven (350°) for 2 hours, or until tender. Thicken gravy, if desired (page 195).

CORN STUFFING

4 slices dry bread, cut ¾ in. thick
1 small onion, minced
2 tablespoons butter or margarine
1 egg, well beaten
½ cup whole-kernel corn

1 pimento, minced
¾ teaspoon salt
⅛ teaspoon pepper
½ teaspoon Ac'cent
1 teaspoon poultry seasoning

Soak bread in enough cold water to cover until soft; squeeze dry. Cook onion in butter or margarine until soft, but not brown. Combine with all remaining ingredients; mix well.

SUGGESTED MENU: Buttered lima beans and stewed tomatoes with the steak; endive salad. For dessert, loganberry roly-poly with whipped cream.

FLANK MIGNONETTES

6 Servings

1 flank steak (2 to 2 ½ lbs.)   6 to 8 slices bacon

Use tenderizer for flank steak as directed on page 19. Roll up like jelly roll. Tie or skewer. Cut crosswise in 2-inch slices. Wrap each slice with bacon strips. Broil about 4 inches from source of heat, allowing 10 to 12 minutes per side.

SUGGESTED MENU: Set the French mood with onion soup. With the mignonettes, serve glazed yams, green peas and a hot bread such as cornsticks. Add a water cress salad. For dessert, chocolate chiffon pie.

FLANK STEAK WITH APPLE STUFFING

6 Servings

1 flank steak (about 2 to 2 ½ lbs.)   salt and pepper
  apple stuffing   1 cup water
2 tablespoons fat or salad oil

Spread a thin slice of flank steak with apple stuffing. Roll up; tie securely. Sear in hot fat or salad oil. Add salt, pepper and water. Cover and bake in moderate oven (350°) for 2 hours.

APPLE STUFFING

Makes about 3 cups

1 tablespoon onion, minced   2 cups tart apples, finely chopped
2 tablespoons butter or margarine   beef stock to moisten
1 cup small bread cubes
  salt and pepper

Brown onion in butter or margarine. Add remaining ingredients; mix well.

SUGGESTED MENU: With the steak serve potatoes au gratin, buttered broccoli and mashed Hubbard squash. Add a green salad. For dessert, steamed chocolate pudding with foamy sauce.

NEW ENGLAND BOILED DINNER

6 Servings

4 lbs. brisket corned beef   6 potatoes, quartered
6 medium-size onions   1 head cabbage, cut in wedges
6 carrots, halved   1 No. 303 can (1 lb.) sliced beets

Cut corned beef into portion-size pieces, place in kettle and cover with water. Simmer until tender or about 3 ½ hours. Remove meat to hot platter and keep hot. Boil onions, carrots and potatoes in the broth for 30 minutes or until done. Add cabbage during last 15 minutes of cooking. Heat beets separately and season. Arrange vegetables around corned beef on platter with beets in separate serving dish.

SUGGESTED MENU: Add a Waldorf salad with cream mayonnaise to double as both salad and dessert.

BOILED BEEF

3 lbs. fresh beef brisket
1 carrot, sliced
½ cup celery, chopped

1 tablespoon salt
¼ teaspoon pepper
6 whole cloves

Put brisket in deep kettle. Add vegetables and seasonings. Cover with water. Cover kettle, and simmer (do not boil) for 3 hours. Serve hot with horse-radish sauce. Save meat broth for use in gravy or as stock for soup.

SUGGESTED MENU: Buttered spaghetti, fried green tomatoes and sliced carrots accompany the beef. Add a green salad. For dessert, canned cling peaches and chocolate loaf cake.

WESTERN BOILED DINNER

10 to 12 Servings

1 corned brisket or rump of beef (5 to 6 lbs.)
1 cup water
1 cup sauterne or other white table wine
½ cup white wine vinegar
3 bay leaves
1 teaspoon oregano

2 teaspoons allspice
2 garlic cloves
2 tablespoons instant minced onion or
½ cup chopped raw onion
2 or 3 stalks celery
1 sprig parsley

Place all ingredients in a deep heavy kettle, and bring to boil. Cover and simmer gently until meat is fork-tender or about 3 to 4 hours. Cook vegetables (such as carrots, turnips, cabbage, etc.) separately and serve on platter surrounding meat. Meat may be served hot or cold.

Note: If meat should have tendency to be too salty, simmer for half an hour or so, well covered with water; discard water and proceed as directed in recipe.

SUGGESTED MENU: Add a tomato aspic salad with cooked salad dressing. For dessert, coffee chiffon pie.

BEEF BRISKET WITH SAUERKRAUT

8 Servings

4 lbs. beef brisket
  boiling water
1 tablespoon salt
¼ teaspoon pepper
2 tablespoons onion, minced

¼ cup brown sugar, firmly packed
1 cup mild vinegar
1 qt. sauerkraut
1 peeled raw potato, grated

Place meat in deep kettle. Add enough boiling water to cover, then salt, pepper and onion. Simmer for 1 hour. Add brown sugar, vinegar and sauerkraut. Continue cooking for about 1 ½ hours or until meat is tender. Add grated potato and cook for 10 minutes longer.

SUGGESTED MENU: With the meat, home-fried potatoes, baby limas and crisp celery. For dessert, whipped fruit gelatin.

GLAZED BEEF BRISKET

8 to 10 Servings

4 to 5 lbs. beef brisket
    1 medium-size onion, quartered
    8 peppercorns
2 ⅛ teaspoons salt
    2 jars (5 oz. ea.) strained applesauce and
    apricots (baby food)

2 teaspoons lemon juice
¼ cup brown sugar
whole cloves

Cover meat with water. Add onion, peppercorns and part of your salt (2 teaspoons). Cover tightly and simmer for 3 to 4 hours or until tender. Remove meat; place in shallow baking dish. Combine strained applesauce and apricots, lemon juice, brown sugar and remaining salt. Glaze meat with part of fruit mixture. Decorate with whole cloves. Bake in moderate oven (350°) for 15 minutes, or until glaze is set. Heat remaining fruit mixture; serve as sauce for meat.

SUGGESTED MENU: Mashed sweet potatoes, buttered Swiss chard and a green salad complete the main course. For dessert, deep-dish pear pie.

BRISKET OF BEEF WITH HORSE-RADISH SAUCE

8 Servings

3 to 4 lbs. beef brisket
    salt and pepper
1 onion, minced
1 tablespoon butter or margarine
1 tablespoon flour

1 cup milk
½ cup fresh horse-radish
1 tablespoon lemon juice
1 tablespoon minced pimento

Place beef in deep kettle; season with salt and pepper. Add onion and enough cold water to cover. Bring to boil. Reduce heat, cover and cook for 3 hours or until tender. Melt butter or margarine and blend in flour. Add milk; cook until mixture begins to thicken. Mix horse-radish, lemon juice and pimento and add to sauce. Cook and stir over low heat for 2 or 3 minutes. Season to taste with more salt and pepper. Cut meat in thick slices. Cover with hot sauce and serve immediately.

SUGGESTED MENU: With the beef serve hashed-brown potatoes, Harvard beets and buttered Brussels sprouts. For dessert, floating island pudding.

BEEF PUT-TOGETHER

4 Servings

1 lb. boneless stewing beef, cut in 1-in. cubes
3 tablespoons fat or salad oil
1 medium-size onion, sliced
1 green pepper, sliced
1 cup celery, diced
1 cup carrots, diced

1 can condensed tomato soup
1 ½ teaspoons salt
⅛ teaspoon pepper
½ cup cooked peas
2 cups cooked rice

Brown meat in fat or oil. Add onion and green pepper. Cook for 5 minutes, and add celery, carrots, tomato soup and seasonings. Cover and cook slowly for about 1 hour, or until meat and vegetables are done. Add cooked peas; serve over hot, cooked rice.

SUGGESTED MENU: Add a salad of lettuce wedges and hot rolls. For dessert, rhubarb pie.

OCTOBER STEW

4 to 5 Servings

1 lb. beef stew meat
2 tablespoons fat or salad oil
1 ½ teaspoons salt
½ cup onion, chopped
1 cup cooked lima beans
1 cup whole-kernel corn

1 can (8 oz.) mushrooms, sliced
1 cup carrots, diced
1 cup canned tomatoes
1 cup elbow macaroni
½ bay leaf
1 cup water

Cut beef into 1-inch cubes. Brown in hot fat or oil in heavy kettle. Add remaining ingredients and cover. Simmer (do not boil) for about 1 ½ hours, or until beef is tender. Stir to blend.

SUGGESTED MENU: This is a whole meal in itself, needing only coleslaw or a salad to round it out. For dessert, canned or frozen pineapple chunks and crisp cookies.

BEEF RAGOUT

6 Servings

3 cups raw potatoes, cubed
1 bunch carrots, quartered
2 large onions, sliced
2 lbs. lean stewing beef, cubed
¼ cup fat or salad oil
1 cup canned tomatoes

1 ¼ cups strong coffee
½ cup water
2 cups cooked peas
salt and pepper
3 tablespoons flour

Combine potatoes, carrots and onions. Brown cubed beef in fat or oil; add vegetable mixture, tomatoes, 1 cup coffee (keeping ¼ cup) and water. Simmer for 2 hours. Add peas. Season to taste with salt and pepper. Blend flour and remaining ¼ cup coffee. Add and stir over low heat until gravy thickens.

SUGGESTED MENU: A salad of mixed greens completes the main course. For dessert, chocolate coconut tapioca cream.

SAVORY BEEF RAGOUT

8 Servings

3 lbs. stewing beef (chuck or round)
$^2/_3$ cup flour
$^1/_4$ cup fat or salad oil
2 teaspoons salt
$^1/_4$ teaspoon pepper
3 cups boiling water

1 can (8 oz.) tomato sauce
8 medium-size onions, peeled
6 medium-size carrots, thinly sliced
1 pkg. (10 oz.) frozen peas
$^1/_8$ teaspoon marjoram
$^1/_3$ cup cold water

Cut meat in 1-inch cubes and coat with half of flour ($^1/_3$ cup). Heat fat or oil in heavy sauce pot or Dutch oven over high heat and brown meat on all sides. Stir in salt, pepper, boiling water and tomato sauce. Reduce heat to low and simmer covered for 4 hours or until meat is almost tender. Add onions; cover and cook 30 minutes longer. Add carrots and peas; continue to cook 20 minutes or until meat and vegetables are tender. Stir in marjoram. Blend remaining $^1/_3$ cup flour and cold water. Stir in with other ingredients and cook slowly until thickened. Season with additional salt and pepper if necessary.

SUGGESTED MENU: To complete the main course add hot, buttered French bread and a crisp salad. For dessert, fresh fruit in season and cheese.

GOURMET BEEF STEW

6 Servings

2 lbs. stewing beef (boneless chuck)
$^1/_2$ cup flour
3 tablespoons fat or salad oil
2 teaspoons salt
$^1/_4$ teaspoon pepper
1 can (8 oz.) tomato sauce
1 can No. 303 (1 lb.) peas (undrained)
  boiling water

6 medium-size potatoes, pared
6 medium-size carrots, scraped
6 medium-size onions, peeled
1 teaspoon oregano
$^1/_2$ cup cold water

Cut beef in 1-inch cubes. Coat cubes with half of the flour ($^1/_4$ cup). Heat fat or oil in Dutch oven or heavy sauce pot. Add meat and brown well on all sides; stir often to brown evenly. Add salt, pepper and tomato sauce. Drain peas, reserving their liquid, then set them aside. Measure liquid and add enough boiling water to make 3 cups. Stir into stew. Cover, reduce heat to low, and simmer stew for about 1 $^1/_2$ hours or until meat is almost tender. Add potatoes, carrots and onions. Cover and cook for 30 minutes more or until meat and vegetables are tender. Add oregano and peas. Cook 2 or 3 minutes longer. Blend remaining $^1/_4$ cup flour with the cold water, and slowly stir into stew. Bring to boil and cook until thickened, stirring constantly. Turn stew into a large heated serving dish.

SUGGESTED MENU: Hot, crusty rolls and a tossed salad complete the main course. For dessert, apricot-prune upside-down cake.

WESTERN BEEF

2 lbs. stewing beef, diced
2 to 3 tablespoons lemon juice
2 teaspoons salt
2 to 3 teaspoons chili powder
1/3 cup flour, sifted

2 tablespoons fat or salad oil
1 cup ripe olives, pitted
1 pkg. (8 oz.) cooked noodles
parsley or water cress, chopped

Sprinkle beef with lemon juice; let stand for 1 hour. Mix salt, chili powder and flour; roll meat in flour mixture until all flour is absorbed by meat. Brown thoroughly in hot fat or oil. Add just enough hot water to cover meat and simmer for 2 hours, adding more water if needed. Add olives 20 minutes before serving. Allow liquid to cook down to gravy consistency. Serve on hot buttered noodles; sprinkle with chopped parsley or water cress.

SUGGESTED MENU: Add a salad of sliced tomatoes, cucumbers, celery and shredded lettuce, tossed with French dressing. For dessert, a bowl of fresh fruit and a tray of assorted cheese.

TOMACARONI STEW

6 Servings

1½ lbs. chuck or round steak, cut in cubes
1 tablespoon fat or salad oil
1½ cups onions, chopped
1 garlic clove, minced
1 teaspoon salt

¼ teaspoon pepper
2 No. 303 cans (1 lb. ea.) tomatoes
1 can (8 oz.) peas (undrained)
1 can (4 oz.) mushrooms (undrained)
1 cup elbow macaroni

Heat fat or oil and brown meat cubes. Remove meat and cook onions and garlic until golden brown. Put meat back with onions and garlic. Add salt, pepper and tomatoes. Cover and simmer for 1½ to 2 hours, or until meat is tender. Add undrained peas and mushrooms. Stir in macaroni. Cover and cook for 15 minutes, or until macaroni is tender.

SUGGESTED MENU: A crisp salad of greens is all that it takes to complete this hearty main course. Add hot poppy-seed rolls if you wish. For dessert, coconut custard pie.

CHUCK-WAGON BEEF STEW

6 Servings

3½ lbs. chuck (rump or arm), cut in cubes
2 tablespoons flour
2 tablespoons fat or salad oil
1½ cups water or consomme

2 medium potatoes, cubed and parboiled
3 carrots, sliced
6 small onions, peeled

Use meat tenderizer according to directions on page 19. Dust beef cubes with flour. Heat fat or oil in Dutch oven and brown meat well in hot fat or oil. Add liquid. Simmer over low heat for about 2 hours or until tender. Add vegetables during last 15 minutes of cooking. Cook until tender.

SUGGESTED MENU: Add a salad of tomato wedges and water cress. For dessert, rhubarb pie.

HEARTY BEEF SOUP

Makes about 4 quarts

1 lb. lean stewing beef, cut in 1-in. pieces (chuck, shin, neck)
1 beef knucklebone, cracked
6 cups water
1 No. 303 can (1 lb.) tomatoes
2 cups potatoes, diced
2 cups carrots, diced
1 cup celery, diced

½ cup onion, chopped
¼ cup pearl barley
6 whole cloves
1 bay leaf
1 tablespoon salt
1 teaspoon sugar
⅛ teaspoon pepper
1 cup white turnips, diced

Place all ingredients in deep kettle; cover. Heat soup mixture to boiling, then reduce heat and simmer for 1½ to 2 hours, or until meat is tender. Remove bones. Chill overnight. Skim off fat and reheat. Serve piping hot.

SUGGESTED MENU: This soup is a meal-in-a-dish, needing only hot, crusty French bread and a green salad to make it a complete main course. For dessert, coconut cream pie.

SAVORY ROAST

6 Servings

1 chuck or rump roast (about 4 lbs.)
½ cup small stuffed olives
1 large garlic clove
    seasoned flour
2 tablespoons fat or salad oil

1 can condensed tomato soup
1 can (8 oz.) tomato sauce
1 can (3 or 4 oz.) chopped mushrooms (undrained)

Trim meat and wipe with damp cloth. Use sharp paring knife to make 1-inch-deep cuts on all sides of roast. Insert whole olive or sliver of garlic in each cut. Rub with seasoned flour. Heat fat or oil in Dutch oven and brown meat on all sides. Add remaining ingredients, including liquid from mushrooms. Bake in moderate oven (325°) until tender, or about 2½ to 3 hours, depending on size of roast.

SUGGESTED MENU: Mashed potatoes, fried parsnips and green beans with the roast. For dessert, butterscotch-banana pie.

SPICED POT ROAST

10 to 12 Servings

5 lbs. beef chuck
2 tablespoons fat or salad oil
1 tablespoon cinnamon
2 teaspoons ginger
2 tablespoons sugar

1 tablespoon vinegar
2 cups tomato juice
⅔ cup chopped onion
1½ teaspoons salt
    dash pepper

Brown meat on all sides in fat or oil. Combine remaining ingredients; pour over meat. Cover and simmer for 3 hours, or until meat is tender. Thicken gravy, if desired (page 195).

SUGGESTED MENU: Serve mashed potatoes, buttered carrots and glazed onions with the pot roast. Add a green salad. For dessert, lemon chiffon pie.

CAPE COD POT ROAST

8 to 10 Servings

2 tablespoons fat or salad oil
4 to 5 lbs. beef chuck, boned and rolled
½ cup seasoned flour
1 cup fresh cranberries

4 cups water
3 tablespoons brown sugar
¼ teaspoon nutmeg

Heat fat or oil in large kettle; dredge beef with seasoned flour; brown well on all sides in hot fat or oil. Add cranberries and water. Bring to a boil. Cover and simmer for 3 hours or until beef is tender. Strain gravy, measure and thicken (page 195). Add brown sugar and nutmeg. Stir over low heat until sugar dissolves. Season to taste with salt and pepper.

SUGGESTED MENU: Parslied potatoes, glazed carrots and a green salad complete the main course. For dessert, Indian pudding with cream.

KETTLE ROAST

8 Servings

3 lbs. beef chuck, boned and rolled
3 teaspoons salt
¼ teaspoon pepper
⅛ teaspoon allspice
¼ cup flour

¼ cup fat or salad oil
2 tablespoons brown sugar
3 tablespoons vinegar
3 cups hot water

Dredge beef with mixture of salt, pepper, allspice and flour. Brown in hot fat or oil, then sprinkle with brown sugar. Pour in vinegar and part of hot water (one cup). Cover and simmer for 2½ hours or until tender. Pour off all but 4 tablespoons of drippings. Add remaining hot water (2 cups); bring to boil. Thicken gravy (page 195).

SUGGESTED MENU: Serve buttered broad noodles, braised onions and sliced carrots with the roast. Serve coleslaw instead of salad. For dessert, apple pan dowdy.

COFFEE BEEF STEW

6 Servings

3 lbs. beef chuck
  seasoned flour
3 tablespoons fat or salad oil
6 potatoes
6 medium onions
1 bunch carrots

1 teaspoon salt
¼ teaspoon pepper
1 teaspoon sugar
5 cups boiling water
1 cup strong coffee

Cut beef in one-inch cubes; dredge with seasoned flour; brown on all sides in fat or salad oil. Pare and quarter potatoes and peel onions. Scrape carrots, cut in quarters lengthwise and add to meat with remaining ingredients. Simmer for 2½ hours, or until meat is tender. Thicken gravy, if desired (page 195).

SUGGESTED MENU: Serve sliced tomatoes with chive mayonnaise as an accompaniment to the stew. For dessert, raisin custard rice pudding.

OVEN STEW

2 slices bacon, diced
2 large onions, sliced
1 ½ lbs. round steak, cubed
  sugar
  flour
1 can condensed tomato soup

1 cup water
  salt, pepper and paprika
4 carrots, sliced
6 small onions
6 small potatoes

Brown bacon in hot frying pan; remove to casserole. Add sliced large onions and beef to hot bacon fat; sprinkle with a little mixed flour and sugar. Stir and cook until browned, then add to casserole with bacon. Add soup, water and seasonings to fat remaining in pan. Bring to quick boil and pour over beef. Cover and bake in moderate oven (350°) for about 2 hours. Add vegetables; cover and continue baking 1 hour longer.

SUGGESTED MENU: Begin with chilled vegetable juice. Serve hot yeast rolls and a cucumber salad with the stew. Pineapple fritters with lemon sauce for dessert.

STEAK ROLLS

¼ lb. bulk sausage
1 small onion, minced
2 tablespoons parsley, chopped
2 cups bread crumbs
½ teaspoon salt
½ teaspoon pepper
  stock or water to moisten

8 slices round steak, ½ in. thick
3 tablespoons fat or salad oil
¼ cup ketchup
1 tablespoon lemon peel, grated
1 tablespoon onion, grated
¼ cup water

Cook sausage, onion and parsley in heavy skillet or Dutch oven until sausage separates and browns. Add crumbs, seasonings and enough stock or water to make a moist stuffing. Spread stuffing evenly on slices of round steak. Roll and tie, or secure with toothpicks. In same skillet, heat fat or oil and brown meat rolls on all sides. Combine remaining ingredients to make a sauce. Pour over meat rolls. Cover and cook over moderate heat for about 1 hour, or until very tender. Add liquid, if necessary, during cooking.

SUGGESTED MENU: With the steak rolls serve mashed Hubbard or butternut squash, frozen asparagus spears and lettuce wedges with Russian dressing. Lemon meringue pie for dessert.

BAKED BEEF SLICES IN TOMATO SAUCE

1 ½ lbs. round steak, 1 in. thick
¹/₃ cup butter or margarine
8 small white onions, peeled
  salt and pepper
1 cup water

¼ cup vinegar
1 tablespoon sugar
1 cup canned tomatoes
⅛ teaspoon allspice

Cut steak in slices ½ inch thick. Sauté in butter or margarine with onions until brown.

Transfer to roasting pan. Combine remaining ingredients; pour over meat and onions. Bake in moderate oven (325°) for 1 hour and 15 minutes.

SUGGESTED MENU: Serve buttered spaghetti with the steak. Add asparagus tips and a salad of water cress and sliced cucumbers. For dessert, pineapple ambrosia.

TENDER SWISS STEAK   8 to 10 Servings

3 lbs. round steak, 2 in. thick   ½ cup fat or salad oil
  salt and pepper   2 onions, sliced
  flour   2 cups cooked tomatoes

Use meat tenderizer (page 19). Season and flour the meat. Heat fat or oil in heavy skillet. Brown onions in hot fat or oil, then remove them and brown steak on both sides. Place onions on top of steak; add tomatoes. Cover and cook slowly for 2½ to 3 hours, or bake in moderate oven (350°). Remove steak to hot platter; serve with gravy made from drippings in skillet (page 195).

SUGGESTED MENU: With the steak serve creamed potatoes and spinach with mushrooms. Add a crisp salad. For dessert, lemon meringue pie.

SWISS STEAK SUPREME   6 to 8 Servings

2 lbs. top round steak, 1 in. thick   1 cup canned tomatoes
½ cup flour   1 pkg. (10 oz.) frozen peas
1 teaspoon salt   2 large onions, peeled and cut in ½-in. slices
⅛ teaspoon pepper   1 pkg. (8 oz.) cooked noodles
2 tablespoons fat or salad oil

Cut steak into portion-size pieces. Combine flour, salt and pepper. Pound flour mixture into meat, using the edge of a heavy saucer or use meat tenderizer as directed on page 19 and omit flour mixture. Heat fat or oil in large skillet over low heat. Brown meat on both sides. Add tomatoes. Cover skillet and cook for about 1 hour. Add peas. Place some of onion slices on top of meat, saving as a garnish enough for 1 or 2 slices per serving. Continue to cook, covered, about ½ hour longer or until meat and onions are fork-tender. Serve on hot cooked noodles with remaining slices of onion on top of each portion of meat. Pour pan drippings over all.

SUGGESTED MENU: With the steak and noodles serve Mexican-style corn and chopped spinach. Add raw carrot sticks. For dessert, spice layer cake.

SWISS STEAK CHILI

6 Servings

2 lbs. round steak, 1 ½ in. thick
½ cup flour
½ teaspoon salt
  dash pepper
2 tablespoons fat or salad oil

3 cups hot water
1 tablespoon chili powder
¼ cup cold water
½ cup sliced ripe olives

Use meat tenderizer (page 19). Cut into strips 4×2 inches. Combine flour, salt and pepper; dredge strips in flour mixture. Brown on all sides in fat or oil. Add hot water, cover and simmer for 45 minutes. Blend chili powder with cold water; mix with olives and add to steak. Simmer 20 minutes longer.

SUGGESTED MENU: With the steak serve mashed potatoes, buttered kale and whole-kernel corn. For dessert, lemon snow with custard sauce.

SWISS STEAK ROYALE

4 Servings

1 ½ lbs. round steak, ½ in. thick
1 garlic clove
¼ cup flour
1 teaspoon paprika
1 teaspoon salt
¼ teaspoon pepper

¼ cup fat or salad oil
¼ cup sliced onions
1 can (4 oz.) mushrooms (undrained)
½ cup water or bouillon
½ cup sour cream

Cut steak into 4 pieces. Use meat tenderizer (page 19). Rub each piece on both sides with cut garlic clove. Combine flour, paprika, salt and pepper; pound into steak with edge of plate. Brown steak on both sides in fat or oil. Top with onions and mushrooms. Add water or bouillon. Cover and cook over low heat until tender, or about 2 hours, adding more liquid as needed. Remove steak to warm platter. Spoon off excess fat and add sour cream to liquid in pan; stir to blend. Dilute to right consistency with water, if necessary. Reheat meat in sauce.

SUGGESTED MENU: Mashed potatoes, green peas cooked with spring onions (scallions) and a tomato salad accompany the steak. For dessert, cherry pie.

BEEFSTEAK PIE

6 Servings

5 tablespoons flour
1 teaspoon paprika
⅛ teaspoon pepper
1 teaspoon salt
⅛ teaspoon ginger
⅛ teaspoon nutmeg
1 lb. round steak, cubed

¼ cup fat or salad oil
1 cup onions, finely chopped
2 ½ cups hot water
1 ½ cups potatoes, diced
  pastry for 1-crust pie
  cream

Combine flour, seasonings and spices. Dredge meat cubes in flour mixture; brown on all sides in hot fat or oil. Add any leftover flour mixture. Add onions; cook until lightly browned. Add water, cover and simmer for 45 minutes. Add potatoes and simmer 15 minutes longer or until potatoes are tender. Pour into greased deep 10-inch pie pan.

Cover with pastry. Cut a few gashes in pastry to release steam. Brush with cream. Bake in hot oven (425°) for 25 to 30 minutes, or until pastry is golden brown.

SUGGESTED MENU: With the pie serve buttered mixed carrots and green beans. Add crisp celery. For dessert, Spanish cream with strawberry sauce.

WEST COAST PEPPER STEAK   4 Servings

2 lbs. round steak, 1 in. thick
3 large onions, sliced
3 tablespoons salad oil

4 green peppers, seeded and cut in strips
1 garlic clove, minced

Use specially-seasoned meat tenderizer according to directions on page 19. Do not add salt. Pierce both sides deeply with sharp fork to insure penetration and seal in juices and flavor. Let stand at room temperature for 1 hour or cover loosely and refrigerate overnight. Heat 2 of your 3 tablespoons of oil and cook onions in heavy skillet until tender; remove to plate. Cook pepper and garlic until tender, but do not overcook; remove to plate. Cook steak in remaining hot oil (one tablespoon) until done to your taste: 5 to 6 minutes per side for rare, 6 to 7 minutes for medium. Return onions and peppers to skillet; reheat over low heat. Arrange onions on one end of steak platter and peppers on other.

SUGGESTED MENU: Spanish rice, summer squash and cucumber salad with the steak. For dessert, raspberry tapioca parfait.

STROGANOFF SPAGHETTI   4 Servings

1 lb. round steak, cut in 1-in. cubes
  seasoned flour
2 tablespoons fat or salad oil
$^1/_3$ cup onion, chopped
1 garlic clove, minced
1 can (3 oz.) mushrooms, chopped (undrained)
1 cup sour cream

1 can (8 oz.) tomato sauce
2 teaspoons Worcestershire sauce
$^1/_8$ teaspoon pepper
3 $^1/_2$ teaspoons salt
3 qts. boiling water
8 oz. spaghetti
Parmesan cheese

Dredge meat with seasoned flour. Heat fat or oil in large skillet over medium heat and brown meat in it on all sides. Add onion, garlic and drained mushrooms (reserve liquid). Cook for 5 minutes. Add sour cream, tomato sauce, mushroom liquid, Worcestershire sauce, pepper and a small part of the salt ($^1/_2$ teaspoon), saving the rest for cooking with the spaghetti. Mix well. Stirring occasionally, cook over low heat for 1 hour or until meat is tender. If sauce becomes too thick during cooking, add $^1/_2$ cup of water. Serve the Stroganoff sauce over cooked spaghetti. Sprinkle with Parmesan cheese.

To cook spaghetti, add remaining salt (3 teaspoons or 1 tablespoon) to rapidly-boiling water. Add spaghetti gradually, so that water continues to boil. Cook uncovered until tender, stirring occasionally. Drain in colander.

SUGGESTED MENU: Just a tossed salad with this hearty, satisfying dish. For dessert, strawberry chiffon pie.

SAVORY ROUND STEAK

4 Servings

1½ lbs. round steak, ½ in. thick
¼ cup flour
½ teaspoon salt
⅛ teaspoon pepper
¼ teaspoon garlic salt

3 tablespoons fat or salad oil
¾ cup water
¼ cup onion, chopped
¹/₃ cup cheddar cheese, grated
2 tablespoons parsley, chopped

Cut steak into 8 pieces. Pound to thickness of about ¼ inch. Mix together flour, salt, pepper and garlic salt. Dredge steak in seasoned flour. Brown in fat or salad oil. Pour off drippings. Add water and onion. Cover tightly and simmer for 1½ hours, or until tender. Sprinkle cheese and parsley over meat. Cover and simmer for 2 to 3 minutes, or until cheese is melted.

SUGGESTED MENU: Serve scalloped potatoes, beet greens and mashed Hubbard squash with the steak. For dessert, applesauce.

STEAK SMOTHERED WITH ONIONS

4 Servings

3 tablespoons fat or salad oil
1 lb. round steak, ¾ in. thick
¼ cup seasoned flour
½ cup water

4 medium-size onions, sliced
1 teaspoon salt
⅛ teaspoon pepper

Heat fat or oil in heavy skillet. Cut steak into 4 pieces. Dip each piece in seasoned flour. Brown in hot fat. Add water. Cover and cook slowly for about 1 hour. Add onions, salt and pepper. Cover and continue cooking for another 30 minutes, or until meat is fork-tender and onions are done.

SUGGESTED MENU: Corn pudding and Harvard beets with the steak. Add raw carrot sticks and celery. For dessert, baked applesauce and spice cookies.

STEAK LOUISIANA

4 to 6 Servings

1½ lbs. round steak, 1 in. thick
　seasoned flour
3 tablespoons fat or salad oil
2 medium-size onions, thinly sliced
1 No. 303 can (1 lb.) tomatoes
1 cup tomato juice

1 tablespoon Parmesan cheese, grated
1 green pepper, cut into rings
4 medium-size Louisiana yams, peeled and
　sliced ¾ in. thick
salt and pepper

Dredge meat in seasoned flour. Heat fat or oil over low heat. Add onion slices and cook until golden brown. Remove onion and brown meat well on both sides. Add tomatoes, tomato juice, cheese and green pepper rings. Top with onions. Cover and cook over low heat until meat is tender or about 1 hour. Add yam slices. Cover and continue cooking until yams are tender or about 15 minutes. Season to taste with salt and pepper.

SUGGESTED MENU: With the steak and yams serve buttered mixed vegetables and a green salad. For dessert, pineapple refrigerator cake.

STEAK CASSEROLE
4 Servings

1 ½ lbs. round steak
3 tablespoons butter or margarine
2 medium-size onions, sliced
6 small potatoes, sliced

1 cup bouillon
⅛ teaspoon pepper
dash garlic salt

Cut steak in slices ½ inch thick. Brown quickly on both sides in butter or margarine. Remove from pan and cook onion slices until lightly browned. Put a layer of steak slices in shallow baking dish, add a layer of onions, then a layer of potatoes; repeat. Combine bouillon, pepper and garlic salt; pour over all. Cover with foil. Bake in moderate oven (350°) for about 2 hours. Remove foil during last half hour.

SUGGESTED MENU: Serve mashed Hubbard or butternut squash with the meat dish. Add a tossed salad. For dessert, apple tapioca with cream.

LONE-STAR BEEF STEW
6 Servings

¼ cup butter or margarine
½ cup flour
¾ cup ketchup
1 teaspoon salt
¼ teaspoon pepper

4 cups water
juice of 1 lemon
2 lbs. round steak, cubed
6 small potatoes, halved
6 small onions

Melt butter or margarine. Add flour; blend. Stir in ketchup, salt and pepper. Add water and lemon juice. Stir over low heat until thickened. Add meat, potatoes and onions. Cover and simmer for 2½ hours.

SUGGESTED MENU: A tossed green salad and hot buttered corn bread make this meal complete. For dessert, deep-dish pie made of berries in season.

KANSAS SWISS STEAK
6 Servings

1 ½ lbs. top round, 1 in. thick
1 tablespoon dry mustard
½ cup flour
salt and pepper
3 tablespoons fat or salad oil

1 cup onions, sliced
½ cup carrots, diced
1 No. 303 can (1 lb.) tomatoes
1 tablespoon brown sugar
1 tablespoon Worcestershire sauce

Spread steak on flat surface. Combine mustard and flour. Spread over steak and pound in thoroughly. Sprinkle with salt and pepper to taste. Brown on both sides in hot fat or oil in heavy skillet, Dutch oven or small roaster. Combine remaining ingredients and spread over meat. Cover and bake in slow oven (325°) for 1 ½ hours, or until very tender.

SUGGESTED MENU: With the Swiss steak serve fluffy mashed potatoes, and buttered green beans. For dessert, baked apples and cream.

GLORIFIED BEEF STEW WITH HERB DUMPLINGS   6 Servings

2 lbs. round steak
½ cup seasoned flour
2 tablespoons fat or salad oil
4 medium-size onions, sliced
½ cup tomato juice
3 cups boiling water
2 teaspoons Ac'cent

1 teaspoon salt
few drops Tabasco
6 carrots
½ cup leftover coffee
1 pkg. (12 oz.) frozen lima beans
1 teaspoon sugar
herb dumpling batter

Cut beef in 1-inch cubes. Dredge with seasoned flour and brown in hot fat or salad oil. Add onions, tomato juice, water, Ac'cent, salt and Tabasco. Simmer for 1 hour. Cut carrots in chunks and add. Simmer for another hour. Add coffee, lima beans and sugar and simmer ½ hour longer. Drop dumpling batter by spoonfuls on top of stew, being sure each spoonful rests on a piece of meat or vegetable. Cook uncovered for 10 minutes. Cover and cook for 10 more minutes. Thicken gravy, if desired (page 195).

For herb dumplings follow dumpling recipe on package of biscuit mix, adding ¼ teaspoon each of marjoram and savory before adding liquid.

SUGGESTED MENU: A crisp salad completes the main course. For dessert, queen of puddings.

COUNTRY-FRIED STEAK   4 Servings

1 lb. round steak, cut ½ in. thick
1 teaspoon salt
¼ cup flour

1 tablespoon fat or salad oil
2 tablespoons water

Use tenderizer for steak (page 19). Cut into portion-size pieces. Sprinkle with salt and roll in flour. Brown in hot fat or oil. Add water, cover and simmer for 15 to 20 minutes. Remove steak to platter; pour drippings over steak.

SUGGESTED MENU: Rutabaga fluff (yellow turnips and potatoes mashed together), buttered green beans and crisp celery complete the main course. For dessert, steamed spice pudding with lemon sauce.

CUBED BEEF WITH HERBS   4 to 6 Servings

4 tablespoons butter or margarine
1 small onion, chopped
½ garlic clove, chopped
1 teaspoon salt
¼ teaspoon pepper
½ teaspoon rosemary
½ teaspoon thyme

1½ lbs. round steak, ½ in. thick and cubed
seasoned flour
1 can (10½ oz.) condensed beef bouillon
1¼ cups water
6 tablespoons flour
1 pint sour cream

Melt butter or margarine in saucepan. Add onion, garlic and seasonings. Cook over low heat for 5 minutes. Coat cubed meat with seasoned flour, add and brown. Make consommé by mixing condensed beef bouillon with water. Pour in, cover tightly and cook slowly for about 1 hour or until meat is tender. Thicken broth with flour. Stir in sour cream just before serving.

SUGGESTED MENU: With the beef serve buttered, fluffy rice or buttered noodles, Harvard beets and broccoli. Add a tossed salad. For dessert, coffee jelly.

BRAISED STEAK   4 to 5 Servings

2 tablespoons fat or salad oil
1 ½ lbs. round steak, ¾ in. thick
1 onion, chopped

½ green pepper, chopped
1 jar (3 ½ oz.) pimento olives, sliced (undrained)
1 can condensed tomato soup

Heat fat or oil in heavy skillet. Cut steak into portion-size pieces; brown with onion and green pepper in hot fat or oil. Add olives, with brine in which they are packed, and tomato soup. Cover tightly and cook slowly for about 1 ½ hours, or until steaks are fork-tender.

SUGGESTED MENU: With the braised steak serve mashed potatoes and peas cooked with sliced celery. Add a tossed salad. For dessert, chocolate bread pudding with cream.

RANCHERO PLANKED STEAK   6 Servings

4 lbs. round steak or chuck, 1 ½ in. to 2 in. thick
1 pkg. (10 oz.) frozen peas
1 pkg. (12 oz.) frozen green beans, French cut
1 No. 303 can (1 lb.) small whole beets
6 small tomatoes (sprinkled with bread crumbs and broiled)

3 cups mashed potatoes (whipped with 2 tablespoons butter or margarine, 2 eggs, salt and pepper to taste)
butter or margarine

Use specially-seasoned meat tenderizer according to directions on page 19. Do not add salt. Pierce both sides deeply with sharp fork to insure penetration and prevent juice loss. Let stand at room temperature for 1 hour or cover loosely and refrigerate overnight. Prepare vegetables and potatoes. Oil and heat plank. Broil steak until done to your taste. For 1 ½-inch steak: 7 to 8 minutes per side for rare, 10 minutes for medium. For 2-inch steak 10 to 12 minutes per side for rare, 12 to 15 minutes for medium. Using a pastry tube, make a border of potatoes around the heated plank. Place cooked steak in center of plank. Arrange vegetables, putting one red and one green on each end of plank. Separate vegetables with frilly row of mashed potatoes. Brush steak with butter or margarine; place entire plank under broiler for just a minute to brown potatoes and make everything piping hot. Serve the planked-steak dinner at once, carving at the table in thick, diagonal slices.

SUGGESTED MENU: Add a salad or assorted raw-vegetable relishes to round out the main course. For dessert, butterscotch cream pie.

STEAK PROVENÇAL   4 Servings

1 lb. round steak
¾ cup fine bread crumbs
¼ teaspoon pepper
½ cup evaporated milk
⅓ cup fat or salad oil

1 No. 303 can (1 lb.) tomatoes (undrained)
1 No. 303 can (1 lb.) whole-kernel corn (undrained)
1 medium-size onion, sliced
1 green pepper, cut in strips

Use meat tenderizer according to directions on page 19. (If you don't use tenderizer, steak must be cooked an additional 20 minutes.) Pierce steak all over with fork, then cut into ¼-inch slices. Let stand 30 to 40 minutes at room temperature. Combine bread crumbs and half of the pepper (⅛ teaspoon). Dip meat slices in bread crumb mixture, then in evaporated milk and then in bread crumbs again. Brown about ¼ of the meat at a time in hot fat or oil over medium heat. Return all browned meat to skillet, cover tightly and cook over very low heat for 8 minutes. Place on warm platter; keep hot. Drain tomato and corn liquid into skillet; add onion and green pepper. Boil liquid rapidly until reduced to about ½ cup. Add tomatoes, corn and remaining ⅛ teaspoon pepper. Heat to serving temperature. Serve with steak.

SUGGESTED MENU: Hot, crusty French bread and cucumber slices in sweetened vinegar with the steak and vegetables. For dessert, strawberries and cream.

BEEFSTEAK CASSEROLE   4 Servings

1 lb. beef (round steak or chuck), ¼ in. thick
2 teaspoons salt
1 teaspoon paprika
2 tablespoons flour
2 tablespoons fat or salad oil

1 small onion, sliced
3 potatoes, sliced
1 cup cooked or canned tomatoes
1 tablespoon ketchup

Cut steak into 4 pieces. Season with half of salt (1 teaspoon) and paprika. Flour thoroughly and brown in hot fat or oil in heavy skillet. Transfer to baking dish. Cover meat with onion and potatoes. Mix tomatoes, rest of salt (one teaspoon) and ketchup; pour over onion and potatoes. Cover and bake in a moderate oven (350°) until meat is tender when pierced with a fork, or about 1¼ hours. Add water, if needed.

SUGGESTED MENU: With the casserole serve hot, buttered French bread and a tossed salad. For dessert, jelly roll.

BAKED KANSAS STEAK   4 Servings

1 lb. round steak, ½ in. thick
salt and pepper

¼ cup butter or margarine
½ cup flour

Wipe steak dry and cut into 4 pieces. Sprinkle generously with salt and pepper. Cream butter or margarine and mix with flour until smooth. Spread over each piece of steak. Place pieces in small roasting pan or baking dish. Cover and bake in moderate oven (350°) for 1 hour, or until very tender. Remove cover during last 15 minutes of baking.

SUGGESTED MENU: Begin with chilled tomato juice. Serve baked, parslied carrots and mashed potatoes with the steak. For dessert, canned pear halves and chocolate cookies.

BEEF IN RED WINE   4 to 6 Servings

2 lbs. round steak
1 teaspoon salt
1 can condensed bouillon
¼ cup lemon juice
⅛ teaspoon cloves
½ small bay leaf, crumbled
¾ cup port wine

1 tablespoon instant minced onion or ¼ cup raw onion, finely chopped
⅛ teaspoon garlic powder or 1 garlic clove, crushed
1½ tablespoons cornstarch
¼ cup light or dark seedless raisins

Rub heated skillet with fat trimmed from steak; brown steak. Transfer to casserole; add all remaining ingredients except cornstarch and raisins. Bake in moderate oven (350°) for about 2 hours, or until steak is tender. Transfer steak to hot platter; keep warm. Thicken gravy with cornstarch mixed with a little cold water. Add raisins and simmer for a few minutes. Serve with steak.

SUGGESTED MENU: Mashed potatoes, broccoli au gratin and raw carrot sticks complete the main course. For dessert, frozen raspberries and sponge cake.

GOURMET BEEF BIRDS   6 Servings

⅓ cup flour
2 teaspoons salt
¼ teaspoon pepper
2 lbs. top round steak, ½ in. thick
1½ cups bread crumbs
¼ cup raisins

¼ cup celery, finely chopped
1 cup apple, chopped
2 teaspoons prepared mustard
¼ teaspoon sage
1 cup apple juice
3 tablespoons fat or salad oil

Combine flour, most of salt (1½ teaspoons) and pepper. Pound seasoned flour into steak. Cut steak into 6 portions. Mix together crumbs, raisins, celery, apple, mustard, sage, remaining salt (½ teaspoon) and 1 tablespoon of the apple juice. Place about ⅓ cup apple mixture on each piece of steak. Roll like jelly roll and fasten with wooden picks or skewers. Brown meat slowly in hot fat or oil. Pour off drippings. Add rest of apple juice. Cover tightly and cook slowly for 1½ hours, or until meat is tender. Thicken cooking liquid for gravy, if desired (page 195).

SUGGESTED MENU: Mashed potato cakes, glazed carrots and creamed spinach with the meat. For dessert, sliced oranges and brownies.

PARTY POT ROAST

8 to 10 Servings

1 blade pot roast (about 5 lbs.)
2 teaspoons salt
¼ teaspoon pepper
1 garlic clove
3 tablespoons fat or salad oil
¾ cup water
1 can condensed tomato soup

¼ cup ketchup
1 tablespoon Worcestershire sauce
1 large onion, diced
3 tablespoons brown sugar
½ teaspoon dry mustard
3 tablespoons lemon juice

Rub meat with salt, pepper and garlic. Brown on all sides in hot fat or oil. Add water, soup, ketchup, Worcestershire sauce and onion. Cover and simmer for 2 hours. Combine remaining ingredients; spread over meat. Cover and cook 1 hour longer, or until meat is tender. Thicken gravy, if desired (page 195).

SUGGESTED MENU: Serve buttered noodles and zucchini Parmesan with the pot roast. Add a beet salad. For dessert, orange chiffon cake.

BLADE POT ROAST WITH VEGETABLES

6 Servings

½ cup flour
1 teaspoon salt
1 teaspoon Ac'cent
¼ teaspoon pepper
1 blade pot roast with bone, 2 in. thick (about 3 lbs.)

2 tablespoons fat or salad oil
3½ cups water
12 small carrots
12 small onions

Combine first 4 ingredients, using only half of each. Coat pot roast with this mixture, place in Dutch oven or kettle and brown slowly on each side in hot fat or oil. Pour off excess fat. Add part of water (1 cup). Slip a low rack under meat to prevent sticking. Cover kettle and simmer for 2½ hours. It may be necessary to add more water in order to keep at least ½ inch in bottom of kettle. Add vegetables. Cook 45 minutes longer, or until meat and vegetables are fork-tender. Arrange meat and vegetables on hot platter; keep warm. Add 2 more cups water to liquid in kettle. Combine rest of first 4 ingredients and blend to smooth paste with last ½ cup water. Add to liquid in kettle. Stir over low heat until smooth and thickened. Serve with pot roast.

SUGGESTED MENU: Pumpernickel bread and beet and horse-radish relish complete the main course. For dessert, cranberry chiffon pie.

BLADE POT ROAST OF BEEF

6 Servings

½ cup flour
1½ teaspoons salt
¼ teaspoon pepper
1 blade pot roast of beef, 3 to 4 lbs.
2 tablespoons fat or salad oil

water (a little more than 1 cup)
18 small carrots, scraped
12 small onions, peeled
2 cups fresh green beans, in 1-in. pieces

Combine half of the flour (¼ cup) with salt and pepper; coat meat on all sides. Heat fat or oil in Dutch oven or heavy sauce pot over high heat. Add meat; brown well on both sides. Pour off excess fat or oil. Add part of water (one cup); cover. Reduce heat to low and simmer for 2½ hours, adding more water if necessary to keep ½ inch of liquid in bottom of pan. Add carrots, onions and beans; cook 30 minutes longer, or until meat and vegetables are fork-tender. Arrange meat and vegetables on platter; keep warm. Measure liquid in pan; add enough water to make 2 cups liquid. Return to pan. Combine remaining flour with a little cold water to make a smooth paste; stir slowly into liquid. Bring to a boil; stir constantly until thickened.

SUGGESTED MENU: Add a salad of sliced tomatoes. For dessert, frosted devil's food cake.

SPICY BEEF POT ROAST
10 to 12 Servings

2 tablespoons fat or salad oil	2 cups tomato juice
4 to 5 lbs. beef (boned rump or sirloin tip)	1 cup onion, chopped
1 tablespoon cinnamon	1½ teaspoons salt
2 teaspoons ginger	⅛ teaspoon pepper
2 tablespoons sugar	½ cup cold water
1 tablespoon vinegar	¼ cup flour

Heat fat or oil in Dutch oven or sauce pot over high heat. Add meat; brown well on all sides. Combine cinnamon, ginger, sugar, vinegar, tomato juice, onion, salt and pepper. Pour over meat. Bring to boiling, then reduce heat to low and simmer covered for about 3 hours, or until meat is tender. Place meat on platter; keep warm. Measure liquid in pan; add a little water, if necessary, to make 2 cups. Return to pan. Blend cold water with the flour to make a smooth paste. Slowly stir into liquid. Bring to boil and cook until thickened, stirring constantly.

SUGGESTED MENU: Fluffy mashed potatoes, buttered carrots and green beans vinaigrette accompany the pot roast. For dessert, coffee ice cream with caramel sauce and toasted almonds.

SPICY TOMATO POT ROAST
8 to 10 Servings

4 lbs. beef pot roast	¼ teaspoon pepper
¼ cup fat or salad oil	2 teaspoons salt
2 medium-size onions, sliced	½ teaspoon ginger
1 can (8 oz.) tomato sauce	⅛ teaspoon cloves
1 cup water	⅛ teaspoon allspice

Brown meat on all sides in hot fat or oil in Dutch oven or heavy kettle. Add onions, tomato sauce, water and seasonings. Cover tightly. Simmer for about 3 hours or until tender, adding more water if necessary.

SUGGESTED MENU: Fried sweet potatoes, beet greens and buttered whole-kernel corn with the pot roast. For dessert, raspberry gelatin whip with cream.

POT ROAST WITH VEGETABLES

4 Servings (with meat for a second meal)

1 tablespoon fat or salad oil
3 to 4 lbs. beef (boned rump or sirloin tip)
2 teaspoons salt
⅛ teaspoon pepper
¼ to ½ cup hot water

4 medium-size onions
8 small carrots
4 medium-size potatoes
3 tablespoons flour
¹/₃ cup cold water

Heat fat or oil in Dutch oven or heavy sauce pot. Brown meat well on all sides. Sprinkle with salt and pepper; add hot water. Cover and simmer for about 2½ to 3 hours, or until meat is almost tender, adding more water during cooking, if necessary. Add onions and cook for 10 minutes. Add carrots and potatoes. Continue cooking 30 to 35 minutes longer. When meat and vegetables are tender, place them on a hot platter and keep warm. Measure liquid in the pan and add water, if necessary, to make 1½ cups. Blend flour and cold water; slowly stir into hot liquid. Bring to boil and cook until thickened, stirring constantly. Serve with meat.

SUGGESTED MENU: Nothing more is needed for the main course except a green salad and any preferred bread. For dessert, chilled canned pears and gingersnaps.

HERB POT ROAST

6 Servings

1 arm-bone pot roast, (about 4 lbs.)
1 garlic clove
2 tablespoons olive or salad oil
½ cup green onions, chopped
2 tablespoons wine vinegar
2 teaspoons salt

1 teaspoon oregano
¼ teaspoon powdered ginger
½ cup chili sauce
1 beef bouillon cube
½ cup hot water

Brown meat and garlic in hot oil. Remove garlic. Add chopped onions, vinegar, salt, oregano, ginger and chili sauce. Dissolve bouillon cube in hot water and pour over all. Bring to boiling point, then reduce heat and simmer until meat is very tender, or 2½ to 3 hours.

SUGGESTED MENU: Serve the pot roast with buttered rice, green beans and mushrooms and a tossed green salad. For dessert, orange pudding-cake.

CALIFORNIA BEEF POT ROAST

6 to 8 Servings

3 to 4 lbs. beef pot roast (either round bone or blade bone)
2 teaspoons salt
1 teaspoon pepper
½ cup flour
¼ cup salad oil

1 No. 303 can (1 lb.) tomatoes
2 medium-size onions, sliced
½ cup ripe olives, sliced
½ teaspoon chili powder
1 large ripe avocado, sliced
lemon juice

Season pot roast with salt and pepper and dredge in flour. Brown in hot salad oil in heavy skillet. Add tomatoes, onions, olives and chili powder. Cover and simmer for 2 to 2½ hours or until meat is tender. Remove meat from sauce, slice and keep hot.

Skim fat from sauce and pour sauce over meat on platter. Top with sliced avocado dipped in lemon juice to prevent darkening.

SUGGESTED MENU: Some buttered noodles and green salad with the pot roast. For dessert, coffee Bavarian cream.

SHERRIED BEEF   4 Serving

1 lb. lean boneless beefsteak
3 tablespoons salad oil
3 medium-size onions, sliced
2 tablespoons soy sauce
1 bouillon cube
½ cup water

2 tablespoons cornstarch
1 teaspoon wine vinegar
¼ cup dry sherry
1 can (6 oz.) sliced mushrooms (undrained)
2 cups hot cooked rice

Cut beef into thin strips; brown quickly in hot oil. Set aside. Sauté onions, adding more oil if needed. Set aside. Combine soy sauce, bouillon cube, water and cornstarch. Add to pan drippings and cook, stirring constantly, until mixture is thickened. Put back meat and onions and add vinegar, sherry and mushrooms (including liquid). Heat thoroughly. Serve over hot cooked rice.

SUGGESTED MENU: With the beef and rice serve minted carrots and spinach soufflé. Add an endive salad. For dessert, cubed coffee jelly and cream.

SKILLET STEAKS   4 Servings

1 garlic clove, chopped
¼ cup salad oil
4 boneless sirloin steaks, cut very thin (8 oz. ea.)
¼ cup butter or margarine
1 teaspoon dry mustard

½ teaspoon salt
¼ cup parsley, chopped
1 tablespoon lemon juice
1 teaspoon Worcestershire sauce
¼ teaspoon pepper

Add garlic to salad oil. Let stand for 10 minutes, then brush on both sides of steaks. Combine butter or margarine, mustard and salt in heavy skillet. Add parsley; heat until butter bubbles. Place steaks in skillet and turn at once to coat both sides with butter or margarine. Cook slowly for 5 minutes. Do not brown. Turn steaks; cook 5 minutes more; remove to hot platter. Stir lemon juice into butter or margarine remaining in skillet. Add Worcestershire sauce and pepper. Heat well and pour over steaks. Serve at once.

SUGGESTED MENU: Scalloped potatoes, green peas and summer crookneck squash with the steaks. Add a salad of iceberg lettuce chunks. For dessert, deep-dish peach pie.

SMOTHERED BEEF AND MUSHROOMS   6 Servings

1 ½ lbs. fillet of beef tenderloin, about 2 ½ in.
    in diameter, cut in 12 to 14 thin slices
¼ cup butter or margarine
2 tablespoons onion, minced
2 tablespoons flour
1 cup water
3 cans (4 oz. ea.) mushrooms, sliced
    (undrained)

2 tablespoons sherry
¾ teaspoon salt
⅛ teaspoon pepper
2 cups mashed potatoes
1 egg, beaten

Sauté beef slices quickly on both sides in butter or margarine; set aside. Sauté onion in butter left in skillet. Stir in flour; blend until smooth. Add water and mushrooms with their liquid. Cook and stir until sauce is smooth and thickened. Add sherry, salt and pepper. Place slices of fillet and sauce in alternate layers in 1 ½-quart casserole, ending with mushroom sauce. Combine potatoes with egg and top casserole with mixture. Bake in hot oven (425°) for 20 minutes, or until potatoes are tipped with brown.

SUGGESTED MENU: With the beef serve wax beans with dill or dillseed, Harvard beets and a green salad. For dessert, broiled grapefruit halves with honey.

COUNTRY STEAK DINNER   4 Servings

4 cube steaks, ½ lb. ea.
¾ cup fine bread crumbs
    salt and pepper
½ cup evaporated milk
3 tablespoons fat or salad oil
1 onion, finely chopped

2 tablespoons flour
1 teaspoon salt
⅛ teaspoon pepper
2 cups canned tomatoes (undrained)
2 cups canned or frozen whole-kernel corn

Roll steaks in crumbs seasoned with a little salt and pepper. Dip in evaporated milk and roll again in crumbs. Brown slowly in hot fat or oil in heavy skillet. Cover and continue cooking over low heat for 10 to 12 minutes or until meat is tender. Remove steaks to warm serving dish. Add onion to fat remaining in skillet; brown quickly. Stir in flour, salt and pepper. Add ½ cup juice drained from tomatoes. Cook and stir mixture over low heat until it begins to thicken. Add drained tomatoes and corn. Heat quickly. Pour around steaks in serving dish.

SUGGESTED MENU: Hot raised rolls or baking-powder biscuits are very good with this delicious, one-dish meal. Add a crisp salad. Chocolate pudding and sugar cookies for dessert.

BARBECUED STEAK SANDWICH PLATTER   4 Servings

4 cube steaks
¼ cup ketchup
¼ cup vinegar
1 ½ tablespoons salad oil

2 tablespoons Worcestershire sauce
2 tablespoons water
½ teaspoon salt
4 slices buttered toast

Have meat at room temperature. Place in shallow bowl. Combine all remaining ingredients except bread; mix well. Pour over cube steaks; let stand for about 15 minutes. Drain and reserve sauce. Place steaks on broiler rack about 2 inches below heat. Broil for 4 to 5 minutes on each side, spooning sauce over meat as it broils. Place steaks on buttered toast and serve at once.

SUGGESTED MENU: With the sandwiches serve cucumber and onion slices in sweetened vinegar, tomato wedges and carrot sticks. For dessert, raspberry sundaes.

CUBED STEAKS, WESTERN STYLE

6 Servings

½ cup green pepper, diced
½ cup onion, chopped
1 pimento, chopped
2 tablespoons fat or salad oil
1 can (6 oz.) tomato paste
½ cup black olives, chopped
¼ cup sharp cheddar cheese, grated

¼ cup fine bread crumbs
1½ teaspoons salt
2 teaspoons chili powder
¼ teaspoon pepper
6 minute steaks, cubed
¾ cup water

Cook green pepper, onion and pimento in hot fat or salad oil until onion is tender but not brown. Add tomato paste, olives, cheese, bread crumbs, salt, chili powder and pepper; mix well. Spread steaks with half of this mixture. Roll as for a jelly roll and fasten with wooden picks. Place in shallow baking pan, folded side down. Mix remaining sauce with water and pour over steaks. Bake in moderate oven (375°) for 45 minutes, or until steaks are tender.

SUGGESTED MENU: With these savory steak rolls serve French-fried potatoes, Mexican corn and a green salad. For dessert, chilled fresh apples and Camembert cheese.

VALLEY STEAK WITH MUSHROOMS

4 Servings

2 lbs. beef shoulder steak
¾ cup flour
½ teaspoon dried tarragon leaves
½ teaspoon salt

beef suet (about ¼ lb.)
1 can (8 oz.) mushrooms
3 tablespoons butter or margarine
green pepper rings

Place steak flat on board and pound in flour mixed with seasonings. Pound all of seasoned flour into steak, covering both sides with the mixture. Cut steak in 4 pieces. Chop beef suet and fry in heavy skillet. Add steak pieces; brown quickly on both sides. Reduce heat and cook until done to your taste, turning several times. Remove steak to warm platter. Put mushrooms and butter or margarine in skillet; cook rapidly for 5 minutes. Serve steak garnished with mushrooms and green pepper rings. Liquid in pan may be thickened for gravy, if desired (page 195).

SUGGESTED MENU: Serve creamed potatoes and perfection gelatin salad with the steak. For dessert, fresh fruit, crackers and cheese.

PORCUPINE BALLS IN TOMATO SAUCE

4 Servings

1 lb. ground beef (chuck or round)
3 tablespoons onion, chopped
¼ cup uncooked rice
¼ cup cracker crumbs
⅓ cup milk
1 teaspoon salt

⅛ teaspoon pepper
2 tablespoons fat or salad oil
1 can condensed tomato soup
½ cup water
1 can (4 oz.) mushroom stems and pieces (undrained)

Combine beef, onion, rice, crumbs, milk and seasonings. Shape with hands into 1-inch balls. Fry slowly in hot fat or oil in heavy skillet. Turn to brown evenly. Add soup mixed with water. Cover and simmer for about 1 hour. Remove meat to hot platter. Stir mushrooms and liquid into gravy in pan; heat. Serve in a bowl with the meat balls.

SUGGESTED MENU: Mashed potatoes and green bean succotash with the meat balls and gravy. Add a salad of romaine lettuce with a snappy dressing. For dessert, steamed fruit pudding.

BEEF PATTIES DE LUXE

4 Servings

1 lb. lean ground beef
½ to ¾ cup light cream
1 teaspoon onion, minced
1 teaspoon parsley, minced

salt and pepper
½ cup sharp cheese, grated
mushroom sauce

Mix meat, cream, onion and parsley. Sprinkle with salt and pepper. Lightly shape into 4 generous patties and place in shallow greased baking pan. Broil for 5 to 6 minutes on each side. Top with grated cheese and return to broiler for 2 to 3 minutes, or until cheese melts and bubbles. Serve hot with mushroom sauce.

SUGGESTED MENU: Try these with fluffy curried rice, lettuce and tomato salad and chunks of toasted peasant bread. Add fresh fruit compote, cookies and coffee.

APPLESAUCE MEAT BALLS

6 Servings

1 lb. lean ground beef
½ cup applesauce
½ cup soft bread crumbs
1 egg, beaten
seasoned flour

1 to 2 tablespoons fat or salad oil
¼ cup ea. celery, green pepper and carrot, thinly sliced or diced
1 onion, thinly sliced
1 cup tomato juice

Combine beef, applesauce, bread crumbs and egg. Shape mixture into small balls. Roll in seasoned flour and brown in hot fat or oil. Use a slotted spoon to skim meat balls from frying pan and place in shallow casserole. Heat pan drippings and stir in prepared vegetables, tomato juice and more seasoning, if desired. Bring to rapid boil and pour over meat balls. Cover and bake in moderate oven (350°) for 40 minutes.

SUGGESTED MENU: These are good served with parslied noodles, cabbage salad, bran muffins and coffee. For dessert, try thin slices of poundcake spread with your favorite jam and topped with unsweetened whipped cream.

BAKED HAMBURG STEAK

1 ½ cups bread crumbs
½ cup milk
1 ½ lbs. lean ground beef
1 small onion, chopped
2 eggs, beaten

1 ½ teaspoons salt
¼ teaspoon pepper
½ teaspoon poultry seasoning
4 hard-cooked eggs
1 cup tomato sauce

Soak crumbs in milk. Combine them with meat, onion, beaten eggs and seasonings. Mixture will be moist, but firm enough to hold its shape. Place hard-cooked eggs end-to-end lengthwise on top of meat and shape meat mixture up around eggs. Place meat roll in baking pan; pat smooth. Pour tomato sauce over top of roll. Bake in moderate oven (350°) for 1 hour. When cut, slices will have a circle of egg in the center.

SUGGESTED MENU: Serve with buttered lima beans, new potatoes in their jackets and a tossed salad. Prunes in cream for dessert.

OLD ENGLISH BURGERS

1 ½ lbs. lean ground beef
1 pkg. onion soup mix
2 tablespoons parsley, chopped
¼ teaspoon pepper
¼ teaspoon poultry seasoning
¼ cup chili sauce
5 eggs

1 tablespoon water
1 ½ cups all-purpose flour, sifted
1 ½ teaspoons baking powder
1 teaspoon salt
1 ½ cups milk
3 tablespoons butter or margarine, melted

Combine ground beef, soup mix, parsley, pepper, poultry seasoning and chili sauce. Take one of your 5 eggs, beat slightly and blend with water. Add to meat mixture and mix thoroughly. Form into 24 balls. Place in well-greased baking dish 12×18 inches. Mix and sift flour, baking powder and salt. Beat your 4 remaining eggs until foamy and mix well with milk and butter or margarine. Add dry ingredients all at once to egg mixture. Beat with rotary beater (or low speed on mixer) until smooth and well blended. Pour batter over meat balls. Bake in moderate oven (350°) for 50 to 60 minutes or until golden brown. Serve hot, with canned beef gravy if desired.

SUGGESTED MENU: Serve creamed onions and buttered asparagus with this interesting meat dish. Add a sliced beet and onion salad. For dessert, fruit gelatin whip.

SPEEDLOAF

4 Servings

1 lb. lean ground beef
1 teaspoon Ac'cent
1 ½ teaspoons salt
¼ teaspoon pepper
⅛ teaspoon ea., oregano and thyme
⅔ cup evaporated milk

⅔ cup fine bread crumbs
3 tablespoons fat or salad oil
2 tablespoons onion, finely chopped
1 No. 303 can (1 lb.) whole-kernel corn (undrained)
1 No. 303 can (1 lb.) lima beans (undrained)

Break up meat with fork in mixing bowl. Sprinkle Ac'cent, part of salt (1 teaspoon), half of pepper (⅛ teaspoon) and herbs over surface of meat. Toss lightly to distribute seasonings. Add evaporated milk and bread crumbs; mix lightly. Shape meat mixture into a large patty. Brown patty in hot fat or oil on both sides. Add onion and cook until tender, but not brown. Drain corn and bean liquid into skillet; simmer until liquid is reduced to about ½ cup. Add corn, lima beans and remaining salt and pepper. Heat to serving temperature.

SUGGESTED MENU: A crisp salad completes the main course. For dessert, sliced bananas with cream and chocolate cookies.

THREE-LAYER CASSEROLE

4 to 6 Servings

4 tablespoons butter or margarine, melted
1 lb. lean ground beef
1 medium-size onion, chopped

1 No. 303 can (1 lb.) cream-style corn
3 cups mashed potatoes

Put half of butter or margarine (2 tablespoons) in skillet with meat and onion. Cook until brown, stirring often to break up pieces of meat and brown evenly. Spread meat in greased 2-quart casserole; cover with corn and hot, seasoned, mashed potatoes. Top with remaining butter or margarine (2 tablespoons). Heat in moderate oven (350°) for 20 minutes or until brown.

SUGGESTED MENU: Add sliced tomatoes, cucumbers and onions in French dressing. For dessert, drained canned pears with chocolate sauce and whipped cream.

OPEN-FACE BURGERS

4 Servings

1 lb. lean ground beef
1 teaspoon salt
¼ teaspoon pepper
¼ teaspoon Ac'cent
2 tablespoons onion, minced

3 to 4 tablespoons milk or cream
4 hamburger buns
prepared mustard
butter or margarine

Mix meat lightly with seasonings, onion and milk or cream. Split buns; spread bottom halves with mustard. Spread meat mixture so that it completely covers bottom half of each bun. Broil about 5 to 6 inches from heat for 8 to 10 minutes. Top each broiled patty with thin pat of butter or margarine and remaining half bun.

SUGGESTED MENU: Serve a vegetable aspic salad with the buns. For dessert, instant chocolate pudding with cream.

BEEF DILLBURGERS

6 Servings

1 ½ lbs. lean ground beef
2 tablespoons onion, minced
1 ½ teaspoons salt
¼ teaspoon pepper
3 large dill pickles

6 slices beef bacon
1 tablespoon fat or salad oil
6 frankfurter buns
butter or margarine

Mix beef, onion and seasonings. Cut pickles in halves lengthwise. Shape some of meat mixture around each pickle half to make a long meat roll. Wrap slice of beef bacon around each meat roll. Brown on all sides in hot fat or oil. Drain most of fat or oil from pan. Cover and simmer over low heat for 20 to 25 minutes. Serve on toasted frankfurter buns spread with butter or margarine.

SUGGESTED MENU: Serve potato chips and sliced tomatoes in French dressing with the dillburgers. Canned white cherries and brownies for dessert.

STUFFED PEPPERS

4 Servings

4 large green peppers
1 lb. lean ground beef
1 cup rolled oats
1 egg, beaten

1 onion, chopped
½ cup tomato juice
2 tablespoons Worcestershire sauce
salt and pepper

Cut peppers in halves lengthwise; seed, wash and drain. Combine remaining ingredients; use to stuff pepper cases. Place in shallow greased pan and add water to depth of 1 inch. Bake in moderate oven (350°) for 1 hour.

SUGGESTED MENU: Serve creamed potatoes and buttered asparagus spears with the stuffed peppers. For dessert, grapefruit halves.

MACARONI-BEEF CASSEROLE

4 Servings

1 lb. lean ground beef
2 tablespoons fat or salad oil
1 medium-size onion, chopped
1 No. 303 can (1 lb.) tomatoes
1 tablespoon ketchup
1 tablespoon steak sauce

¼ cup green pepper, chopped
1 pkg. (8 oz.) elbow macaroni
2 tablespoons parsley, chopped
salt and pepper
1 can condensed cream of mushroom soup
1 cup cheddar cheese, grated

Brown beef in hot fat or oil in heavy skillet until all red color disappears. Add onion, tomatoes, ketchup, steak sauce and green pepper. Simmer for 30 minutes. Cook macaroni according to directions on package. Combine macaroni, parsley and beef mixture in baking dish. Season to taste. Gently spoon cream of mushroom soup into mixture, lifting from bottom. Sprinkle grated cheese over top. Bake in moderate oven (350°) for 30 minutes, or until top is bubbly and brown.

SUGGESTED MENU: Serve hot garlic bread and any favorite green salad with the casserole. For dessert, chilled grapes with blue cheese.

HAMBURGER-NOODLE CASSEROLE

6 Servings

2 tablespoons fat or salad oil
1 onion, chopped
1 lb. lean ground beef
1 can condensed tomato soup
1 cup water

½ pkg. (4 oz.) uncooked noodles
salt and pepper
1 No. 303 can (1 lb.) cream-style corn
1 can (8 oz.) sliced mushrooms
1 cup sharp cheese, shredded

Heat fat or oil in heavy skillet and fry onion in it until lightly browned. Add meat; cook and stir until all pinkness disappears. Pour in soup, water and noodles. Cook until noodles are tender, stirring often. Season to taste. Add corn and mushrooms and stir. Transfer to casserole. Top with shredded cheese. Bake in moderate oven (350°) for about 45 minutes.

SUGGESTED MENU: A crisp salad is a sufficient complement for this one-dish meal. For dessert, pumpkin pie.

STEAK OLIVETTE

6 Servings

1 small onion, minced
1 ½ lbs. lean ground beef
1 teaspoon salt
dash pepper

1 No. 303 can (1 lb.) tomatoes
½ cup sharp cheddar cheese, grated
12 stuffed olives, sliced
6 strips bacon

Combine onion, beef, salt and pepper and pack in 8-inch square pan. Drain tomatoes and spread over meat mixture. Sprinkle cheese over tomatoes and dot with olives. Top with bacon strips. Bake in moderate oven (350°) for 45 minutes.

SUGGESTED MENU: Serve home-fried potatoes and sautéed parsnips with the meat. Add a salad of iceberg lettuce and French dressing. For dessert, broiled grapefruit with honey.

MOCK STEAK

6 Servings

2 teaspoons Worcestershire sauce
1 teaspoon salt
dash pepper
½ cup ketchup
2 lbs. lean ground beef

1 cup bread crumbs
¼ cup onion, chopped
3 cups mashed potatoes
1 can (4 oz.) button mushrooms
2 cups green peas

Combine Worcestershire sauce, salt, pepper and ketchup. Blend with meat, crumbs and onion. Heat plank in moderate oven (350°); grease well. Shape meat mixture on plank to resemble a T-bone steak. Bake at 350° for 45 minutes. Spoon border of mashed potatoes around meat. Garnish with drained mushrooms. Return to hot oven (450°) to brown potatoes. Add hot peas.

SUGGESTED MENU: Hot biscuits and a tossed salad round out the main course. For dessert, steamed spice pudding with lemon sauce.

HAMBURGER CASSEROLE

4 to 6 Servings

1 lb. lean ground beef
1 teaspoon onion salt
  salt and pepper
2 teaspoons prepared mustard
2 teaspoons Worcestershire sauce
2 tablespoons fat or salad oil

1 can beef gravy
1 can (8 oz.) tomato sauce
1 No. 303 can (1 lb.) green peas
1 No. 303 can (1 lb.) onions
1 ½ cups biscuit mix

Combine first 5 ingredients. Form into 8 patties and brown in hot fat or oil. Remove patties and heat gravy and tomato sauce in pan. Arrange patties, peas and onions in casserole. Add gravy. Make biscuits according to directions on package; place on casserole. Bake in hot oven (450°) for 20 minutes.

SUGGESTED MENU: Bake additional biscuits to serve separately. Add a salad of sliced oranges and onion rings on romaine lettuce. For dessert, a two-crust grapefruit pie.

WINEBURGERS

6 Servings

1 medium-size onion, minced
1 tablespoon butter or margarine
1 lb. lean ground beef
2 tablespoons flour
1 can condensed tomato soup

$^1/_3$ cup Burgundy or claret wine
½ teaspoon Worcestershire sauce
1 teaspoon (or more) chili powder
  salt and pepper
6 hamburger buns

Cook onion in butter or margarine until soft, but not brown. Add meat and cook, stirring with fork, until all pinkness disappears. Sprinkle flour over meat; blend well. Add soup and wine. Cook, stirring constantly, until mixture boils and thickens. Add seasonings. Simmer uncovered for about 10 minutes, stirring frequently. Cut thin slice from top and hollow out inside of each bun. Brush inside with more butter or margarine; toast under broiler to a golden brown, heating bun lids at the same time. Fill shells with hot meat mixture and put lids in place. Serve at once.

SUGGESTED MENU: Begin with cream of pea soup and cheese crackers. Follow up with the wineburgers. For dessert, chocolate pudding with cream.

CRUSTY HAMBURGERS

4 to 6 Servings

1 ½ lbs. lean ground beef
1 egg, well beaten
3 tablespoons seasoned flour

½ cup fine bread crumbs
4 tablespoons bacon fat

Shape beef into cakes. Dip in egg, roll in seasoned flour and dip in egg again. Roll in bread crumbs and fry in hot bacon fat until hamburgers are golden brown.

SUGGESTED MENU: Whipped potatoes, buttered Brussels sprouts and pickled beets with the hamburgers. Add a green salad. For dessert, devil's food layer cake.

BEEFBURGER-BANANA GRILL   2 Servings

½ lb. lean ground beef
1 small egg
1 tablespoon onion, chopped
¾ teaspoon salt
⅛ teaspoon pepper

¼ cup milk
½ cup all-bran
4 strips bacon
2 firm bananas, peeled
   butter or margarine, melted

Combine beef, egg, onion and seasonings. Pour milk over bran. Heat broiler. Combine meat mixture and bran. Shape into 4 patties, 1 inch thick. Wrap bacon slice around each and fasten with wooden pick. Place on shallow pan and broil 3 inches below heat source for about 5 minutes. When they are brown, turn patties and place bananas on pan. Brush with butter or margarine and broil with patties for another 5 minutes or until patties are brown and bananas are tender. Serve hot.

SUGGESTED MENU: Buttered rice, scalloped tomatoes and a green salad augment the grill. For dessert, cherry gelatin whip.

CURRIED MEAT BALLS   6 to 8 Servings

1 can (1 lb. 12 oz.) tomatoes (undrained)
¾ cup soft bread crumbs
1½ lbs. lean ground beef
¼ cup onion, chopped
1½ teaspoons salt

¼ cup flour
3 tablespoons fat or salad oil
½ teaspoon sugar
2 teaspoons curry powder

Drain ½ cup juice from tomatoes, reserving remaining juice and tomatoes, and pour over bread crumbs. Add beef, onion and salt; mix thoroughly. Shape mixture into 24 balls, using a rounded tablespoon. Coat meat balls with flour; brown in hot fat or salad oil. Pour off drippings. Add tomatoes and remaining juice, sugar and curry powder. Simmer for 20 minutes.

SUGGESTED MENU: Mashed potatoes and onions au gratin with the meat balls. Add a crisp tossed salad. For dessert, fudge cake squares.

PARMESAN MEAT BALLS WITH MUSHROOM SAUCE   4 Servings

1 lb. lean ground beef
1 egg
¼ cup fine bread crumbs
2 tablespoons Parmesan cheese, grated
1 teaspoon salt

2 tablespoons butter or margarine
1 can condensed cream of mushroom soup
$^1/_3$ cup sherry
½ cup water
2 tablespoons parsley, minced

Combine beef, egg, crumbs, cheese and salt; mix well. Take up mixture by rounded teaspoonfuls and shape into balls. Melt butter or margarine in large, heavy skillet. Add meat balls; brown on all sides. Pour off all but about 1 tablespoon drippings. Blend mushroom soup, sherry, water and parsley and pour over meat balls. Cover and simmer for 20 minutes, stirring occasionally. Add a little more water if sauce is too thick.

SUGGESTED MENU: Baked potatoes, buttered broccoli and sliced carrots with the meat balls. Add a salad of shredded lettuce. For dessert, lemon flake layer cake.

HAMBURG EN BROCHETTE

6 Servings

1 ½ lbs. lean ground beef
  ½ teaspoon salt
  dash pepper
  ½ cup soft bread crumbs
  ½ cup evaporated milk
3 to 4 strips bacon
1 medium-size onion, thinly sliced

Combine meat, salt, pepper, bread crumbs and milk. Shape into small balls about 1 ½ inches in diameter. Cut bacon in 1 ½-inch pieces. Place meat balls, bacon pieces and onion slices alternately on 12 short metal skewers, beginning and ending with meat balls. Broil for 10 to 12 minutes, turning once.

SUGGESTED MENU: Begin with tomato juice. With the meat serve baked sweet potatoes and scalloped eggplant. For dessert, cranberry pie.

SUMMER-TIME MEAT LOAVES

4 Servings

1 lb. lean ground beef
½ cup dry bread crumbs
¹/₃ cup non-fat evaporated milk
1 egg, slightly beaten
3 tablespoons cold water
¼ cup green pepper, finely chopped
3 tablespoons onion, finely chopped
½ teaspoon salt
4 stuffed olives, finely chopped
2 gherkin pickles, finely chopped

Combine all ingredients; mix well. Divide into 4 parts and mold each portion into loaf. Place on greased shallow baking pan. Bake in moderate oven (375°) for about 35 minutes. Allow to cool, then chill.

SUGGESTED MENU: With the cold meat loaves serve a salad of cooked vegetables, deviled eggs and coleslaw. For dessert, red raspberry shortcake.

BROILED INDIVIDUAL MEAT LOAVES

4 Servings

1 lb. ground beef chuck
2 eggs, slightly beaten
1 cup fine bread crumbs
¹/₃ cup onions, minced
2 tablespoons ketchup
¼ cup sweet mixed pickles, chopped
1 ½ teaspoons salt
½ teaspoon dry mustard
2 tablespoons milk

Combine all ingredients; mix thoroughly. Divide mixture into 4 parts, and shape into rectangular loaves, each 1 inch thick. Place on broiler pan and broil 3 or 4 inches from source of heat for 10 to 15 minutes, or until done, turning only once.

SUGGESTED MENU: Creamed potatoes with chives, grilled tomatoes and buttered zucchini squash accompany the meat loaves. Add coleslaw. For dessert, butterscotch pudding with sliced bananas and cream.

BOTTOMS-UP MUSHROOM MEAT LOAF

4 to 6 Servings

2 medium-size onions
1 tablespoon salad oil
½ cup water
2 tablespoons ketchup
1 can (4 oz.) mushrooms, sliced
2 soda crackers

1 egg, slightly beaten
1 lb. lean ground beef
1 teaspoon salt
½ teaspoon pepper
1 garlic clove, minced
paprika

Slice one of the onions and cook in hot oil until tender. Stir in half of water (¼ cup), ketchup and mushrooms; heat. Place in bottom of small loaf pan.

Soak crackers in remaining water (¼ cup). Mince your other onion and toss together with crackers, egg, meat, salt, pepper and garlic. Shape into loaf and place in pan on top of mushroom mixture. Sprinkle with paprika. Bake in moderate oven (350°) for 1 hour and 15 minutes. Invert on serving platter.

SUGGESTED MENU: Baked sweet potatoes, green peas and eggplant Creole with the meat loaf. Add a salad of shredded lettuce. For dessert, pineapple upside-down cake.

LAYERED RICE AND MEAT LOAF

4 Servings

1 pkg. (5¼ oz.) precooked rice
¹/₃ cup onion, chopped
1 tablespoon parsley, chopped
½ cup bread, finely diced
½ cup milk
1 lb. lean ground beef

1 egg, slightly beaten
1 teaspoon salt
dash of pepper
1 teaspoon Worcestershire sauce
¼ cup ketchup

Prepare rice as directed on package. Add part of the onion (1 tablespoon) and parsley. Meanwhile, soak bread in milk. Add meat, egg, salt, pepper, Worcestershire sauce, ketchup and remaining onion. Place layer of meat mixture in bottom of greased loaf pan, 8×5×3 inches. Add rice and rest of meat mixture in alternating layers. Make 2 layers of rice and 3 layers of meat, ending with meat. Bake in moderate oven (350°) for 45 minutes. Serve on platter.

SUGGESTED MENU: With the meat loaf serve cauliflower with browned crumbs, chopped kale and beet relish. For dessert, fruit compote.

BACON-LATTICED MEAT LOAF

6 to 8 Servings

1½ lbs. lean ground beef
1 cup parsley, chopped
1 cup onion, chopped
1½ teaspoons salt
¼ teaspoon pepper

1 teaspoon Ac'cent
1½ teaspoons Worcestershire sauce
½ cup fine bread crumbs
1 cup water
6 slices bacon, partially cooked

Combine all ingredients except bacon; blend well. Pack into loaf pan, 8×5×3 inches. Bake in slow oven (325°) for 45 to 50 minutes. Arrange half-cooked bacon lattice-fashion over top of meat loaf. Continue baking 10 to 15 minutes longer, or place under broiler heat until bacon is crisp.

SUGGESTED MENU: Serve Spanish rice and creamed mushrooms with the meat loaf. Add a tossed salad. For dessert, rhubarb pie and cheese.

MARSHFIELD MEAT LOAF   8 to 10 Servings

2 lbs. lean ground beef
2 cups soft bread crumbs
2 eggs, well beaten
2 teaspoons salt
1 tablespoon prepared mustard

¼ cup prepared horse-radish
1 large onion, minced
2 teaspoons Worcestershire sauce
2 to 3 drops Tabasco
1 cup ketchup

Combine all ingredients except ½ cup of the ketchup. Pack in greased loaf pan 8×5×3 inches. Bake in moderate oven (350°) for 1 hour and 15 minutes. Garnish meat with remaining ½ cup ketchup.

SUGGESTED MENU: Baked yams and scalloped zucchini squash with the meat loaf. Add lettuce wedges with Thousand Island dressing. For dessert, pumpkin pie.

BEEF PINWHEEL   8 Servings

½ cup onion, chopped
2 tablespoons fat or salad oil
2 lbs. lean ground beef
1 teaspoon salt
1 cup soft bread crumbs

2 teaspoons Worcestershire sauce
¼ cup milk
bread stuffing
mashed potatoes

Cook onion in hot fat or oil until tender. Combine with beef, salt, crumbs, Worcestershire sauce and milk; mix well. Form an oblong about 10×14 inches by rolling between 2 sheets of wax paper. Remove top paper and spread surface with stuffing. Roll up firmly. Place on heat-proof platter. Bake in moderate oven (325°) for 1 hour and 15 minutes. With pastry bag and rose tip, press out rosettes of mashed potato around meat. Return to oven to brown for about 15 minutes.

BREAD STUFFING

½ cup onion, minced
¼ cup butter or margarine
4 cups soft bread crumbs

½ teaspoon salt
dash pepper
¼ teaspoon oregano

Brown onion in butter or margarine. Combine all ingredients.

SUGGESTED MENU: Serve mashed butternut squash and green peas with the meat loaf. Add an endive and celery salad. For dessert, pineapple refrigerator cake.

UPSIDE-DOWN MEAT LOAF   6 Servings

¾ cup packaged bread stuffing
½ cup milk
⅓ cup ketchup
1 medium-size onion, chopped
1½ lbs. lean ground beef
¾ teaspoon salt

dash pepper
¾ teaspoon Ac'cent
few drops Tabasco
½ teaspoon Worcestershire sauce
3 to 4 canned cling peach halves
currant jelly

Empty stuffing into large bowl. Combine milk and ketchup. Pour over stuffing and let stand for 15 minutes or until stuffing is soft. Add remaining ingredients except two peaches and jelly; mix until well blended. Arrange peach halves, cut side down, in greased loaf pan; cover with meat mixture. Bake in moderate oven (350°) for 1 hour. Serve on platter. Fill centers of peach halves with currant jelly.

SUGGESTED MENU: Scalloped potatoes, buttered asparagus and a tossed salad with the meat loaf. For dessert, baked custard.

WYOMING MEAT LOAF   12 to 14 Servings

3 lbs. lean ground beef
1 lb. ground pork
1 medium-size onion, finely chopped (about ½ cup)
½ green pepper, chopped (about ½ cup)
1 cup celery, diced

3 eggs
1 cup cooked oatmeal
1½ cups cracker crumbs
½ cup ketchup
4 teaspoons salt
¼ teaspoon pepper

Combine all ingredients. Mix well. Pack in 2 greased loaf pans 8×5×3 inches. Bake in moderate oven (350°) for 1½ hours.

SUGGESTED MENU: With the meat loaf serve Mexican corn and buttered green beans. Add a tossed salad. Wind up with fruit gelatin.

WISCONSIN-STYLE BURGER BALLS   6 to 8 Servings

1½ lbs. lean ground beef
¾ cup rolled oats
¾ cup evaporated milk
¼ cup sour cream
1 large onion, finely chopped
1½ teaspoons salt
¼ teapsoon pepper

4 tablespoons fat or salad oil
2 tablespoons Worcestershire sauce
3 tablespoons vinegar
2 tablespoons brown sugar
1 cup ketchup
½ cup water

Mix meat, oats, evaporated milk, sour cream, onion and seasonings. Shape into balls and fry in hot fat or salad oil. Combine remaining ingredients and pour over meat balls in pan. Reduce heat to simmer; cook for 25 minutes.

SUGGESTED MENU: Serve whipped potatoes and buttered Brussels sprouts with the burgers. Add a stuffed celery salad. For dessert, cherry pie.

WESTERN HASH
6 Servings

2 tablespoons butter or margarine
¼ cup onion, finely chopped
¼ cup green pepper, chopped
1 lb. lean ground beef
1 teaspoon salt
1 teaspoon chili powder

¼ cup molasses
¼ cup prepared mustard
2 tablespoons Worcestershire sauce
¼ cup ripe olives, chopped (optional)
1 No. 303 can (1 lb.) tomatoes
1 cup uncooked rice

Melt butter or margarine in large skillet. Add onion and green pepper. Cook until onion is tender, but not brown. Add ground beef, half of the salt (½ teaspoon) and chili powder. Brown beef, breaking up with a fork. While it is browning, combine molasses and prepared mustard. Stir in Worcestershire sauce. Add to beef mixture with ripe olives, tomatoes and remaining ½ teaspoon salt. Add rice slowly. Cover and reduce heat. Simmer for 25 to 30 minutes or until rice is tender.

SUGGESTED MENU: Add a salad of tomatoes, cucumbers and spring onions, tossed with shredded lettuce and a blue cheese dressing. For dessert, rhubarb and strawberry roly-poly.

TOMATO-CHEESE BURGERS
6 Servings

1 ½ lbs. lean ground beef
1 small onion, chopped
2 tablespoons fat or salad oil
1 ½ teaspoons salt

¼ teaspoon pepper
1 No. 303 can (1 lb.) tomatoes
½ lb. sharp cheddar cheese, diced

Brown beef and onion in hot fat or oil. Pour excess fat from pan. Season beef mixture with salt and pepper. Add tomatoes. Cook for 15 to 20 minutes, or until mixture in pan has absorbed most of the juice. Add diced cheese and cook for about 5 minutes longer. Serve on hot soft buns.

SUGGESTED MENU: Add a salad of cooked vegetables or raw vegetable relishes. For dessert, cherry tarts.

OLIVE CHEESEBURGERS
8 Servings

1 ½ cups soft bread crumbs
3 tablespoons olive brine
3 tablespoons water
1 teaspoon Ac'cent
⅛ teaspoon pepper

1 ½ lbs. lean ground beef
prepared mustard
1 dozen large stuffed olives
8 slices (½-lb. pkg.) Swiss cheese

Combine first 5 ingredients; mix well. Add ground beef and form into 8 large patties. Broil on one side for about 7 minutes, with meat about 3 inches below source of heat. Turn, spread with mustard and cover with sliced olives. Top each patty with slice of cheese. Broil 5 minutes longer, or until cheese melts and is delicately browned.

SUGGESTED MENU: With the cheeseburgers serve fried sweet potatoes and scalloped mixed vegetables. Add a salad of water cress vinaigrette. For dessert, Boston cream pie.

WEST COAST CHEESEBURGERS

6 Servings

1 tablespoon instant minced onion or
¼ cup raw onion, finely chopped
¼ cup fine bread crumbs
1 egg
⅓ cup milk
1 teaspoon salt

1 teaspoon prepared mustard
1 lb. lean ground beef
6 sticks American cheese (about ¼ × ¼ × 5 in.)
6 frankfurter buns
butter or margarine

Combine onion, crumbs, egg, milk, salt and mustard; mix well. Add beef; mix thoroughly with fork. Divide into 6 portions. Shape each into a log around a stick of cheese, enclosing cheese completely. Place on shallow baking pan. Bake in hot oven (400°) for about 20 minutes or until well browned. Meanwhile, split and toast buns and spread with butter or margarine. Place cheeseburger log in each toasted bun. Serve at once.

SUGGESTED MENU: Serve tomato soup in cups as a beverage with the cheeseburgers. Add sliced cucumbers and onion rings in a sharp dressing. For dessert, blueberry pie.

THREE-DECKER HAMBURGERS

6 Servings

2 lbs. lean ground beef
  salt and pepper
½ lb. blue cheese
¼ cup onion, minced

½ teaspoon Worcestershire sauce
  few drops Tabasco
  strong, cold coffee
6 hamburger buns

Season beef with salt and pepper. Form into 12 thin patties. Break up cheese and add onion, Worcestershire sauce and Tabasco. Beat until well blended. Add enough coffee to make soft, spreading consistency; spread between hamburger patties, sandwich-fashion. Broil, turning once. Serve on hot, toasted hamburger buns.

SUGGESTED MENU: Serve cream of mushroom soup as a beverage with the hamburgers. Try Waldorf salad with cream mayonnaise as both salad and dessert.

STUFFED MEAT ROLL WITH MUSHROOM SAUCE

6 Servings

4 tablespoons butter or margarine
2 tablespoons onion, minced
4 cups soft bread crumbs
½ cup celery, finely diced
2 tablespoons parsley, chopped

1 teaspoon salt
¼ teaspoon pepper
1 lb. lean ground beef
¼ cup milk
  mushroom sauce

Melt butter or margarine and add onion; cook until tender, but not brown. Add bread crumbs, celery, parsley, half of salt (½ teaspoon) and half of pepper (⅛ teaspoon). Mix lightly; reserve. Combine beef, milk, remaining salt and pepper; mix in 1 cup of the stuffing. Put wax paper on breadboard; place meat on paper. Flour rolling pin; roll meat into rectangle 9 × 11 inches. Spread remaining stuffing on meat; roll as for jelly roll. Place in shallow baking pan; bake in moderate oven (350°) for 45 minutes.

MUSHROOM SAUCE

1 can (4 oz.) button mushrooms (undrained)   ¼ teaspoon salt
1 tablespoon flour

Drain mushrooms. Add enough water to mushroom liquid to make 1 cup. Add flour and salt to drippings in pan; stir smooth. Add liquid. Cook, stirring constantly, until mixture thickens and comes to a boil. Add mushrooms. Heat to serving temperature.

SUGGESTED MENU: Parslied rice, buttered asparagus cuts and sliced carrots with the meat roll. Add a salad of iceberg lettuce chunks. For dessert, strawberry Bavarian cream.

SUPREME OF BEEF AND RICE   6 Servings

1½ lbs. lean ground beef
2 to 3 tablespoons fat or salad oil
1 teaspoon salt
½ teaspoon pepper
2 medium-size onions, ground
3 carrots, ground

1 green pepper, ground
2 stalks celery, diced
2 bouillon cubes
2 cups hot water
1 cup uncooked rice

Brown meat in hot fat or oil in a large skillet. Season. Add remaining ingredients. Cover and cook over low heat for about 45 minutes.

SUGGESTED MENU: Serve crisp, tender Brussels sprouts and buttered wax beans with the meat dish. For dessert, fresh pears and blue cheese.

ROUND-UP-TIME CHUCK (for a crowd)   25 Servings

½ cup chopped suet
4 large onions, chopped
4 lbs. lean ground beef
salt and pepper

2 tablespoons chili powder
1 lb. dry pinto or kidney beans, cooked tender
2 No. 2½ cans (3½ cups ea.) tomatoes
2 pkgs. (1 lb. ea.) noodles, cooked

Heat chopped suet in skillet and brown onions and beef in it. Season to taste with salt and pepper. Turn mixture into saucepan or kettle large enough to hold remaining ingredients. Stir in chili powder, cooked beans and tomatoes. Cook over low to moderate heat, stirring occasionally, for about 40 minutes. Add cooked noodles and simmer 10 to 15 minutes longer, or until heated thoroughly.

SUGGESTED MENU: Big bowls of salad, a variety of relishes, buttered rolls and lots of coffee with the meat dish. For dessert, layer cake or pie.

SKILLET BEEF 'N HOMINY

6 Servings

3 tablespoons fat or salad oil
1 onion, chopped
1 lb. lean ground beef
½ cup tomato juice (or ketchup)
1 teaspoon salt

1 tablespoon chili powder
1 No. 303 can (1 lb.) hominy
½ cup stuffed olives, sliced
1 cup American cheese, shredded
paprika

Heat fat or oil in heavy skillet. Add onion and beef; fry and stir until beef is no longer pink. Add tomato juice or ketchup, salt, chili powder, hominy and olives. Cover and cook slowly for 20 minutes. Spread cheese over top; sprinkle with paprika (don't stir). Cover and cook 5 minutes more, until cheese is melted. Serve from the skillet.

SUGGESTED MENU: Green bean succotash with the meat. For dessert, melon cup.

SOUTH DAKOTA MEAT LOAF

6 Servings

3 lbs. lean ground beef
½ lb. bulk sausage
1 egg
1 teaspoon salt
1 cup beef broth or stock

dash pepper
1 small onion, chopped
2 cups bread crumbs
1 can condensed tomato soup

Combine all ingredients; pack lightly in large, greased loaf pan. Bake in moderate oven (325°) for 1½ hours.

SUGGESTED MENU: With the meat loaf serve Lyonnaise potatoes, red cabbage and apple slaw. For dessert, frosted angel cake.

RANCH MEAT LOAF

10 to 12 Servings

1 onion, chopped
¾ cup celery, sliced
¼ cup fat or salad oil
⅓ cup green pepper, minced
2 teaspoons salt
2 eggs

3 cups soft bread crumbs
½ cup water
2 lbs. lean ground beef
½ cup tomato juice
2 tablespoons butter or margarine, melted

Brown onion and celery in hot fat or oil in heavy skillet. Combine with green pepper, salt, eggs, bread crumbs, and water to make stuffing. Add half this stuffing (1½ cups) to meat, mixing well. Pat out half this meat mixture in greased 2-quart loaf pan. Cover meat with remaining stuffing and top with rest of meat mixture. Bake in moderate oven (350°) for 1¼ hours. Combine tomato juice and butter or margarine. After loaf has cooked for 15 minutes, pour half tomato mixture over meat. After another 15 minutes, cover meat with remaining mixture.

SUGGESTED MENU: Serve baked yams and cream-style corn with the meat loaf. Add a green salad. For dessert, baked pears and hermit cookies.

QUICK TAMALE-PIE CASSEROLE

4 Servings

1 lb. lean ground beef
1 onion, thinly sliced
3 tablespoons fat or salad oil
3 large tamales, sliced

2 cans (8 oz. ea.) seasoned tomato sauce
1 No. 303 can (1 lb.) whole-kernel corn
1 cup sharp cheese, grated

Brown beef and onion in hot fat or oil. Mix in sliced tamales, tomato sauce and corn. Turn into greased casserole; top with grated cheese. Bake in moderate oven (350°) for 30 minutes.

SUGGESTED MENU: Hot biscuits and a tossed green salad round out this meal-in-a-dish menu. For dessert, canned Elberta peaches and unfrosted angel cake.

QUICK BEEF AND BEANS

4 Servings

1 onion, minced
3 tablespoons butter or margarine
1 lb. lean ground beef

1 No. 303 can (1 lb.) red kidney beans
2 tablespoons lemon juice or vinegar
salt and pepper

Cook onion in butter or margarine until yellow. Add meat and cook, breaking up with fork, until no pink color remains and meat begins to brown. Add beans and lemon juice or vinegar; season with salt and pepper. Simmer for 20 minutes.

SUGGESTED MENU: Crisp, buttered French bread and a tossed salad with the beef and beans. Top off with fresh fruit and cheese.

PLANKED PATTIES

4 Servings

½ teaspoon Tabasco
½ cup milk
1 cup soft bread crumbs
½ teaspoon salt
1 teaspoon onion, grated

1 lb. lean ground beef
1 No. 303 can (1 lb.) green beans
melted butter or margarine
nutmeg
2 cups mashed potatoes

Mix Tabasco and milk; pour over crumbs. Add salt. Mash crumbs to soft mass in milk. Add onion and ground beef; mix well with fork. Shape into 4 large patties. Brown on one side in lightly greased skillet over moderate heat for about 7 minutes. Place, cooked side down, on center of plank or heat-proof platter. Arrange green beans around patties in a border. Pour a little melted butter or margarine over green beans; sprinkle with nutmeg. Make a border of mashed potatoes around outer rim of plank. Brush with melted butter or margarine. Place plank in broiler with surface of food 3 inches below heat. Broil for 5 minutes or until potatoes are lightly browned.

SUGGESTED MENU: Add jellied perfection salad, hot rolls and a dessert of fresh fruit and cheese.

OKLAHOMA CASSEROLE

6 Servings

1 ½ lbs. lean ground beef
2 tablespoons salad oil
2 teaspoons salt
1 No. 303 can (1 lb.) whole-kernel corn

1 can (3 or 4 oz.) mushrooms, chopped
½-lb. pkg. noodles, cooked
2 cups tomato juice
1 cup cheese, grated

Brown beef in hot oil; sprinkle with salt. Arrange ingredients in large casserole or baking dish in order given, beginning with browned beef and topping off with cheese. Bake in moderate oven (325°) for about 1 hour.

SUGGESTED MENU: This is a meal-in-a-dish, and needs only a green salad or raw vegetable relishes to complete the menu. For dessert, pineapple ambrosia.

NORTHWEST MEAT LOAF

6 to 8 Servings

1 ½ lbs. lean ground beef
1 small onion, chopped
2 teaspoons salt
¼ teaspoon pepper
⅛ teaspoon seasoned salt
1 cup cracker crumbs
1 cup milk

1 egg, beaten
¼ cup tomato soup
½ cup ketchup
3 tablespoons brown sugar
¼ teaspoon nutmeg
1 teaspoon dry mustard

Combine meat, onion, seasonings, crumbs, milk, egg and soup. Turn into greased baking pan and mold into loaf. Mix remaining ingredients; pour over loaf. Bake in moderate oven (350°) for 1 hour.

SUGGESTED MENU: Buttered beets and lima beans with the meat loaf, plus a tossed salad. For dessert, baked apples and cream.

MEAT CAKES TEXARKANA

6 Servings

²/₃ cup seedless raisins
2 cups cooked rice
2 lbs. ground beef chuck
2 teaspoons salt
⅛ teaspoon Tabasco
¹/₃ cup fat or salad oil

1 small garlic clove, minced
¾ cup onion, chopped
3 tablespoons flour
2 tablespoons chili powder
3 cups water

Rinse raisins in hot water; drain. Combine rice, meat, salt and Tabasco; shape into 12 patties. Fry in part of fat or oil (2 tablespoons) until brown on both sides. Remove from skillet. Pour remaining fat or oil into skillet. Add garlic and onion and cook until golden brown. Pour in flour and chili powder; blend well. Add water; cook and stir over low heat until thickened. Add raisins and meat patties; cover and simmer for 15 minutes.

SUGGESTED MENU: Serve buttered green beans and cauliflower au gratin with the meat cakes. For dessert, chocolate pudding.

BARBECUED KANSAS BEEF RING

4 to 6 Servings

2 lbs. lean ground beef
1 ½ cups uncooked rolled oats
1 ½ cups milk
2 small onions, minced (about ⅔ cup)
2 ½ teaspoons salt
¼ teaspoon pepper

2 tablespoons Worcestershire sauce
3 tablespoons vinegar
2 tablespoons sugar
1 cup ketchup
½ cup water

Combine beef, oats, milk, onions, salt and pepper; mix well. Press into greased 5-cup ring mold. Bake in moderate oven (375°) for 20 minutes. Combine remaining ingredients; bring to rapid boil. Turn ring-loaf out into shallow baking pan and pour sauce over it. Return to oven; continue baking for about 45 minutes, basting with sauce in pan several times during cooking.

SUGGESTED MENU: Fill center of meat ring with brown rice and mushrooms. Add buttered kale or other greens and a salad of grated raw carrots and raisins. For dessert, frosted spice cake and raspberries, fresh or frozen.

LAYERED MEAT LOAF

8 Servings

4 cups soft bread crumbs
1 small onion, grated
2 teaspoons poultry seasoning
½ cup butter or margarine, melted

1 teaspoon salt
dash pepper
2 lbs. lean ground beef
1 egg

Combine first 3 ingredients with half of salt (½ teaspoon) and pepper; mix well. Add enough hot water to hold mixture together. Combine remaining ingredients, including remaining salt; mix well. Pack half the meat mixture in loaf pan 8×5×3 inches. Add bread-crumb mixture and top with remaining meat mixture. Bake in moderate oven (375°) for 1 hour.

SUGGESTED MENU: Candied yams and broccoli accompany the meat loaf. Add a salad of tomato aspic. For dessert, baked caramel custard.

HOT-DOG HAMBURGERS (for a crowd)

25 Servings

10 slices bread
1 pint (2 cups) milk
5 lbs. lean ground beef
2 medium-size onions, finely chopped
2 teaspoons salt

1 teaspoon pepper
2 teaspoons Ac'cent
25 slices bacon
25 frankfurter buns, split and toasted

Soak bread in milk; combine with meat, onion and seasonings. Shape into 25 rolls the same length as the buns. Wrap each meat roll in strip of bacon. Bake in moderate oven (350°) until meat and bacon are done as desired. Serve hot in the buns.

SUGGESTED MENU: Serve potato salad garnished with tomato and cucumber slices, beet relish and coleslaw with the hamburgers. For dessert, ice cream and frosted cake squares.

HEARTY CASSEROLE

6 Servings

1½ lbs. lean ground beef
1 teaspoon Ac'cent
1½ teaspoons salt
¼ teaspoon pepper
¼ teaspoon oregano or thyme
2 tablespoons fat or salad oil

2 cups potatoes (about 2 large potatoes), thinly sliced
2 medium-size onions, sliced
1 can (20 oz.) kidney beans
¾ cup chili sauce
2 slices bacon (optional)

Break up meat with fork in mixing bowl. Sprinkle Ac'cent, salt, pepper and oregano or thyme over surface of meat. Toss gently to distribute seasonings. Put meat in skillet. Cook in hot fat or oil, breaking meat up with a fork, just until browned. Layer meat, potato slices, onion slices, kidney beans and chili sauce in a 2½-quart casserole, beginning and ending with meat. If desired, top with a few of the potato slices and 2 slices bacon. Cover; bake in moderate oven (375°) for 40 minutes. Uncover and bake 20 minutes longer.

SUGGESTED MENU: Nothing but a tossed green salad is needed to supplement this one-dish meal. For dessert, cup custard with fruit sauce.

HAMBURGER SOUP

7 Servings

1 lb. lean ground beef
1 large onion, sliced
1 tablespoon fat or salad oil
¼ teaspoon leaf oregano
1½ teaspoons salt

⅛ teaspoon pepper
1 can condensed consommé
1 No. 303 can (1 lb.) tomatoes
1 No. 303 can (1 lb.) lima beans

Cook ground beef and onion in hot fat or oil until browned. Pour off drippings. Add oregano, salt, pepper, consommé and tomatoes. Cover tightly and simmer for 15 minutes. Add lima beans and continue simmering uncovered for 15 minutes.

SUGGESTED MENU: With the soup serve chunks of hot garlic bread. Follow with a green salad. For dessert, prune whip.

HAMBURGER-ONION ROLLS

12 Servings

2 lbs. lean ground beef
2 medium-size onions, grated
dash Tabasco
3 tablespoons chili sauce
2 eggs

2 teaspoons Worcestershire sauce
2 teaspoons prepared mustard
1 teaspoon salt
⅛ teaspoon pepper
12 hamburger rolls

Combine all ingredients except rolls; mix well. Split rolls; spread meat mixture on cut surfaces. Broil for about 10 minutes, with surface of meat 3 inches beneath heating unit or element. Serve at once.

SUGGESTED MENU: Serve pea soup as a beverage with the hamburger-onion rolls. Add a salad of sliced tomatoes and cucumbers. For dessert, deep-dish cherry pie.

FOLD-OVER HAMBURGERS

4 Servings

1 lb. lean ground beef
1 teaspoon salt
⅛ teaspoon pepper
2 teaspoons Worcestershire sauce

4 tablespoons onion, finely chopped
4 thin slices tomato
4 hamburger buns, toasted

Mix ground beef with salt and pepper; flatten into a large square. Divide into 8 equal parts and make a thin patty of each part. Combine Worcestershire sauce and onion. On half the patties place a slice of tomato and a tablespoon of onion mixture. Top with a second patty and pinch edges together. Place in a shallow pan; broil about 15 minutes, turning once. Serve on toasted hamburger buns.

SUGGESTED MENU: Serve cream of broccoli soup as a beverage with the hamburgers. Add a cucumber salad. For dessert, coffee Spanish cream.

DINNER PATTIES

4 Servings

2 lbs. lean ground beef
2 teaspoons salt
¼ teaspoon pepper (optional)
2 tablespoons onion, chopped

½ cup mushrooms, chopped
1 tablespoon fat or salad oil
2 tablespoons butter or margarine
1 tablespoon lemon juice

Sprinkle beef with salt. (Add pepper, if desired.) Brown onion and mushrooms lightly in hot fat or oil; add to beef; mix thoroughly. Shape into 4 large patties 1½ inches thick. Place patties on pan or aluminum foil and broil about 3 inches below source of heat for about 10 minutes on each side or until crispy brown on both sides and rare inside. Combine butter or margarine and lemon juice. Spread on hamburgers.

SUGGESTED MENU: With the patties serve home-fried potatoes, asparagus au gratin and Harvard beets. Fruit salad with cream mayonnaise completes the dinner.

DEVILED HAMBURGERS

6 Servings

1 lb. lean ground beef
2 tablespoons ketchup
1 teaspoon salt
1 tablespoon prepared horse-radish
1 tablespoon onion, minced

1 teaspoon Worcestershire sauce
1 teaspoon prepared mustard
6 hamburger buns, toasted
butter or margarine

Mix first 7 ingredients lightly; shape into 6 patties. Broil quickly on both sides. Serve on hot toasted hamburger buns spread with additional mustard and butter or margarine.

SUGGESTED MENU: Serve with assorted sliced cheeses, dill pickles and coleslaw. For dessert, marble cake slices with ice cream and chocolate sauce.

CHILI BURGUNDIES

6 Servings

1 ½ lbs. lean ground beef
3 tablespoons bacon drippings

2 cans (15 oz. ea.) chili con carne with beans
²⁄₃ cup Burgundy wine

Shape ground beef into cakes; brown well in bacon drippings. While cakes are browning, heat chili con carne to boiling; stir in wine. Pour chili mixture over browned meat cakes. Cover and simmer for 5 minutes.

SUGGESTED MENU: Hot corn bread, grilled tomatoes, sliced cucumber and onion rings in sweetened vinegar accompany the meat. For dessert, peach tapioca cream.

CALIFORNIA MEAT LOAF

6 Servings

¾ lb. lean ground beef
1 large raw potato, peeled and grated
1 ½ teaspoons salt
¼ teaspoon pepper
¼ teaspoon sage

2 tablespoons cream or sour cream
1 cup canned whole-kernel corn
1 large onion, thinly sliced
1 cup canned whole tomatoes

Combine beef, potato, seasonings and cream or sour cream. Spread ½ mixture in greased loaf pan 8 × 5 × 3 inches. Add layer of corn, layer of onion and layer of tomatoes. Sprinkle with seasonings to taste. Cover with remaining meat mixture. Bake in moderate oven (350°) for 1 hour.

SUGGESTED MENU: Add a salad of greens, sliced cucumbers, sliced stuffed olives and cubed Swiss cheese. For dessert, melon wedges served with powdered ginger and sugar.

BEEF ROLLS

12 Servings

2 tablespoons butter or margarine
2 medium-size onions, finely chopped
1 garlic clove, minced
3 lbs. lean ground beef chuck
3 eggs
1 tablespoon prepared mustard
1 ½ teaspoons salt

dash pepper
3 tablespoons salad oil
½ cup dry red table wine
1 tablespoon tomato paste
1 teaspoon cornstarch (optional)
mushroom caps (optional)

Melt butter or margarine in frying pan; add onions and garlic. Cook over low heat for 5 minutes. Combine beef and eggs; add mustard and onion mixture, salt and pepper. Divide mixture in half; shape into 2 rolls about 3 inches in diameter. Place in roasting pan with salad oil. Bake in moderate oven (325°) for 45 minutes to 1 hour. Remove rolls to hot platter; keep warm. Add wine and tomato paste to drippings in roasting pan; stir smooth. Thicken with cornstarch if desired; pour over rolls.

SUGGESTED MENU: Corn pudding and Brussels sprouts with the meat rolls. Add a tossed salad. For dessert, lemon tapioca cream.

BEEF-POTATO WHIRLIGIGS

6 Servings

1 lb. lean ground beef
1 ½ teaspoons salt
¼ teaspoon pepper
1 egg
2 tablespoons fat or salad oil

6 tablespoons bread crumbs
2 tablespoons milk
1 ½ cups potatoes, mashed
1 ½ cups peas, mashed
¼ cup butter or margarine, melted

Combine all except last 3 ingredients. Place between 2 sheets wax paper; press or roll out with rolling pin into rectangular sheet about ½ inch thick. Remove top piece of wax paper; spread half the surface with mashed potatoes. Spread other half with mashed peas. Roll meat firmly, jelly-roll fashion, starting at potato end. Wrap in wax paper; chill. When ready to cook, cut crosswise into 1-inch slices. Place on broiler rack 3 to 4 inches below heat source. Brush with melted butter or margarine. Broil slowly for about 10 minutes. Turn (with pancake turner), brush again with butter or margarine and finish broiling.

SUGGESTED MENU: With the whirligigs serve baked acorn squash and tomato aspic salad. For dessert, chocolate soufflé.

BEEFBURGERS

4 Servings

1 lb. lean ground beef
3 tablespoons ketchup
2 teaspoons prepared mustard
1 ½ teaspoons horse-radish
1 small onion, finely chopped

1 teaspoon salt
½ cup soft bread crumbs
¼ cup top milk or thin cream
1 ½ teaspoons Worcestershire sauce

Combine all ingredients. Shape into 4 large or 8 small patties. Broil on pan 3 inches below source of heat for about 6 minutes on each side for large patties (4 minutes for smaller ones), or until browned outside and moderately well-done inside.

SUGGESTED MENU: Creamed potatoes and peas would be good with the burgers. Add raw carrot sticks and celery. For dessert, deep-dish cherry pie.

BEEF CHILI PATTIES

4 Servings

1 lb. lean ground beef
3 teaspoons salt
⅛ teaspoon pepper
1 egg, beaten
2 tablespoons onion, chopped

2 tablespoons green pepper, chopped
2 tablespoons fat or salad oil
1 No. 303 can (1 lb.) tomatoes
1 can (12 oz.) whole-kernel corn
1 teaspoon chili powder

Combine ground beef, one of your 3 teaspoons of salt, pepper and egg. Shape into 8 small patties; place in baking dish. Cook onion and green pepper in hot fat or oil for 2 minutes. Add tomatoes, corn, chili powder and remaining salt (2 teaspoons); pour over patties. Bake in slow oven (300°) for 30 minutes.

SUGGESTED MENU: Whipped potatoes, buttered baby lima beans and a tossed green salad accompany the patties. For dessert, apple dumplings.

BARBECUED MEAT BALLS AND CORN

4 Servings

1 lb. lean ground beef
½ cup uncooked rolled oats
2 teaspoons salt
⅛ teaspoon pepper
½ cup evaporated milk
2 tablespoons flour

1 teaspoon paprika
2 tablespoons fat or salad oil
½ cup onion, chopped
¼ cup bottled barbecue sauce
1 ¼ cups water
1 No. 303 can (1 lb.) whole-kernel corn

Mix meat, oats, half of salt (1 teaspoon), pepper and milk. Shape into medium-size balls. Combine flour, paprika and remaining salt (1 teaspoon). Roll meat balls in flour mixture. Brown in heavy skillet in hot fat or oil. Reduce heat, add onion and cook for about 5 minutes or until soft. Stir in barbecue sauce and water. Cover and simmer for 45 minutes, turning meat balls several times. Add corn; heat rapidly. Serve at once.

SUGGESTED MENU: Serve potato chips and green beans vinaigrette with the meat balls. For dessert, watermelon slices.

BARBECUED HAMBURGERS

12 Servings

2 ½ lbs. lean ground beef
1 large onion, minced
2 tablespoons fat or salad oil
¼ cup brown sugar

1 cup hot ketchup
1 tablespoon Worcestershire sauce
salt and pepper
12 hamburger buns, toasted

Brown meat and onion in hot fat or oil. Break up meat with fork while cooking. Stir in remaining ingredients. Simmer for about 15 minutes. Spoon over toasted buns.

SUGGESTED MENU: Serve carrot and cabbage slaw with the hamburgers; blueberry dumplings for dessert.

BAKED BEEF AND RICE

6 Servings

1 lb. lean ground beef
1 cup uncooked rice
1 small onion, chopped
2 tablespoons fat or salad oil
1 teaspoon salt
½ teaspoon pepper

1 teaspoon paprika
1 small bottle stuffed olives, sliced
2 cups tomato juice
1 ½ cups boiling water
½ cup cheddar cheese, grated

Cook beef, rice and onion in hot fat or oil until lightly browned. Season with salt, pepper and paprika. Add sliced olives, tomato juice and boiling water. Turn into 1 ½-quart casserole, cover and bake in slow oven (300°) for 1 hour. Uncover, sprinkle with cheese and bake 10 minutes longer, or until cheese is melted.

SUGGESTED MENU: With the casserole serve green peas and mashed yellow turnips. Add small servings of perfection salad. For dessert, coconut cake.

BAKED BEEF AND SAUERKRAUT CASSEROLE
4 Servings

1 lb. lean ground beef
1 egg
2 tablespoons flour
¼ cup onion, finely chopped
1 teaspoon salt

⅛ teaspoon pepper
3 tablespoons fat or salad oil
3 cups sauerkraut
½ cup ketchup

Combine meat, egg, flour, onion and seasonings. Brown in hot fat or oil, breaking up meat mixture as it cooks. Alternate layers of cooked meat and sauerkraut in greased casserole. Spread top with ketchup; cover. Bake in moderate oven (350°) for 1 hour.

SUGGESTED MENU: With the casserole serve baked potatoes and a salad of sliced beets. For dessert, fruit cup and sugar cookies.

BACON-WRAPPED HAMBURGERS
4 Servings

1½ teaspoons Ac'cent
2 teaspoons salt
dash pepper
¼ cup onion, minced
½ cup evaporated milk

¾ cup chili sauce
1 cup whole bran
1½ lbs. lean ground beef
8 strips bacon

Combine first 6 ingredients; mix well. Pour over bran and let stand for 10 minutes or until bran absorbs liquid. Add meat; mix lightly. Form into 8 patties. Wrap bacon strip around each patty; secure with wooden picks. Broil with surface of meat 3 inches below source of heat until bacon is crisp (about 10 minutes), turning once.

SUGGESTED MENU: Serve mashed sweet potatoes, stewed tomatoes and a green salad with the hamburgers. Top off with apple crisp.

BAKED STEAK
4 Servings

1 sirloin or porterhouse steak, 3 in. thick
2 tablespoons butter or margarine
3 onions, chopped
½ cup chili sauce
1 teaspoon parsley, chopped

1 teaspoon Worcestershire sauce
salt and pepper
1 lemon, thinly sliced
paprika

Quickly sear steak on both sides in very hot, dry skillet. Place in baking pan or shallow casserole. In same skillet, melt butter or margarine and cook onions until lightly browned. Spread buttery onions on top of steak. Combine chili sauce, parsley and seasonings. Spread over onions. Top with thin slices of lemon and sprinkle with paprika. Let stand at room temperature for 1 hour. Bake in moderate oven (350°) for 35 to 40 minutes, or until very tender.

SUGGESTED MENU: Baked yams and buttered green beans go well with the steak. Add a tossed salad if desired. For dessert, fruit gelatin with whipped cream.

IMPERIAL TENDERLOIN

12 to 16 Servings

1 beef tenderloin (4 lbs.)
¾ cup melted butter or margarine
1 garlic clove

1 tablespoon Worcestershire sauce
¼ lb. blue cheese

Trim surface of fat from tenderloin. Brush with a little of your melted butter or margarine (¼ cup). Roast on a rack in hot oven (450°) for approximately 45 minutes to one hour or until roast meat thermometer registers 140°. Mash garlic in Worcestershire sauce and combine with blue cheese and rest of melted butter or margarine (½ cup). Remove meat from oven. Spread cheese mixture over top of hot tenderloin and serve immediately.

SUGGESTED MENU: Stuffed baked potatoes, French green beans with almonds and tossed green salad with the beef. For dessert, fruit and toasted crackers.

DEVILED STEAK

6 Servings

beef arm steak, 1 in. thick
¼ cup flour
2 tablespoons fat or salad oil
1 large onion, sliced
1 teaspoon dry mustard

⅛ teaspoon paprika
1 teaspoon salt
⅛ teaspoon pepper
3 tablespoons vinegar
1 cup hot water

Cut steak into individual servings, dredge with flour and brown on both sides in hot fat or oil. Place sliced onion over meat and add seasonings, vinegar and hot water. Cover closely; cook in slow oven (300°) for about 1 hour or until tender. Thicken remaining liquid for gravy (page 195).

SUGGESTED MENU: Scalloped potatoes and buttered asparagus with the steak. Add an orange-avocado salad. For dessert, chocolate chiffon pie.

RED-INDIAN STEW

4 to 6 Servings

2 tablespoons fat or salad oil
1 onion, chopped
½ green pepper, chopped
1 lb. lean beef, coarsely ground
dash chili powder

2 to 3 cups fresh corn, cut from cob
1 can condensed tomato soup
2 teaspoons sugar
1½ teaspoons salt

Heat fat or oil in heavy skillet and cook onion and pepper until soft. Brown meat. Add remaining ingredients and simmer for 1 hour.

SUGGESTED MENU: Hot, crusty rolls, celery, carrot sticks, cucumber sticks and spring onions or scallions accompany the stew. For dessert, berries and cream with sponge cake.

STEAMED SUET PUDDING
10 to 12 Servings

1 cup ground suet
1 cup molasses
1 cup seedless raisins
1 cup dried currants
3 cups flour, sifted
2 teaspoons baking powder

½ teaspoon salt
1 teaspoon cloves
1 teaspoon cinnamon
1 ½ cups milk
¾ cup walnuts, chopped

Combine suet, molasses, raisins and currants. Mix and sift dry ingredients; add to suet mixture alternately with milk, beating well after each addition. Stir in walnuts. Turn into greased 2-quart mold, cover tightly and steam for 3 hours. Serve hot with hard sauce.

MINCEMEAT
Makes 4 quarts

4 lbs. lean round steak
1 lb. suet
1 lb. citron
1 peck apples
4 lbs. seeded raisins

1 gallon cider
2 tablespoons nutmeg
3 ½ lbs. sugar
2 tablespoons cinnamon
1 teaspoon cloves

Cover beef with boiling water and simmer until tender. Let cool in broth. Remove meat; cut fine. (Save broth for soup.) Put suet and citron through fine knife of food chopper. Pare, core and dice apples. Combine all ingredients. Cook slowly for 1 ½ hours, stirring occasionally to prevent sticking. Pour into hot sterilized pint or quart jars; seal so that jars are airtight.

FAVORITES FROM OTHER LANDS

FAVORITES FROM OTHER LANDS

This is a country of immigrants. Some came early, some came later and some are still arriving on our shores. And with these people, carried in their heads or on scraps of paper, come family heirlooms in the form of recipes from all over the world.

These recipes are our heritage. Like the people who brought them, they have gone into the melting pot and emerged somewhat changed, having been adapted to the customs and tastes of their new homeland. Still distinctive and flavorful, they are a decided addition to American cuisine.

BLANQUETTE DE VEAU (FRENCH)   6 to 8 Servings

2 ½ to 3 lbs. veal steak, cubed
   2 tablespoons fat or salad oil
   3 medium-size onions, sliced
   ½ bay leaf
   5 instant chicken bouillon cubes

3 cups water
½ carrot, cut in lengthwise strips
6 sprigs parsley
1 garlic clove
2 celery stalks with leaves

Brown veal cubes in hot fat or oil in heavy skillet, stirring often, until meat is golden brown. Add onions and bay leaf. Cook 3 minutes longer. Crumble bouillon cubes into skillet, add water and bring to a boil. Make a "bouquet garni" of remaining ingredients by tying them together firmly with white string; add and cook for 20 minutes. Remove meat. Simmer gravy for 30 minutes. Take out bouquet garni. Thicken gravy to desired consistency (page 195); add meat; reheat.

SUGGESTED MENU: Mashed potato cakes, baked acorn squash and green peas accompany the veal. For dessert, lattice-top peach pie.

BEEF BOURGUIGNON (FRENCH)   6 Servings

4 tablespoons butter or margarine
3 lbs. round steak, cut in 1 in. cubes
1 garlic clove, crushed
3 onions, sliced
4 tablespoons flour
2 cups Burgundy wine
1 cup water

2 teaspoons salt
½ teaspoon Ac'cent
½ teaspoon pepper
¼ teaspoon marjoram
¼ teaspoon oregano
½ cup strong black coffee

Melt butter or margarine in deep frying pan or chicken fryer. Add cubed round steak; brown on all sides. Add garlic and onions; cook until onions are soft, but not brown. Remove meat and onions from pan. Blend flour with butter or margarine remaining in pan or fryer. Add wine, water, seasonings and coffee. Stir until slightly thickened. Return meat and onions to kettle. Cover, bring to boil and simmer for 1 ½ hours, or until meat is tender.

SUGGESTED MENU: With the beef in its savory sauce serve baked potatoes, buttered green beans and baked butternut squash. For dessert, French pastry.

STEAK AU POIVRE (FRENCH)   6 Servings

2 lbs. boneless steak (round, chuck, sirloin   ¼ cup peppercorns, or very coarse black pepper
tip or rib), 1 to 1½ in. thick   3 tablespoons butter or margarine

Use meat tenderizer according to directions on page 19; do not add salt. Pierce both sides deeply with sharp fork to insure penetration and seal in juices. Let stand at room temperature for 1 hour, or cover loosely and refrigerate overnight. Using a rolling pin, crush peppercorns, or use coarse pepper; press into both sides of steak with heel of hand. (Cracked pepper is deliciously pungent, has a "bite," but is not hot. Its pungence, which is absorbed by the meat, is what makes this dish unusual.) Heat butter or margarine in a skillet and brown steak quickly on both sides. Lower heat and cook until done to taste. For 1-inch steak: 5 to 6 minutes per side for rare, 6 to 7 for medium. For 1½-inch steak: 7 to 8 minutes per side for rare, 10 minutes for medium. Transfer steak to hot platter. Serve at once.

SUGGESTED MENU: French-fried potatoes and corn on the cob with the steak. Add a green salad. For dessert, peach shortcake.

SPAGHETTI WITH MEAT BALLS (ITALIAN)   8 Servings

Sauce	Meat balls
¾ cup onion, minced	1½ lbs. lean ground beef
1 garlic clove, minced	⅛ teaspoon pepper
¼ cup salad oil	¼ teaspoon marjoram
2 cans (6 oz. ea.) tomato paste	⅓ cup parsley, minced
¾ cup water	1 egg, slightly beaten
1 No. 2½ can (3½ cups) tomatoes	1 slice bread, coarsely crumbled
1 bay leaf	hot cooked spaghetti (about 1½ lbs.)
1¼ teaspoons salt	grated Parmesan cheese

Sauté part of minced onion (¼ cup) and garlic with part of oil (1 tablespoon) until lightly browned. Put into sauce pot. Add tomato paste, water, tomatoes, bay leaf and a little of the salt (¼ teaspoon). Bring mixture to boil, then reduce heat to low and simmer. Meanwhile, heat more of oil in the skillet (another tablespoon). Add remaining minced onion (½ cup); cook, stirring occasionally, until soft. Combine with remaining salt (1 teaspoon), and next 6 ingredients. Shape mixture into bite-size balls. Heat remaining oil in skillet. Brown meat balls in oil, turning often to brown evenly. Add browned meat balls to sauce. Cook sauce with meat balls ¾-hour longer or until sauce has thickened and meat balls are cooked. Stir occasionally. Arrange spaghetti on a platter and spoon sauce over it. Arrange meat balls around edge of platter. Serve with grated Parmesan cheese.

SUGGESTED MENU: Just a crisp salad to supplement this hearty main dish. For dessert, melon wedges.

VEAL SCALLOPINI (ITALIAN)   4 Servings

1 lb. veal cutlet	¼ lb. fresh mushrooms, sliced
2 tablespoons seasoned flour	few drops Tabasco
3 tablespoons butter or margarine	¼ cup hot water
1 garlic clove, peeled	¼ cup dry white wine

Slice veal; pound very thin. Season flour with a little salt and pepper; dredge veal. Melt part of butter or margarine (about 1 tablespoon) in skillet; add garlic. Place layer of veal in skillet; cook over high heat for about 2 minutes on each side, turning once to brown evenly. Remove pieces of veal as they brown; keep warm. Repeat with remaining veal, adding more butter or margarine as required. When all meat is browned, lift out garlic and discard. Melt 2 more tablespoons butter or margarine in skillet; add mushrooms. Cook over medium heat until mushrooms are tender and lightly browned, stirring occasionally. Add Tabasco and hot water. Heat and stir gently over low heat to dissolve any browned particles on bottom of skillet. Stir in wine. Lay veal in the sauce. Cover and simmer over low heat for 3 minutes or until veal is fork-tender.

SUGGESTED MENU: Serve French-fried potatoes, eggplant Creole and crisp celery with the veal. For dessert, baked applesauce and ginger cookies.

SCALLOPINI OF BEEF WITH MUSHROOM SAUCE (ITALIAN)   4 Servings

2 ½ lbs. round steak, thinly sliced	1 teaspoon pepper
4 tablespoons fat or salad oil	1 cup red wine
2 small onions, finely chopped	beef suet
1 garlic clove, minced	¼ cup parsley, finely chopped
1 can (3 oz.) broiled mushrooms, sliced	

Use specially-seasoned meat tenderizer according to directions on page 19. Pierce deeply with fork. Allow to remain at room temperature for 15 to 20 minutes. While meat is getting tender, prepare sauce. Heat fat or oil. Add onions and garlic; cook until light brown. Add mushrooms, pepper and wine; simmer for 10 minutes. Rub heated skillet with suet. When sizzling hot, sear beef slices very quickly. They should be rare—1 minute on each side is quite enough. Pour sauce over meat and sprinkle with parsley.

SUGGESTED MENU: Mashed potatoes and buttered Brussels sprouts with the beef. Add a salad of chopped iceberg lettuce with Russian dressing. For dessert, coffee ice cream with chocolate sauce.

OSSOBUCO MILANESE (ITALIAN)   4 Servings

2 tablespoons salad oil
2 tablespoons flour
½ teaspoon salt
⅛ teaspoon pepper
4 veal shinbones, ea. 4 in. long, with meat
½ cup dry white wine
1 cup water
2 tablespoons tomato paste

1 teaspoon Ac'cent
½ cup celery, chopped
1 medium-size carrot, chopped
1 medium-size onion, chopped
1 teaspoon parsley, chopped
½ garlic clove, minced
4 strips lemon peel, 1 in. long
1 instant chicken bouillon cube

Heat oil in deep skillet or Dutch oven. Combine flour, salt and pepper. Dust over veal shinbones and brown them on all sides in hot oil. Add wine; cook slowly until it evaporates. Add water blended with tomato paste and Ac'cent. Cover and simmer for half an hour. Add celery, carrot, onion, parsley, garlic, lemon peel, and more water if necessary. Cover and simmer for half an hour, or until meat and vegetables are tender. Remove veal bones, placing each in a deep soup dish. Crumble chicken bouillon cube into stock in pan; stir until dissolved. Pour an equal amount of soup into each dish.

SUGGESTED MENU: Serve hot, crusty rolls with this hearty soup. Follow up with a salad. For dessert, date squares à la mode.

VEAL CHOPS OREGANO (ITALIAN)   4 Servings

4 tablespoons olive or salad oil
3 green peppers, thinly sliced
1 medium-size onion, chopped
6 stuffed olives, chopped
1 tablespoon capers
1 No. 303 can (1 lb.) tomatoes
½ garlic clove, peeled and chopped

4 loin veal chops, ¾ in. thick
1 tablespoon flour
  salt and pepper
2 tablespoons water
2 tablespoons dry white wine
½ teaspoon oregano

Heat 1 of your 4 tablespoons of oil in saucepan. Add green peppers and onion; cook slowly until peppers are almost tender. Add olives, capers and tomatoes; simmer 20 minutes more. Set aside; keep warm. Heat second tablespoon of oil in a large skillet. Add garlic; cook over low heat until lightly browned. Add to tomato mixture; keep hot. Meanwhile, sprinkle chops with flour. Heat remaining 2 tablespoons of oil in skillet. Add chops and cook over medium heat, turning to brown evenly. When browned, sprinkle with salt and pepper. Reduce heat to low; add water. Cover; simmer for 20 minutes more, or until chops are tender. Put chops on heated platter. Measure wine and oregano into hot skillet. Stir to mix drippings and wine; pour over chops. Top with hot tomato mixture.

SUGGESTED MENU: Buttered macaroni shells and a green vegetable of your choice round out the main course. For dessert, chilled pineapple chunks and ladyfingers.

HAMBURGERS PARMIGIANA (ITALIAN)
6 Servings

2 lbs. lean ground beef
1 egg
1 teaspoon salt
⅛ teaspoon pepper
  dash Tabasco
1 tablespoon Worcestershire sauce

1 can (6 oz.) tomato paste
1 large onion, minced
½ lb. Mozzarella cheese
  grated Parmesan cheese
6 hamburger buns, toasted

Combine beef, egg, salt, pepper, Tabasco and Worcestershire sauce; mix well. Pat out in square about 1 inch thick. Cut into 6 squares. Broil squares on one side for 5 minutes, turn and spread with tomato paste. Sprinkle with onion and top with thin slices of Mozzarella cheese. Sprinkle with grated Parmesan cheese and broil until cheese melts and browns. Serve the hamburgers on halves of toasted buns.

SUGGESTED MENU: Add a salad of grated raw carrots and raisins with cooked salad dressing. For dessert, chocolate chiffon cake à la mode.

LASAGNA (ITALIAN)
6 to 8 Servings

5 cups meat sauce
1 pkg. (1 lb.) lasagna noodles
  boiling salted water

1 lb. ricotta or cottage cheese
½ cup grated Parmesan cheese
½ lb. Mozzarella cheese, thinly sliced

Measure meat sauce. Cook noodles in boiling salted water according to package directions until almost tender; rinse and drain well. Spread half the drained noodles over the bottom of a lightly oiled baking dish 13×9×2 inches. Using half of each of the three kinds of cheese, spread alternate layers on top of noodles, covering each layer with meat sauce. Repeat, starting with noodles and ending with Mozzarella slices. Bake in moderate oven (350°) for 30 minutes or until hot and bubbly.

MEAT SAUCE
Makes about 2 ½ quarts

1 cup onion, chopped
2 garlic cloves, minced
½ cup celery, minced
¼ cup olive or salad oil
2 lbs. ground beef

2 teaspoons sugar
1 teaspoon oregano
1 ½ tablespoons salt
4 No. 303 cans (1 lb. ea.) tomatoes
2 cans (6 oz. ea.) tomato paste

Cook onion, garlic and celery in hot oil over low heat until soft, but not brown. Add beef. Brown over medium heat, breaking up with side of a spoon as it cooks. Stir in remaining ingredients and cover. Bring mixture to a boil. Reduce heat and simmer, stirring frequently, for 3 hours, or until thick. Chill; skim off fat. Store sauce covered in refrigerator or freeze until needed.

SUGGESTED MENU: This is rich eating and needs only a salad or assorted raw vegetable relishes for accompaniment. For dessert, fresh fruit in season.

ROUND STEAK ITALIENNE
5 to 6 Servings

2 lbs. round steak, ½ in. thick
¼ cup flour
1½ teaspoons salt
⅛ teaspoon pepper
3 tablespoons fat or salad oil

1 No. 303 can (1 lb.) tomatoes
½ teaspoon oregano
⅛ teaspoon dry mustard
1 garlic clove, minced

Cut steak into 6 portions. Pound to thickness of ¼ inch. Mix together flour, salt and pepper and dredge meat in seasoned flour. Brown in hot fat or salad oil and pour off drippings. Add tomatoes, oregano, mustard and garlic. Cover tightly and simmer for 1 hour, or until done.

SUGGESTED MENU: With the round steak, spaghetti Parmesan, spinach soufflé and a green salad. For dessert, coffee jelly with cream.

ITALIAN SPAGHETTI
4 to 6 Servings

2 tablespoons olive oil
1 lb. lean ground beef
1 large onion, chopped
1 green pepper, chopped
1 can (6 oz.) tomato paste
1 No. 303 can (1 lb.) tomatoes
½ cup water

2 teaspoons sugar
1 garlic clove, mashed
1 teaspoon salt
few drops Tabasco (optional)
boiling salted water
1 pkg. (8 oz.) spaghetti
grated Parmesan cheese

Heat oil in large skillet. Brown meat and break it into small pieces with the side of a spoon as it browns. Add onion and green pepper. Cook for about 10 minutes, or until tender. Stir in next 4 ingredients. Cover and simmer for about 1 hour, stirring occasionally. Mix garlic and salt; stir into sauce. If you desire a more highly-seasoned sauce, add Tabasco. Cook spaghetti in boiling salted water according to package directions. To serve, arrange spaghetti on heated platter. Pour sauce over it and sprinkle with cheese.

SUGGESTED MENU: To be truly Italian, begin with thin melon wedges and wafer-thin slices of prosciutto ham. Next the spaghetti, with a green salad. For dessert, fresh fruit cup.

MACARONI ITALIA
6 Servings

2 tablespoons fat or salad oil
½ cup onion, chopped
1 garlic clove, minced
1 lb. lean ground beef
1 No. 303 can (1 lb.) tomatoes
1 cup celery, diced
½ cup green pepper, diced
1½ teaspoons salt

¼ teaspoon celery salt
few drops Tabasco
1 teaspoon Worcestershire sauce
1 pkg. (8 oz.) elbow macaroni
boiling salted water
1 can (3 oz.) chopped mushrooms
grated Parmesan cheese

Heat fat or oil in sauce pot. Add onion and garlic; cook, stirring occasionally, until onion is soft, but not brown. Add beef. Cook meat until lightly browned, breaking up with side of a spoon as it cooks. Stir in next 7 ingredients and bring to a boil. Simmer covered for 45 minutes. Meanwhile, cook macaroni in boiling salted water according to package directions; rinse and drain. Add mushrooms to sauce; heat to boiling. To serve, arrange macaroni on large, heated serving platter. Pour meat mixture over macaroni. Sprinkle with cheese.

SUGGESTED MENU: Begin with small servings of Caesar salad. The macaroni dish needs no accompaniment. For dessert, fresh fruit and bel paese cheese.

BEEF POT ROAST ITALIAN   6 to 8 Servings

1 beef chuck pot roast (3 to 4 lbs.)
½ cup flour
½ teaspoon salt
¼ teaspoon pepper
2 tablespoons olive oil
2 medium-size onions, sliced
½ teaspoon oregano

1 beef bouillon cube
1 cup hot water
8 oz. wide noodles
1 garlic clove
2 tablespoons butter or margarine
2 tablespoons parsley, chopped

Cut beef chuck into individual portions and dredge in flour seasoned with the salt and pepper. Heat olive oil and brown meat well in it. Add onion rings and oregano. Dissolve bouillon cube in hot water. Add half of the bouillon (½ cup) as a start, remainder as needed. Cover and simmer for 2 hours or until tender. Cook noodles according to directions on package. Mash garlic clove and mix with butter or margarine. Add parsley and toss with hot cooked noodles. Serve each portion of beef on bed of noodles with sauce.

SUGGESTED MENU: Assorted relishes and broiled tomato halves with the beef. Try fruit and cheese for dessert.

BEEF PASTIES (ENGLISH)   Makes 12 turnovers

pastry for 2-crust pie
1½ lbs. ground round steak
2 cups cooked potatoes, finely diced
1 large onion, finely chopped
⅓ cup parsley, chopped
1½ teaspoons salt
⅛ teaspoon pepper

⅛ teaspoon rosemary
¹/₃ cup butter or margarine
¹/₃ cup lemon juice
1 teaspoon lemon peel, grated
1 egg, beaten
tomato sauce or relish

Roll pastry ⅛ inch thick; cut into 12 6-inch circles. Mix round steak, potatoes, onion, parsley, salt, pepper and rosemary. Put a spoonful of meat mixture on each circle of pastry and dot with butter or margarine. Sprinkle with lemon juice and grated lemon peel. Dampen edges of pastry, fold over and press together; crimp with finger and thumb. Brush with beaten egg. Make 2 small slits in top of each turnover. Bake in hot oven (400°) for 1 hour. Serve hot with tomato sauce or cold with relish.

SUGGESTED MENU: Pack 2 of these turnovers in a lunch box with a container of cole-slaw and a ripe tomato. Add an apple and one or two brownies for dessert.

BEEFSTEAK AND KIDNEY PIE (ENGLISH)   6 Servings

1 beef kidney (about 1 ¼ lbs.)	2 teaspoons salt
1 lb. lean round steak, 1 in. thick	dash pepper
10 small onions	¼ teaspoon savory
2 medium-size potatoes	pastry for 1-crust pie
¼ cup fat or salad oil	

Remove outer membrane of kidney. Split kidney open. Remove all fat and white veins. Soak in cold water for 30 minutes, then drain. Cut kidney and steak into 1-inch cubes. Cut onions in half. Cut pared potatoes into ½-inch cubes. Brown kidney, steak and onion in hot fat or oil in large skillet. Stir frequently to brown evenly. Sprinkle with salt, pepper and savory. Add potatoes and enough water to cover. Simmer until meat is tender, or about 30 to 45 minutes. Add more water if needed. Remove meat and vegetables; thicken gravy with a little flour, if desired (page 195). Pour mixture into 2-quart casserole. Roll out pastry to fit top of casserole; cut slits in several places to allow steam to escape. Bake in hot oven (425°) for about 20 minutes, or until crust is browned. Serve hot.

SUGGESTED MENU: Add a salad of endive and diced iceberg lettuce with cheese dressing. For dessert, a fruit trifle.

CORNED BEEF AND CABBAGE (IRISH)   6 Servings

1 corned beef brisket (4 lbs.)	1 small head cabbage
6 medium-size potatoes	

Put beef in large sauce pot; cover with cold water. Cover sauce pot; bring to a boil over high heat. Reduce heat to medium and cook for 2½ hours or until beef is almost tender. Scrub potatoes and pare a ring around center of each. Cut cabbage in sixths. Put cabbage and potatoes in sauce pot with beef. Bring to a boil. Simmer covered 1 hour longer, or until meat is tender.

SUGGESTED MENU: Add a salad of sliced beets and onion rings. For dessert, apple pie.

RUMP STEAKS ESPAGNOLE   4 Servings

2 tablespoons fat or salad oil	1 green pepper, sliced
1 lb. rump steak, ½ in. thick	1 ½ cups cooked tomatoes
1 teaspoon salt	¼ teaspoon thyme
¼ teaspoon pepper	¼ teaspoon celery salt
flour	1 teaspoon prepared mustard
1 onion, sliced	

Heat fat or oil in heavy skillet. Cut steak into 4 pieces. Season with salt and pepper; dip in flour. Pan-fry onion and green pepper in hot fat or oil until tender; remove from skillet. Brown steaks; top each steak with onion and green pepper. Add remaining ingredients. Cover tightly and cook slowly for 1 hour.

SUGGESTED MENU: Macaroni and cheese, raw carrot sticks and a green salad complete the main course. For dessert, steamed chocolate pudding with whipped cream.

SPANISH POT ROAST

6 Servings

4 lbs. beef round
2 tablespoons olive or salad oil
²/₃ cup onion, minced
¼ cup lemon juice
1 small garlic clove, mashed

3 tablespoons parsley, chopped
5 peppercorns
½ bay leaf
¼ teaspoon tarragon
1 cup unsweetened grape juice

Select a solid piece of meat with very little fat; place in deep crock or container. Combine oil, onion, lemon juice, garlic, parsley and seasonings. Bring to boil, then simmer for 5 minutes; pour over meat. Cover and let stand in cool place for 24 hours, turning often. Heat Dutch oven; then put in the meat, marinade and grape juice and cover. Cook for 2 to 3 hours, turning occasionally. Add a little water if necessary, to keep from sticking.

SUGGESTED MENU: With the pot roast serve instant mashed potatoes, Mexican corn in foil packets and a tossed salad. For dessert, apple turnovers and cubes of cheddar cheese.

SPANISH MEAT BALLS

4 to 6 Servings

1 lb. lean ground beef
1 cup soft bread crumbs
1 egg, beaten
¹/₃ cup onion, minced
¾ teaspoon chili powder

1 teaspoon salt
¾ cup uncooked rice
2 No. 303 cans (1 lb. ea.) tomato juice
½ cup green pepper, minced
1 cup spaghetti, broken up

Mix beef, bread crumbs, egg, onion, and seasonings. Shape into small balls or patties; roll in uncooked rice. Drop into tomato juice which has been heated to boiling point. Add green pepper. Reduce heat at once to a simmer; continue to cook covered, stirring often, for 30 minutes. Stir in broken spaghetti and cook an additional 15 to 30 minutes or until spaghetti is done.

SUGGESTED MENU: Swiss chard, dandelion greens or spinach with the meat balls plus a salad of pickled beets and celery. For dessert, fresh fruit and cheese.

HAMBURGERS HAWAIIAN

4 Servings

1 lb. lean ground beef
1 onion, finely chopped
1 garlic clove, minced

½ cup soy sauce
½ teaspoon ginger, ground

Mix beef and onion. Shape into 8 patties, each ½ inch thick. Combine garlic, soy sauce and ginger; pour over patties. Let stand for 30 minutes. Remove patties from sauce; broil on pan 3 inches from heat source for about 5 to 7 minutes on each side.

SUGGESTED MENU: Buttered rice with lots of chopped parsley stirred in, and asparagus spears au gratin. Combine salad and dessert by serving cottage cheese and canned peaches or pears on greens with cream mayonnaise.

STUFFED FLANK STEAK HAWAIIAN   6 Servings

1 onion, minced
4 tablespoons fat or salad oil
2 cups soft bread crumbs
½ cup pineapple, crushed

½ teaspoon salt
   dash pepper
2 lbs. flank steak
1 cup boiling water

Cook onion in half of hot fat or oil (2 tablespoons) until soft, but not brown. Combine with crumbs, pineapple, salt and pepper; spread on flank steak, which has been tenderized according to instructions on page 19. Roll up tightly; tie with string. Brown roll on all sides in remaining fat or oil (2 tablespoons). Place in baking pan; add boiling water; cover. Bake in moderate oven (325°) for 2 hours. Slice crosswise to serve.

SUGGESTED MENU: Serve French-fried potatoes and buttered green peas with the steak. Add an endive salad with blue cheese dressing. For dessert, pumpkin pie.

SOUTH-SEA BEEF AND PINEAPPLE   6 Servings

1½ lbs. beef, sirloin or rib, cut in 1-in. cubes
1½ teaspoons Ac'cent
¼ cup salad oil
1 can (20 oz.) pineapple chunks (undrained)
2 teaspoons soy sauce
1 tablespoon vinegar
1 cup celery, diced

1 cucumber, thinly sliced
1 tomato, peeled and cut in wedges
1 green pepper, cut in 1-in. squares
1 medium-size onion, sliced
2 teaspoons cornstarch
2 tablespoons water
3 cups hot rice

Sprinkle beef with part of Ac'cent (one teaspoon). Brown beef in hot oil in skillet. Drain pineapple and add pineapple syrup to skillet with soy sauce and vinegar. Bring to boil, then reduce heat and simmer for 15 minutes. Add pineapple chunks and vegetables, sprinkle with remaining ½ teaspoon Ac'cent and cook 5 minutes longer. Combine cornstarch and water; stir until smooth. Add slowly to beef mixture. Cook, stirring constantly, until mixture thickens and comes to a boil. Spoon rice around edge of platter; turn hot mixture into center.

SUGGESTED MENU: You need serve only a few relishes, such as olives and pickles with the beef. For dessert, lemon ice with green crème de menthe.

CHILI CON CARNE   6 to 8 Servings

3 strips bacon
3 medium-size onions
2 lbs. lean ground beef
1 No. 303 can (1 lb.) tomatoes
1 can (1 lb.) kidney beans
3 tablespoons chili powder

2 teaspoons sugar
½ teaspoon salt
¼ teaspoon pepper
   dash cayenne pepper
3 garlic cloves

Dice bacon; fry until crisp, then remove. Fry onions in bacon fat until soft. Add beef and cook until browned. Add tomatoes, beans, chili powder, sugar, salt, pepper and cayenne. Peel garlic cloves and add them. Simmer for 15 minutes. Remove garlic. Add bacon.

SUGGESTED MENU: Rice is the rule with chili con carne. Nothing else is needed except a tossed salad. For dessert, fruit sherbet.

TAMALE BAKE (MEXICAN)   8 Servings

1 cup yellow corn meal	2 onions, chopped
2 cups milk	½ cup salad oil
3 eggs, beaten	1 tablespoon salt
1 No. 2½ can (3½ cups) tomatoes	3 chili peppers
1 No. 303 can (1 lb.) whole-kernel corn	1 teaspoon pepper
1 lb. lean ground beef	2 cups ripe olives, pitted

Combine corn meal, milk and eggs in a saucepan. Cook until very thick. Add tomatoes and corn. Simmer while preparing meat. Brown meat and onions in hot oil; stir in seasonings. Add seasoned meat and onions to corn meal mixture. Stir in ripe olives. Pour all into a large greased baking pan or casserole. Bake in medium oven (375°) for 1 to 1½ hours. This dish may be prepared a day or more in advance, stored in the refrigerator and baked when needed.

SUGGESTED MENU: Serve mustard greens, collard greens or spinach with the tamale pie, and lots of coffee. For dessert, lemon snow pudding.

MEXICAN TAMALE PIE   6 Servings

3 cups boiling water	½ cup onion, chopped
3¼ teaspoons salt	1 tablespoon fat or salad oil
1 cup yellow corn meal	1 tablespoon chili powder
1 lb. lean ground beef	¼ teaspoon pepper
½ cup green pepper, diced, plus several rings	4 medium-size tomatoes, sliced

Combine boiling water with part of salt (1½ teaspoons) in saucepan. Add corn meal gradually, stirring constantly to prevent lumping. Cook and stir over low heat for about 10 minutes or until thick. Cool slightly. Meanwhile, brown beef, onion and diced green pepper in hot fat or oil in heavy skillet over medium heat. Add remaining salt (1¾ teaspoons), chili powder and pepper; mix well. Turn half of the corn meal mush into 10-inch pie pan; spread and press corn meal against bottom and sides of pan. Cover with layer of sliced tomatoes, then with meat mixture. Top with remaining corn meal mush. Garnish with 3 or 4 slices of tomato and several green pepper rings. Bake in moderate oven (375°) for about 25 minutes, or until done.

SUGGESTED MENU: A tossed green salad completes the main course. For dessert, orange sherbet and chocolate cookies.

PAN-AMERICAN MEAT LOAF

6 to 8 Servings

1 egg, beaten
¾ cup strong, cold coffee
½ teaspoon poultry seasoning
1½ teaspoons salt

dash pepper
2 cups soft bread crumbs
1 onion, minced
2 lbs. lean ground beef

Combine egg, coffee, poultry seasoning, salt, pepper and bread crumbs. Let stand for 5 minutes. Add onion and beef; mix well. Pack into greased loaf pan 8 × 5 × 3 inches. Bake in moderate oven (350°) for 1½ hours.

SUGGESTED MENU: Serve meat loaf hot or cold, with asparagus, mayonnaise and tomato-chive salad. For dessert, coffee ice cream with chocolate sauce, cookies and iced coffee.

MEXICAN SHORT RIBS

6 Servings

2 to 3 lbs. short ribs of beef
1 large sweet onion, sliced
½ cup ketchup
½ cup vinegar

2 teaspoons chili powder
1 teaspoon paprika
2½ teaspoons salt

Cut ribs in individual portions. Brown in their own fat in heavy skillet, then place in baking dish or casserole. Spread with layer of onion slices. Combine remaining ingredients; pour over meat and onions. Bake in moderate oven (325°) for 2 to 2½ hours, or until meat is very tender.

SUGGESTED MENU: Serve rice and red or kidney beans and a mixed green salad with the short ribs. For dessert, orange and pineapple ambrosia.

MEXICAN ROLLS

6 Servings

1½ lbs. round steak
1 teaspoon salt
3 tablespoons flour
¼ cup fat or salad oil
⅓ cup chopped onion
1 garlic clove
2 tablespoons chili powder

2 No. 303 cans (1 lb. ea.) tomatoes
2 cups water
1 can (about 1 lb.) kidney beans
6 frankfurters
2 tablespoons butter or margarine
6 frankfurter rolls

Cut steak very fine (do not grind). Sprinkle with salt and flour. Heat fat or oil in frying pan. Add meat, onion and garlic and cook until browned, stirring often. Add chili powder, tomatoes and water. Cover and simmer for 1 hour. Remove garlic. Add kidney beans; cook 20 minutes longer, or until slightly thickened. Split frankfurters; brown in butter or margarine. Split and toast frankfurter rolls. Top rolls with frankfurters; cover generously with meat sauce.

SUGGESTED MENU: With this hearty meat dish only a crisp salad is needed to complete the main course. Baked apples for dessert.

GERMAN POT ROAST

6 to 8 Servings

6 lbs. beef pot roast
3 tablespoons fat or salad oil
¼ cup vinegar
1 bay leaf
1 sprig parsley
1 tablespoon brown sugar

1 tablespoon Worcestershire sauce
  salt and pepper
  boiling water
2 onions
4 carrots
4 stalks celery

Brown meat in hot fat or oil in large heavy skillet or Dutch oven. Add vinegar, seasonings and enough boiling water to barely cover meat. Cook over moderate heat for 1 ½ hours. Add vegetables. Cover tightly and continue cooking over low heat for an additional 2 to 2 ½ hours, or until meat is very tender. To make gravy, remove excess fat from liquid remaining in pan. Put vegetables through food mill or sieve. Strain liquid, add vegetables and thicken (page 195).

SUGGESTED MENU: Potato pancakes and sweet-sour red cabbage with the pot roast. Add celery, black olives and cucumber sticks. For dessert, halves of grapefruit with honey.

BEEF AND SAUERKRAUT DINNER (GERMAN)

6 to 8 Servings

2 lbs. boneless beef, cut in 1-in. cubes
2 tablespoons fat or salad oil
1 teaspoon salt
¼ teaspoon pepper
2 medium-size onions, sliced ¼ in. thick
1 small garlic clove, minced

1 teaspoon dillseed
1 teaspoon paprika
½ cup water
1 cup sour cream
1 can (1 lb. 13 oz.) sauerkraut

Brown beef in hot fat or salad oil. Pour off drippings. Add salt, pepper, onions, garlic, dillseed, paprika and water. Cover tightly and simmer for 2 ½ to 3 hours, or until meat is done. Add sour cream; heat thoroughly. Heat sauerkraut. Serve meat and sauce over sauerkraut. Sprinkle with additional paprika if desired.

SUGGESTED MENU: Riced potatoes, and green beans go with the beef and sauerkraut. For dessert, baked pears.

BAVARIAN POT ROAST

8 Servings

3 to 4 lbs. beef pot roast
  2 tablespoons flour
  2 teaspoons salt
  ¼ teaspoon pepper
  2 tablespoons fat or salad oil

1 medium-size onion, sliced
1 bay leaf
1 teaspoon caraway seed
2 tablespoons vinegar
¼ cup water

Dredge pot roast in flour seasoned with salt and pepper; brown in hot fat or oil. Add remaining ingredients. Cover and simmer 3 hours or longer. Add more water as needed during cooking. Thicken drippings for gravy (page 195).

SUGGESTED MENU: With the pot roast serve mashed potatoes, sweet-sour red cabbage and cucumber salad. For dessert, apple strudel.

GERMAN MEAT BALLS

4 Servings

½ lb. lean ground beef
¼ lb. ground veal
¼ lb. ground pork
1 tablespoon onion, finely chopped
¼ cup fine bread crumbs

1 egg
flour (a little more than 2 tablespoons)
1 can condensed beef bouillon
1 ¼ cups water
½ lemon, sliced

Combine meats, onion, bread crumbs and egg. Shape into 1-inch balls. Roll balls in a little of the flour. Heat bouillon and part of water (1 cup) in a saucepan. Add the meat balls. Simmer for 15 to 20 minutes. Blend rest of flour (2 tablespoons) with remaining ¼ cup water (cold). Add to the meat broth and cook, stirring until thickened. Add sliced lemon.

SUGGESTED MENU: Mashed potatoes, red cabbage and apples and a cucumber salad complete the main course. For dessert, prune whip.

SAUERBRATEN (GERMAN)

10 to 12 Servings

4 to 5 lbs. beef (rump or sirloin tip)
2 cups red wine vinegar
2 cups water
2 medium-size onions, sliced
1 lemon, sliced
10 whole cloves
4 bay leaves

6 peppercorns
2 tablespoons salt
3 tablespoons sugar
8 tablespoons flour
3 tablespoons fat or salad oil
$^1/_3$ cup butter or margarine
8 to 10 gingersnaps, crushed

Place meat in deep bowl. Combine next 8 ingredients; stir in part of sugar (2 tablespoons). Pour marinade over meat. Cover and refrigerate for 2 to 3 days, turning meat often. Lift meat from bowl, pat dry and rub lightly with part of flour (2 tablespoons). Strain marinade; reserve. Heat fat or oil in a sauce pot or Dutch oven. Add meat; brown well on all sides. Pour part of marinade (2 cups) over meat. Cover and bring to a boil, then reduce heat to low and simmer for 3 hours. Melt butter or margarine in saucepan. Blend in remaining 6 tablespoons flour and 1 tablespoon sugar. Continue to heat and stir until rich brown in color. Stir in remaining marinade. Bring to boil and cook and stir until thickened. Pour over meat and simmer covered for 1 hour longer, or until meat is tender. Remove meat from gravy; keep hot. Put gingersnaps in gravy and stir until thickened. Slice hot meat. Arrange on platter and pour gravy over top.

SUGGESTED MENU: Serve potato pancakes, red cabbage and a salad of cut green beans and sliced cucumber with the Sauerbraten. For dessert, cheesecake.

AUSTRIAN VEAL IN ASPIC

8 to 10 Servings

4 lbs. veal shoulder or shank
1 veal knuckle
½ cup carrots, diced
¼ cup celery, diced

1 onion, chopped
boiling water
salt and pepper
3 hard-cooked eggs, sliced

Cover meat, knuckle and vegetables with boiling water; reduce heat and simmer until very tender. Remove meat; dice. Continue cooking broth until reduced to about 1 cup; strain, cool and skim. Combine diced meat and broth; season to taste. Place egg slices in decorative pattern around sides and bottom of mold. Carefully spoon in meat mixture. Cool, then chill until firm. Slice to serve.

SUGGESTED MENU: Begin with hot tomato soup and cheese croutons. Potato salad and coleslaw with the veal in aspic. For dessert, banana tapioca cream.

VEAL RIBLETS HUNGARIAN   6 to 8 Servings

$^1/_3$ cup flour	1 garlic clove, minced
1 $^1/_2$ teaspoons salt	1 cup onion, sliced
$^1/_4$ teaspoon pepper	1 can condensed mushroom soup
1 $^1/_2$ teaspoons paprika	$^3/_4$ cup milk
3 lbs. veal riblets	8 oz. noodles, cooked
2 tablespoons fat or salad oil	

Mix together flour, salt, pepper and paprika and dredge riblets in seasoned flour. Brown in hot fat or salad oil. Pour off drippings. Combine garlic, onion, soup and milk; pour over riblets. Cover tightly and simmer for 2 hours. Serve riblets and mushroom sauce over noodles.

SUGGESTED MENU: Sweet-sour beets, buttered green beans and sliced tomatoes in chive French dressing with the riblets. For dessert, hot gingerbread with whipped cream cheese topping.

VEAL PATTIES HUNGARIAN   4 to 5 Servings

1 lb. veal shoulder, ground	$^1/_4$ cup fat or salad oil
1 garlic clove, finely chopped	1 teaspoon Kitchen Bouquet
2 tablespoons parsley, chopped	2 tablespoons flour
1 teaspoon salt	1 can (3 oz.) broiled mushrooms, sliced
dash pepper	1 $^1/_2$ cups sour cream
$^1/_4$ cup milk	1 pkg. (6 oz.) broad noodles
1 egg, beaten	boiling salted water
$^1/_2$ cup fine bread crumbs	2 tablespoons poppy seeds

Combine veal, garlic, parsley, seasonings, milk, egg and crumbs. Mix thoroughly and shape in small cakes. Heat fat or oil; add Kitchen Bouquet. Brown meat cakes in mixture, then remove. Stir in flour. Add mushrooms and sour cream. Cook until thickened, stirring constantly. Return meat cakes to pan, cover and cook over low heat for about 20 minutes. Cook noodles in boiling salted water according to directions on package. Drain and sprinkle with poppy seeds. Serve on hot platter around meat cakes and gravy.

SUGGESTED MENU: Scalloped zucchini and tomatoes to accompany the meat patties and noodles. Add lettuce wedges with a sharp dressing. For dessert, pineapple cheese-cake.

VEAL STEAK PAPRIKA (AUSTRIAN)   6 Servings

¼ cup flour
1 tablespoon paprika
1 teaspoon salt
1 veal steak, 1 ½ in. thick
3 medium-size onions, thinly sliced
2 tablespoons fat or salad oil

1 cup water
  almond noodles
1 cup sour cream
2 tablespoons dry sherry
¼ teaspoon oregano

Combine flour, paprika and salt; dredge veal thoroughly in this mixture. Cook onions in hot fat or oil over low heat until soft and golden brown; remove from pan. Place veal in same pan and brown well on both sides. Top with onions. Put any remaining flour mixture in pan with water. Cover and simmer until veal is tender, or about 1 hour. Remove veal and onions to platter. Surround with almond noodles; keep warm. Add sour cream, sherry and oregano to pan; stir to blend. Heat to serving temperature and serve separately.

ALMOND NOODLES

¼ cup butter or margarine
½ cup slivered blanched almonds
1 tablespoon paprika

1 tablespoon poppy seeds
1 pkg. (6 oz.) egg noodles, cooked

Melt half the butter or margarine (⅛ cup). Add almonds and cook until golden brown. Combine remaining butter or margarine (⅛ cup), paprika and poppy seeds. Add to hot cooked noodles, tossing with a fork until thoroughly mixed.

SUGGESTED MENU: Brussels sprouts and shoe-string beets go well with the veal steak and noodles. For dessert, apricot whip.

POLISH MEAT-CABBAGE ROLLS   4 Servings

8 large cabbage leaves
  boiling water
1 lb. lean ground beef
2 teaspoons salt
¼ teaspoon pepper

1 cup cooked rice
1 cup milk
2 tablespoons salad oil
2 tablespoons brown sugar
½ cup water

Cover cabbage leaves with boiling water. Drain, dry and spread flat. Mix meat, seasonings, rice and milk. Place spoonful of meat mixture on each cabbage leaf. Roll up and secure with wooden picks. Arrange rolls in greased baking dish. Add oil, sugar and water. Bake in a moderate oven (350°) for 50 minutes, or until done.

SUGGESTED MENU: With the cabbage rolls serve dark rye bread or salt sticks, dill pickles, and buttered green peas. For dessert, prune-filled, rolled dessert pancakes sprinkled with powdered sugar.

WIENER SCHNITZEL HOLSTEIN (AUSTRIAN)   4 Servings

4 veal cutlets (about 6 oz. ea.)
¼ cup flour
1 teaspoon salt
  dash pepper
1 egg, beaten

1 cup fine bread crumbs
¼ cup butter or margarine
4 anchovy fillets
1 dill pickle, sliced lengthwise
4 fried eggs

Flatten cutlets or pound with meat hammer until very thin. Combine flour, salt and pepper and coat meat with flour mixture. Dip in the slightly-beaten egg, then in bread crumbs. Heat butter or margarine in skillet and fry meat in it over medium heat until golden brown and tender, turning to brown on both sides. Place cutlets on heated platter with a fried egg on top of each. Garnish with anchovies and pickle slices.

FRIED EGGS

2 tablespoons butter or margarine
4 eggs

1 teaspoon water

Heat 2 tablespoons butter or margarine in a skillet over medium heat. Slip 4 eggs in the skillet, one at a time. Add water. Cover and cook for 2 to 3 minutes, or until whites are firm but tender.

SUGGESTED MENU: Serve home-fried potatoes, sweet-sour red cabbage and lima beans with the meat. For dessert, coffee ice cream and fudge cake.

SWEET-SOUR SHORT RIBS OF BEEF (MIDDLE EUROPEAN)   6 to 8 Servings

1 cup ketchup
1 cup water
1 tablespoon sugar
1 tablespoon prepared horse-radish
1 teaspoon dry mustard
1 tablespoon vinegar
1 teaspoon salt

¼ teaspoon pepper
2 medium-size onions, sliced
1 tablespoon Worcestershire sauce
3 lbs. short ribs of beef, cut in individual
  portions
  flour
3 tablespoons fat or cooking oil

Combine first 10 ingredients in deep bowl to make a marinade. Put short ribs into bowl. Cover and chill for 6 hours, turning short ribs occasionally. Lift out short ribs; drain well. Reserve marinade. Dip short ribs in flour to coat thoroughly. Heat fat or oil in large skillet or Dutch oven over medium heat; brown meat on all sides. Add marinade. Cover and simmer for 1½ hours, or until meat is tender. If desired, thicken the pan liquid to make a gravy (page 195).

SUGGESTED MENU: Egg noodles, mashed yellow turnips and green peas accompany the beef. Crisp celery instead of salad. For dessert, apricot upside-down cake.

PAPRIKA BEEF (MIDDLE EUROPEAN)

6 Servings

2 lbs. round steak, ½ in. thick
1 ½ teaspoons paprika
1 garlic clove, peeled
2 tablespoons fat or oil

1 cup water
2 tablespoons Worcestershire sauce
1 cup sour cream

Use tenderizer according to directions on page 19. Rub beef with part of paprika (½ teaspoon). Brown garlic in hot fat or oil, then remove. Brown meat on both sides. Add water and Worcestershire sauce. Cover and simmer for 1 ½ hours. Add sour cream and remaining paprika (one teaspoon); simmer 10 minutes longer. Thicken gravy if desired (page 195).

SUGGESTED MENU: Serve buttered noodles with poppy seeds, fried eggplant and sliced tomatoes with the paprika beef. For dessert, apple strudel.

SWEET-SOUR STEAK (MIDDLE EUROPEAN)

4 Servings

4 cube steaks (about 4 oz. ea.)
  seasoned flour
1 onion, chopped
3 tablespoons fat or salad oil
2 tablespoons vinegar

1 tablespoon brown sugar
½ cup ketchup
2 tablespoons Worcestershire sauce
¼ cup water

Dip steaks in seasoned flour; brown with chopped onion in hot fat or oil. Add remaining ingredients. Cover and cook slowly until steaks are fork-tender, or about 20 minutes.

SUGGESTED MENU: Buttered broad noodles, chopped kale and sliced carrots go with the steak. For dessert, stewed prunes with lemon and stick cinnamon; shortbread cookies.

BOHEMIAN POT ROAST

6 to 8 Servings

7 tablespoons flour
⅛ teaspoon pepper
3 to 4 lbs. arm or blade pot roast
3 tablespoons fat or salad oil

¾ cup water
1 No. 303 can (1 lb.) tomatoes
1 pkg. (1 ½ oz.) onion soup mix

Mix together part of flour (4 tablespoons) and pepper. Dredge pot roast with seasoned flour, then brown in hot fat or salad oil. Pour off drippings. Add part of water (½ cup), tomatoes and onion soup mix. Cover tightly and simmer for 3 to 4 hours, or until tender. Remove pot roast to hot platter. Mix together remaining water (¼ cup) and flour (3 tablespoons). Add to cooking liquid; cook and stir until thickened. Serve gravy with pot roast.

SUGGESTED MENU: Mashed or parslied potatoes, fried eggplant and a green salad complete the main course. For dessert, chocolate cream roll.

ROMANIAN MEAT BALLS

4 Servings

1 lb. lean ground beef	⅛ teaspoon paprika
1 onion, minced	2 tablespoons fat or salad oil
¼ cup crushed corn flakes	¼ cup water
1 egg	1 tablespoon sugar
1½ teaspoons salt	¼ cup raisins
⅛ teaspoon pepper	juice of 1 lemon

Mix beef, onion, corn flakes, egg and seasonings. Shape mixture into 8 meat balls. Brown in skillet in hot fat or oil. Mix remaining ingredients and add. Cover and simmer over low heat for 35 to 40 minutes.

SUGGESTED MENU: With the meat balls serve buttered rice, and green beans with mushrooms. Add raw carrot sticks and celery. For dessert, fresh fruit and cheese.

DUTCH TREAT DINNER

6 Servings

1 medium-size onion, finely chopped	2½ lbs. sauerkraut
¼ cup fat or salad oil	¼ teaspoon pepper
2 lbs. beef chuck, cubed	1½ cups water
1 teaspoon paprika	2 tablespoons sugar
1 teaspoon salt	1 cup sour cream

Cook onion in Dutch oven in hot fat or oil until lightly browned. Add beef, paprika and salt to onion and simmer for ½ hour. Rinse sauerkraut. Add pepper and water and simmer for ½ hour, stirring occasionally. Add sauerkraut mixture and sugar to beef mixture and simmer ½ hour longer. Stir in sour cream.

SUGGESTED MENU: Hashed-brown potatoes and buttered lima beans complement the meat dish. Add romaine salad. For dessert, Dutch apple cake.

DUTCH BEEF BIRDS

6 Servings

4 lbs. rolled rib roast	3 to 4 dill pickles
salt and pepper	flour
prepared mustard	2 tablespoons fat or salad oil
2 large sweet onions	

Use a very sharp knife to cut uncooked roast into thin slices. Spread meat slices flat; sprinkle with salt and pepper to taste, then dot with prepared mustard. Cut onions into paper-thin slices. Place a few onion slices on each slice of meat. Put a long sliver of pickle at one end and roll up neatly. Secure rolls with wooden picks, or tie with thread. Dust with flour and brown in hot fat or oil. Remove meat rolls to shallow, greased casserole. Bake in moderate oven (350°) for 30 to 45 minutes, or until tender.

SUGGESTED MENU: With the beef birds serve buttered noodles, mashed Hubbard squash and tiny French peas ("petits pois"). For dessert, Edam cheese and crackers.

BEEF STROGANOFF (RUSSIAN) 6 Servings

3 lbs. Bermuda onions*
2 lbs. sirloin steak
1 lb. mushrooms
1 cup butter or margarine
1 can condensed tomato soup

1 can (6 oz.) tomato paste
1 cup sour cream
1 teaspoon salt
dash pepper
1 teaspoon Worcestershire sauce

Put onions through food chopper, using coarse knife, then drain, saving juice. Cut meat in very thin slices; trim off excess fat. Slice mushrooms and brown with meat in butter or margarine. Add onions; remove from heat. Combine soup, tomato paste, sour cream, seasonings and onion juice; add to meat mixture. Cover and simmer for 1 hour.

SUGGESTED MENU: Rice is the traditional companion for Stroganoff, unless you prefer kasha (buckwheat groats). Add any green vegetable and a tossed salad. For dessert, fresh fruit and cheese.

ECONOMY BEEF STROGANOFF (RUSSIAN) 4 Servings

1½ lbs. lean beef (bottom round or chuck)
3 tablespoons fat or salad oil
1 can (8 oz.) mushrooms (undrained)
1 large onion, sliced
2 tablespoons flour

2 cups beef bouillon or consommé
¼ cup dry sherry
2 tablespoons tomato paste
1 teaspoon dry mustard
²/₃ cup sour cream

Remove all fat and gristle from meat. Cut into strips 2½ × ¾ × ½ inch thick. Use specially seasoned meat tenderizer according to directions on page 19. Do not add salt. Pierce strips clear through with a sharp fork. This insures penetration of the tenderizer and seals in meat juices. Let strips stand at room temperature for about 15 minutes. Set electric skillet to high heat (or use regular heavy skillet); heat 2 of your 3 tablespoons of fat or oil. Drain mushrooms and reserve liquid. Cook with onion for about 15 minutes, or until brown; remove to dish. Add remaining fat or oil (1 tablespoon) to skillet. When sizzling hot, sear beef strips very quickly. They must be rare—1 minute per side is sufficient. Remove meat to dish and add flour to skillet; brown well. Add bouillon or consommé and mushroom liquid, stirring constantly to make a smooth sauce. Blend in sherry, tomato paste and mustard. Return beef, onions, and mushrooms to skillet. Cover and simmer for 10 to 15 minutes. Fold in sour cream 5 minutes before serving.

SUGGESTED MENU: Serve with buttered noodles blended with basil and poppy seeds, black bread and cucumber salad. Baba au rhum or strudel for dessert.

---

*Be sure you use *sweet* onions — Bermuda or Spanish.

DANISH MEAT BALLS

4 Servings

1 lb. lean ground beef
2 tablespoons onion, finely chopped
1 egg, beaten
½ cup fine bread crumbs
⅔ cup milk
2 teaspoons salt
¾ teaspoon pepper

⅛ teaspoon allspice
¼ teaspoon nutmeg
1 teaspoon brown sugar
   flour (a little more than 2 tablespoons)
4 tablespoons fat or salad oil
1 cup light cream or bouillon
⅓ cup water

Have beef ground very fine (at least twice). Combine with onion, egg, crumbs, milk, one of the 2 teaspoons of salt, part of the pepper (⅛ teaspoon), allspice, nutmeg and brown sugar; mix thoroughly. Shape into balls 1½ inches in diameter and roll in a little of the flour. Fry in hot fat or oil over medium heat until well browned on all sides. Remove meat balls from frying pan and add cream or bouillon in their place. Mix the remaining 2 tablespoons of flour with water to make a smooth paste; stir until thick. Season with rest of salt (1 teaspoon) and pepper (¼ teaspoon). Return meat balls to pan. Cover and cook for 20 minutes.

SUGGESTED MENU: Whipped potatoes, buttered asparagus and carrot slaw to go with the meat balls. For dessert, grapes, Danish blue cheese and crisp rye wafers.

DANISH GOULASH

4 to 5 Servings

1 lb. beef (shoulder or round)
2 tablespoons fat or salad oil
2 teaspoons salt
⅛ teaspoon pepper
1 medium-size onion, thinly sliced
2 bay leaves

1 tablespoon brown sugar
2¼ cups water
2 tablespoons flour
1 tablespoon paprika
1 tablespoon vinegar

Cut beef into ½-inch cubes. Brown lightly in hot fat or oil in heavy skillet. Add salt and pepper. Cover with onion slices, bay leaves and brown sugar. Pour most of water (2 cups) over all. Cover and simmer (do not boil) for 1½ hours. Remove bay leaves. Combine flour, paprika, remaining ¼ cup water and vinegar; stir into bubbling stew. Stir and cook for about 10 minutes to thicken.

SUGGESTED MENU: With the goulash serve parslied potatoes, chopped spinach with mushrooms and raw carrot sticks. For dessert, lemon snow with custard sauce.

NORWEGIAN MEAT BALLS

2 lbs. lean ground beef
small piece suet
1 large raw potato
1 small onion
2½ teaspoons salt
¼ teaspoon pepper

⅛ teaspoon nutmeg or mace
1 teaspoon baking powder
1 cup heavy cream
1 egg
¼ cup butter or margarine

Put meat, suet, potato and onion through meat grinder two or three times. Add all remaining ingredients except butter or margarine; mix well. Shape into small balls and brown in skillet in hot butter or margarine. Cover and cook over low heat for about 30 minutes, or until meat balls are well-done. Remove meat balls to a warmed serving dish. Thicken liquid remaining in pan for gravy (page 195); pour over meat balls.

SUGGESTED MENU: Begin with a small plate of hors d'oeuvres (sardines, pimento olives, pickled herring and coleslaw, for example). With the meat balls serve cauliflower with browned crumbs, sliced beets and light rye bread. For dessert, baked custard with caramel sauce.

SWEDISH MEAT BALLS

6 Servings

1 lb. lean ground beef
1 cup soft bread crumbs
1 cup milk
1 egg, well beaten
2 medium-size onions, chopped
2 teaspoons salt

⅛ teaspoon pepper
¼ teaspoon nutmeg
fat or salad oil
1 cup hot water
1 tablespoon flour
2 tablespoons cold water

Combine first 8 ingredients; mix well. Form into 1-inch balls. Brown on all sides in a little fat or oil. Remove from pan; keep warm. Add hot water to drippings in skillet; stir to mix. Put flour in a small bowl; stir in cold water. Mix well and stir into hot mixture. Bring to a boil; cook and stir until thick. Return meat balls to skillet. Cover and cook 30 minutes, adding more water, if necessary.

SUGGESTED MENU: Serve baked beans, coleslaw and sliced pickled beets with the meat balls. For dessert, Swedish pancakes with lingonberries.

SWEET AND PUNGENT MEAT BALLS (CHINESE)

4 Servings

3 large green peppers
1 lb. lean ground beef
1 egg, beaten
2 tablespoons flour
1½ teaspoons salt
dash pepper
¼ cup salad oil

1 cup chicken bouillon
4 slices canned pineapple, diced
12 maraschino cherries
3 tablespoons cornstarch
2 teaspoons soy sauce
½ cup vinegar
½ cup light corn syrup

Cut green peppers in sixths. Make 16 small meat balls. Combine egg, flour, part of salt (½ teaspoon) and pepper; dip meat balls in this batter. Heat salad oil; add remaining salt (1 teaspoon). Fry meat balls in hot oil, turning to brown on all sides. Remove from pan; drain off all but 1 tablespoon of oil. Put in part of bouillon ($^1/_3$ cup), pineapple, cherries and green pepper; simmer for 10 minutes. Blend cornstarch, soy sauce, vinegar, corn syrup and remaining bouillon ($^2/_3$ cup). Add to pineapple mixture. Cook slowly, stirring, until thickened. Pour over meat balls.

SUGGESTED MENU: Rice and tea complete the main course. For dessert, preserved kumquats, diced, on vanilla ice cream.

ORIENTAL PEPPER STEAK   6 Servings

1 ½ lbs. beef (sirloin or rib), cut in thin strips	1 teaspoon soy sauce
1 ½ teaspoons Ac'cent	2 green peppers, cut in strips
¼ cup salad oil	1 medium-size onion, sliced
1 cup bouillon	2 tomatoes, peeled and cut in wedges
½ teaspoon sugar	2 teaspoons cornstarch
¼ teaspoon ginger	2 tablespoons water

Sprinkle beef with part of Ac'cent (1 teaspoon). Brown beef in hot oil in skillet. Add bouillon, sugar, ginger and soy sauce. Bring to a boil, then reduce heat and simmer for 15 minutes. Add vegetables; sprinkle with remaining ½ teaspoon Ac'cent; cook 5 minutes longer. Combine cornstarch and water; stir until smooth. Add slowly to beef mixture. Cook, stirring constantly, until mixture thickens and comes to a boil.

SUGGESTED MENU: Rice, of course, and tea. Dessert can be hearty—deep-dish blueberry pie à la mode, for example.

STEAK ORIENTALE   4 Servings

1 ½ lbs. round steak, 1 in. thick	2 cups water
2 medium-size onions, sliced	1 cup sour cream
1 teaspoon curry powder	2 teaspoons prepared horse-radish
1 teaspoon powdered ginger	salt and pepper

Use meat tenderizer according to directions on page 19. Cut steak in 2-inch squares; place in deep skillet. Add onions, spices and water; simmer for about 45 minutes, or until onions are tender. Combine sour cream and horse-radish; add. Season to taste with salt and pepper. Heat thoroughly, but do not allow to boil.

SUGGESTED MENU: Rice or mashed potatoes are equally good with this meat dish, along with glazed carrots and a green salad. For dessert, grapefruit halves.

ORIENTAL CASSEROLE   8 Servings

1 ½ lbs. lean ground beef
  2 cups onion, coarsely chopped
  1 cup celery, sliced
  2 tablespoons fat or salad oil
  ⅛ teaspoon pepper

¹/₃ cup soy sauce
²/₃ cup uncooked rice
1 can (4 oz.) water chestnuts (undrained)
1 can (4 oz.) mushroom stems and pieces (undrained)

Cook beef, onion and celery in hot fat or salad oil until meat is lightly browned; pour off drippings. Add pepper, soy sauce and rice to the meat mixture. Drain water chestnuts and mushrooms, reserving liquid. Add enough water to the liquid to make 2 cups. Heat liquid to boiling point. Add hot liquid, water chestnuts and mushrooms to meat mixture. Mix lightly. Pour mixture into a greased 2-quart casserole. Cover tightly and bake in moderate oven (350°) for 1 hour.

SUGGESTED MENU: With the casserole serve grilled tomatoes and broccoli au gratin. For dessert, banana tapioca cream.

BEEF MANDARIN (CHINESE)   6 Servings

¼ cup salad oil
1 lb. beef chuck
1 ½ teaspoons Ac'cent
¼ teaspoon pepper
1 No. 2 can (2 cups) pineapple chunks (undrained)
1 cup celery, cut in ½-in. sections
1 can (12 oz.) apricot nectar
1 cup brown sugar
½ cup cider vinegar

2 cups juice drained from fruit
1 teaspoon salt
1 tablespoon soy sauce
3 tablespoons cornstarch
¼ cup water
1 large green pepper, cut in strips
3 tomatoes, cut in wedges
1 can (11 oz.) mandarin oranges (undrained)
12 blanched almonds

Heat salad oil in heavy skillet or electric skillet. Cut meat in 2-inch squares, ¼ inch thick. Season with Ac'cent and pepper. Sauté meat in hot salad oil for about 2 minutes on each side, until lightly browned but not dry. Lower heat; add pineapple and celery; stir carefully. Cover and cook for about 3 minutes. Combine apricot nectar with brown sugar and vinegar. Add liquid drained from pineapple and mandarin oranges (below), using water if necessary to make 2 cups of liquid. Stir in salt and soy sauce. Mix cornstarch with water; blend into liquid mixture, mixing thoroughly. Place in heavy cooking pan over moderate heat and cook until mixture becomes thick and transparent, *stirring constantly*. Remove from heat at once; pour over mixture in skillet. Carefully turn ingredients in skillet to mix with the sauce. Add green pepper, tomato wedges and mandarin oranges. Cover; cook about 5 minutes, or until heated through. Lift ingredients carefully with large spoon or spatula so as not to break tomatoes. Serve topped with almonds.

SUGGESTED MENU: Hot, buttered rice is all that is required. For dessert, prune snow and ladyfingers.

TERIYAKI (JAPANESE)   6 Servings

2 lbs. sirloin steak or tenderized round steak,   **1 medium-size onion, finely chopped**
  thinly sliced   **2 tablespoons sugar**
2 teaspoons powdered ginger   **½ cup soy sauce**
2 garlic cloves, minced   **¼ cup water**

Cut steak into portion-size pieces. Combine ginger, garlic, onion, sugar, soy sauce and water. Stir over low heat until sugar dissolves, then pour over meat. Let stand for 2 hours; drain. Broil for 3 to 5 minutes on each side.

SUGGESTED MENU: Rice is traditional, but you may prefer mashed potatoes or buttered noodles. Spinach and mashed Hubbard squash with pineapple go well with this dish. For dessert, a compote of cooked or canned fruits.

SUKIYAKI (JAPANESE)   8 Servings

1½ lbs. sirloin steak   **1 green pepper, cut in thin strips**
  2 tablespoons salad oil   **1 cup celery, sliced**
¼ cup sugar   **1 can (10½ oz.) bamboo shoots, thinly sliced**
¾ cup soy sauce   **1 can (6 oz.) broiled mushrooms, sliced (un-**
¼ cup water or mushroom stock   **drained)**
  2 medium-size onions, thinly sliced   **1 bunch scallions with tops cut in 1-in. lengths**

Cut steak in thin, diagonal slices about 2 × ½ inches and brown lightly in hot oil. Combine sugar, soy sauce and water or stock from canned mushrooms (below); add half of this to meat. Push meat to one side; add onions, green pepper and celery and cook for a few minutes. Add remaining soy sauce mixture, bamboo shoots and mushrooms. Cook for 3 to 5 minutes. Add scallions and cook 1 minute longer; stir well. Serve at once.

SUGGESTED MENU: Rice, cooked dry and fluffy in the Oriental manner, is always served with sukiyaki. Tea, of course. And for dessert, go occidental with a chocolate refrigerator cake.

VEAL

VEAL

Veal, with its delicate flavor, is one of the most versatile of meats because it combines so well with other foods of varied flavors. Perhaps this is why veal is used in so many French and Italian dishes which feature flavorful sauces.

As veal is young beef, it has very little fat. For this reason, broiling is not recommended. It is best when roasted, braised or stewed, and should always be well-done.

TOMATO-VEAL ROLLS
6 Servings

6 veal cutlets (1 ½ lbs.)
½ cup bread crumbs
1 can (4 oz.) mushrooms, sliced or pieces and stems (undrained)
¼ teaspoon sage
1 tablespoon parsley, minced
1 tablespoon liquid drained from mushrooms
1 teaspoon salt
¼ teaspoon pepper
1 cup onion, minced
3 tablespoons olive or salad oil
¼ cup flour
1 No. 303 can (1 lb.) solid-pack tomatoes
1 bay leaf
½ cup water

Have meat pounded very thin. Combine next 5 ingredients, along with half of the salt (½ teaspoon) and half of the pepper (⅛ teaspoon) to make stuffing. Spread stuffing on each of 6 cutlets. Roll up each and tie with string. Cook onion in hot oil until soft and golden. Coat meat rolls with flour and brown with onion. Add tomatoes, bay leaf, remaining salt (½ teaspoon) and remaining pepper (⅛ teaspoon). Cook covered over low heat for 1 hour and 15 minutes, or until fork-tender. Stir occasionally, adding a little of the water each time to keep sauce from sticking. Turn meat rolls halfway through cooking.

SUGGESTED MENU: Whipped potatoes, French-fried eggplant and buttered carrots with the meat. Apricot pie for dessert.

FLORIDA VEAL COLLOPS
4 to 6 Servings

2 lbs. veal
2 eggs, beaten
1 cup cracker crumbs
salt and pepper
fat

Cut veal in small pieces about the size of an oyster. Dip in beaten egg, then in cracker crumbs seasoned with salt and pepper. Fry in shallow fat (2 inches deep) heated to 390° until golden brown. Drain on absorbent paper.

SUGGESTED MENU: Mashed potatoes, green beans cooked with minced onion and coleslaw complete the main course. For dessert, apple-banana brown Betty.

SAVORY VEAL CUTLET

6 Servings

6 tablespoons salad oil
1 tablespoon vinegar
½ teaspoon salt
½ teaspoon paprika
1 bay leaf
1 garlic clove, mashed

2 lbs. veal cutlet
4 tablespoons flour
1 cup water
1 cup canned tomatoes
1 teaspoon sugar

Combine part of salad oil (4 tablespoons), vinegar, salt, paprika, bay leaf and garlic; pour over veal cutlet. Let stand for at least 4 hours, turning occasionally. Drain, then brown in remaining salad oil (2 tablespoons). Remove cutlet and cut in portion-size pieces. Blend flour into oil remaining in skillet. Add water, tomatoes, sugar and marinade. Cook and stir over low heat until thickened. Add cutlet, cover and simmer for 1 hour, or until tender.

SUGGESTED MENU: Serve hashed-brown potatoes, buttered Brussels sprouts and raw carrot sticks with the veal. For dessert, sherried grapefruit halves.

VEAL BIRDS

4 Servings

½ lb. pork sausage meat
2 cups soft bread crumbs (firmly packed)
1 small onion, grated
8 thin slices veal (about 1 lb.)
¼ cup flour

½ teaspoon salt
  dash pepper
2 chicken bouillon cubes
1 ½ cups hot water
¼ cup cold water

Break up sausage meat in skillet. Cook over medium heat for 10 minutes, stirring occasionally with fork. Meanwhile, combine crumbs and onion. Lift sausage meat from skillet with wide, slotted spatula, leaving fat. Add sausage meat to crumb mixture to make stuffing; mix well. Place spoonful of stuffing in center of each slice of veal. Roll up firmly; secure with wooden picks. Combine flour, salt and pepper; dredge meat rolls with seasoned flour. Save any remaining flour mixture. Brown rolls on all sides in sausage fat over medium heat. Drain off any fat remaining in skillet. Dissolve bouillon cubes in hot water; pour into skillet and cover. Cook over low heat for 40 minutes. Thicken gravy in skillet with remaining seasoned flour blended with cold water. Add extra flour if necessary (see page 195). Season to taste with more salt and pepper.

SUGGESTED MENU: Whipped potatoes, braised celery and broccoli with the veal birds. Grapefruit, pineapple and red apple salad with cream mayonnaise for dessert.

ALABAMA "TURKEY" LEGS

4 Servings

1 lb. veal steak or cutlet
  seasoned flour
1 cup evaporated milk

½ cup fine bread crumbs
3 tablespoons fat or salad oil
¾ cup water

Cut veal steak or cutlet into strips 2 × 3 inches. Thread on skewers, using 3 to 4 strips to a skewer. Press firmly into shape of drumstick. Roll in flour, dip in milk, then roll in crumbs and sauté in hot fat or oil. Add water. Bake in a moderate oven (325°) for 1 hour. Add milk left after dipping and reduce heat to low (275°). Bake 15 minutes longer.

SUGGESTED MENU: With the mock turkey legs serve creamed potatoes and peas. Add an orange and onion ring salad. For dessert, ice cream and plain cake.

DAKOTA CUTLETS   4 Servings

1 ½ lbs. veal steak
1 egg, slightly beaten
1/3 cup milk
1 teaspoon salt

1 cup fine cracker crumbs
3 tablespoons fat or salad oil
1 cup boiling water or stock

Cut veal into 4 pieces. Combine egg, milk and salt. Dip veal in egg mixture, then in crumbs. Brown in hot fat or oil. Add boiling water or stock; cover. Bake in a moderate oven (350°) for 1 hour.

SUGGESTED MENU: Hashed-brown potatoes, buttered zucchini squash and raw carrot sticks with the veal. For dessert, strawberry chiffon pie.

SUNDAY VEAL   6 Servings

1 ½ lbs. veal cutlet, ½ in. thick
  fine bread crumbs
1 egg, beaten
  water (a little more than 1 cup)
1 onion, sliced
¼ cup fat or salad oil
1 ½ teaspoons paprika

1 ½ teaspoons salt
⅛ teaspoon pepper
1 cup sour cream
½ cup blanched almonds, sliced
2 tablespoons butter or margarine
1 pkg. (6 oz.) noodles, cooked

Cut veal into individual portions. Dip pieces in crumbs, then in egg beaten with a little of the water, then in crumbs again. Cook veal pieces and onion in hot fat or oil, turning veal to brown on both sides. Reduce heat; add seasonings and rest of water (1 cup). Cover and simmer for 1 hour. Add sour cream; mix. Spoon gravy over meat while heating thoroughly. Brown almonds in butter or margarine; stir into cooked noodles. Serve veal and gravy in a ring of noodles.

SUGGESTED MENU: With the veal-noodle dish serve sweet-sour cucumber slices, new potatoes in jackets and asparagus spears. For dessert, strawberries and cream.

BREADED VEAL STEAK

4 to 6 Servings

1 veal steak, 1 in. thick
½ cup buttermilk
½ cup fine bread crumbs

2 tablespoons fat or salad oil
1 cup tomato juice
salt and pepper

Dip meat first in buttermilk, then in crumbs. Chill breaded veal for several hours. Heat fat or oil in skillet and brown veal in it, turning once to brown evenly. Add tomato juice and salt and pepper to taste. Cover and simmer over low heat for 1 hour, or until tender. Add more tomato juice, if necessary, to keep meat moist. Thicken gravy (page 195), if desired.

SUGGESTED MENU: Parslied potatoes, buttered green beans and raw cauliflower salad complete the main course. For dessert, date squares à la mode.

VEAL CUTLETS IN CREAM GRAVY

4 Servings

2 lbs. veal cutlets
salt and pepper
2 eggs, beaten
fine bread crumbs
3 tablespoons fat or salad oil

1 cup cream
1 tablespoon flour
2 tablespoons cold water
crisp cooked bacon

Cut veal in individual portions; wipe dry. Sprinkle with salt and pepper; dip in beaten egg, then in crumbs. Sauté in hot fat or oil. When pieces are well browned on both sides, remove to hot platter. Add cream to pan. Blend flour with cold water and mix with cream. Stir over low heat to make a smooth gravy; pour gravy over meat. Garnish with crisp bacon slices.

SUGGESTED MENU: French-fried potatoes, buttered beets and a mixed green salad with the veal. For dessert, lemon gelatin whip with orange sections.

VEAL SWISS STEAK

6 to 8 Servings

2 lbs. veal steak (1½ in. thick)
salt and pepper
flour
2 tablespoons fat or salad oil

1 cup onions, sliced
¼ cup green pepper, diced
¼ cup celery, diced
1 cup tomato juice

Use meat tenderizer (page 19); season well with salt and pepper. Coat both sides with flour. Brown in hot fat or oil in heavy skillet. Add vegetables and tomato juice. Cover and simmer for about 1½ hours, or until veal is fork-tender.

SUGGESTED MENU: Browned rice, buttered asparagus spears and grated carrot salad round out the main course. For dessert, fruit fritters with orange sauce.

VEAL IN MUSHROOM SAUCE
6 Servings

1 egg, slightly beaten
10 tablespoons (⅝ cup) milk
1 teaspoon salt
  dash pepper

6 veal chops
1 cup fine bread crumbs
2 tablespoons fat or salad oil
1 can condensed mushroom soup

Combine egg, 2 of the 10 tablespoons of milk, salt and pepper. Dip chops in bread crumbs, then in egg, then in crumbs again. Brown on both sides in hot fat or salad oil. Combine mushroom soup and remaining milk (8 tablespoons or ½ cup) and add. Cover and simmer for 45 minutes.

SUGGESTED MENU: With the veal chops serve parslied potatoes, buttered beets and cooked shredded cabbage. For dessert, coconut cream pie.

VEAL CHOPS CALIFORNIA
6 Servings

1 garlic clove
6 loin veal chops
  seasoned flour
3 tablespoons fat or salad oil
1 No. 303 can (1 lb.) tomatoes

2 medium-size onions, thinly sliced
1 lb. fresh mushrooms, sliced
3 tablespoons butter or margarine
¼ cup sherry
¼ cup ripe olives, sliced

Peel garlic clove and rub over inner surface of frying pan; discard garlic. Dredge chops in seasoned flour. Brown on both sides in hot fat or salad oil. Add tomatoes and onions. Simmer for 1½ hours. Cook mushrooms in butter or margarine until golden brown. Add with sherry and olives and simmer 15 minutes longer.

SUGGESTED MENU: With the chops serve baked potatoes, buttered zucchini and sliced carrots. For dessert, lemon tapioca cream.

VEAL CHOPS SUPREME
6 Servings

6 loin veal chops
2 tablespoons butter or margarine
¼ teaspoon nutmeg
1 can chicken broth
1 cup tomato juice

¼ teaspoon rosemary
⅛ teaspoon white pepper
1 teaspoon salt
  dash powdered cloves
2 tablespoons parsley, minced

Brown chops on both sides in butter or margarine; sprinkle with nutmeg. Combine chicken broth and tomato juice; add 1 cup of this mixture to chops with rosemary, pepper, salt and cloves. Simmer for 10 minutes, then add remaining liquid. Cover and simmer 40 to 50 minutes longer or until chops are tender. Remove chops to platter. Thicken sauce (page 195) and pour over chops. Sprinkle with parsley.

SUGGESTED MENU: Serve buttered spaghetti and broccoli with the chops. Add carrot slaw. For dessert, stewed rhubarb and cookies.

GLAZED ROLLED VEAL SHOULDER
6 Servings

3 to 4 lbs. veal shoulder, boned and rolled
  1 can (12 oz.) apricot nectar
  ½ cup brown sugar

2 tablespoons frozen concentrated grapefruit
juice

Place veal on rack in open roasting pan. Insert meat thermometer so that bulb reaches center of roast. Do not add water. Do not cover. Roast in slow oven (300°) for 1 ½ hours. During this cooking time, prepare apricot glaze. Combine apricot nectar, grapefruit juice and brown sugar; simmer for about 10 minutes. Cool. Remove veal from oven after roasting for 1 ½ hours and spoon about ¹/₃ of glaze over it. Continue roasting for 20 minutes. Spoon another ¹/₃ of glaze over veal and roast for another 20 minutes. Then coat the veal with remaining glaze and continue roasting until meat thermometer registers 170°. Allow about 40 minutes per pound for roasting. Serve drippings as sauce with veal.

SUGGESTED MENU: Baked yams, creamed spinach and a tossed salad accompany the veal. For dessert, mocha tapioca cream.

VEAL LOAF
6 Servings

1 ¼ lbs. veal shoulder, ground
  ¾ lb. beef chuck, ground
  2 tablespoons parsley, minced
  1 tablespoon onion, grated
  1 cup soft bread crumbs

½ cup evaporated milk
1 egg
1 teaspoon salt
⅛ teaspoon pepper
few drops Tabasco

Combine all ingredients; mix well. Pack into greased loaf pan 8 × 5 × 3 inches; cover with aluminum foil. Bake in moderate oven (375°) for 1 hour and 15 minutes, removing foil after 45 minutes.

SUGGESTED MENU: Baked stuffed potatoes, green beans with mushrooms and tomato aspic salad with the veal loaf. For dessert, honey baked apples.

SAVORY MEAT LOAF
6 to 8 Servings

1 egg, beaten
¾ cup coffee
¼ teaspoon oregano
1 ½ teaspoons salt
  dash cayenne

2 cups soft bread crumbs
1 medium-size onion, minced
1 lb. veal shoulder, ground
1 lb. pork shoulder, ground

Combine egg, coffee, oregano, salt, cayenne and bread crumbs. Let stand for 5 minutes. Add onion and meats; mix well. Pack into greased loaf pan. Bake in moderate oven (350°) for 1 ½ hours.

SUGGESTED MENU: Potatoes baked in cheese sauce, okra Creole and a green salad with the meat loaf. For dessert, mocha chocolate-chip ice cream.

PEACH-GLAZED MEAT LOAF 8 Servings

1 lb. smoked ham, ground
1½ lbs. veal shoulder, ground
2 eggs, well beaten
1 cup milk
½ teaspoon salt
⅛ teaspoon pepper

1 cup fine bread crumbs
whole cloves
1 No. 2½ can (3½ cups) cling peach halves
(undrained)
½ cup brown sugar, firmly packed
2 tablespoons vinegar

Combine first 7 ingredients. Shape into loaf in shallow ungreased baking pan. Insert whole cloves in diagonal pattern on top of loaf. Bake in moderate oven (350°) for 1½ hours. Meanwhile, drain peaches and mix peach syrup, brown sugar and vinegar in saucepan. Simmer for 5 minutes, stirring until sugar is dissolved. Baste the loaf every 20 minutes, using approximately half the syrup. Stud peaches with cloves, heat in remaining syrup and use as garnish.

SUGGESTED MENU: Baked sweet potatoes, buttered cauliflower and French-cut green beans with the meat loaf. Try a chicory salad with Roquefort dressing. For dessert, raisin pie.

MEAT LOAF DE LUXE 6 Servings

1 egg, beaten
¾ cup milk
2 cups soft bread crumbs
1 teaspoon poultry seasoning
1½ teaspoons salt
dash pepper

1 onion, minced
1 lb. veal shoulder, chopped
1 lb. pork shoulder, chopped
5 to 6 strips bacon
1 can broiled mushrooms (optional)

Combine first 6 ingredients in bowl. Let stand for 5 minutes. Add onion and chopped meats; mix well. Line an 8- × 5- × 3-inch loaf pan with bacon, stretching strips across width of pan. Lightly pack meat mixture into pan. Bake in moderate oven (350°) for 1½ hours. Remove from oven and drain off fat. Invert meat loaf on baking sheet. Raise oven temperature to very hot (450°). Return meat loaf to oven for about 10 minutes, or until bacon is crisp. Heat some canned broiled mushrooms, if desired, and use to garnish top of meat loaf.

SUGGESTED MENU: Serve baked potatoes with sour cream and chives with the meat loaf. Add scalloped tomatoes and a green salad. Top off with grapes in lime gelatin.

CREAMY MUSHROOMS AND VEAL

4 Servings

2 lbs. veal shoulder, boned and cut in small pieces
2 tablespoons butter or margarine
½ cup onion, minced
¼ teaspoon garlic salt
¾ teaspoon salt

dash pepper
2 teaspoons paprika
2 beef bouillon cubes
1½ cups boiling water
1 can (4 oz.) mushrooms
1 pint sour cream

Sauté veal in butter or margarine until golden. Add onion and sauté until golden and tender. Add garlic salt, salt, pepper, paprika, bouillon cubes, water and mushrooms. Cook covered over low heat for about 50 minutes, or until meat is very tender. Slowly stir in sour cream. Heat thoroughly, but do not boil.

SUGGESTED MENU: Buttered green noodles, broiled tomatoes and French-fried cauliflower with the meat. For dessert, frozen fruit and cream cheese salad.

VEAL RAGOUT

6 Servings

3 lbs. veal shoulder or breast
3 cups boiling water
1 bay leaf
5 peppercorns
½ teaspoon salt
3 medium-size onions, sliced
4 carrots, sliced

1 cup celery, sliced
⅛ teaspoon rosemary
1 can (4 oz.) button mushrooms (undrained)
¼ cup flour
½ cup water
corn meal dumplings
parsley, chopped

Cut veal in 2-inch cubes. Place in Dutch oven or heavy sauce pot. Add boiling water, bay leaf, peppercorns and salt. Cover and simmer for 1 hour. Add vegetables to veal and simmer 45 minutes longer. Add rosemary and undrained mushrooms. Combine flour and water. Blend until smooth, then stir slowly into boiling stew. Prepare dumplings (cook as directed below). Lift out cooked dumplings and turn stew into serving dish. Place dumplings on top. Garnish with chopped parsley.

CORN MEAL DUMPLINGS

Makes 6 large dumplings

¼ cup all-purpose flour
1 teaspoon baking powder
½ teaspoon salt
1 cup yellow corn meal

1 egg, beaten
½ cup milk
1 tablespoon butter or margarine, melted

Sift together flour, baking powder and salt; stir in corn meal. Combine egg and milk; add. Stir in melted butter or margarine. Drop by spoonfuls into stew. Each dumpling should rest on meat or vegetable. Cover and cook for 15 minutes.

SUGGESTED MENU: You need only a tossed salad to complete the main course. For dessert, sliced bananas with custard sauce.

BARBECUED VEAL

6 Servings

4 to 5 lbs. veal shoulder
½ cup ketchup
½ cup onion, chopped

2 lemons, thinly sliced
salt and pepper

Place veal in roasting pan. Cover with layers of ketchup, onion and lemon and sprinkle with salt and pepper. Roast in moderate oven (350°) for 3 hours, or about 45 minutes per pound.

SUGGESTED MENU: Scalloped sweet potatoes and apples and buttered Brussels sprouts with the veal. Lettuce wedges with French dressing. For dessert, lemon sherbet and gingersnaps.

BRAISED VEAL SHANKS

2 Servings

2 veal shanks (¾ to 1 lb. ea.)
1 teaspoon salt
  dash pepper
¼ cup flour
¼ cup fat or salad oil

1 cup water
1 tablespoon vinegar
¼ cup celery, chopped
¼ cup onion, chopped
½ cup carrots, sliced

Wipe shanks with damp paper towel. Season with salt and pepper and roll in flour to coat evenly. Brown well in hot fat or oil in heavy skillet. Add water, vinegar and vegetables. Cover and bake in moderate oven (350°) for about 2 hours or until the meat is fork-tender. If necessary, add more water to keep shanks moist. Uncover and bake 15 to 20 minutes longer, or until the gravy around the shanks is thick. Serve hot.

SUGGESTED MENU: Baked potatoes, buttered broccoli and green-pepper slaw complete the main course. Apple-cranberry pie for dessert.

VEAL BIRDS IN MUSHROOM GRAVY

6 Servings

2 veal round steaks, ½ in. thick
$^1/_3$ cup celery, chopped
$^1/_3$ cup walnuts, chopped
$^1/_3$ cup stuffed olives, chopped

2 tablespoons fat or salad oil
1 can condensed mushroom soup
½ cup milk
½ teaspoon paprika

Cut veal into 6 pieces. Pound to about ¼-inch thickness. Mix together celery, walnuts and olives; spoon about 2 tablespoonfuls on each piece of veal. Roll like jelly roll and fasten with wooden picks or tie with string. Brown meat slowly in hot fat or salad oil. Pour off drippings. Mix together mushroom soup, milk and paprika. Add to veal birds. Cover tightly and simmer for 45 minutes, or until meat is tender.

SUGGESTED MENU: Spanish rice, buttered cauliflower and green beans vinaigrette with the meat. Lemon snow pudding with custard sauce for dessert.

SOUR-CREAM VEAL LOAF

6 to 8 Servings

1 ½ lbs. veal, ground
½ lb. pork, ground
2 tablespoons onion, minced
2 carrots, ground

1 ½ teaspoons salt
⅛ teaspoon pepper
½ cup sour cream

Combine all ingredients; mix thoroughly. Pack into loaf pan 8 × 5 × 3 inches; bake in moderate oven (350°) for 1 ½ hours. Thicken drippings for gravy (see page 195).

SUGGESTED MENU: With the meat loaf serve baked potatoes, broccoli and salad of sliced oranges. For dessert, apple pie.

SUMMER VEAL LOAF

4 to 6 Servings

1 lb. veal round steak, ground
1 veal knuckle
  salt and pepper

4 hard-cooked eggs, sliced
parsley

Simmer veal and veal knuckle in enough water to cover until meat is very tender. Remove from liquid; continue boiling liquid until it is reduced to about half original volume. Season meat with salt and pepper to taste; chop or grind coarsely. Arrange some of egg slices in bottom of loaf pan. Add a little of the stock and chill until set. Spread half of veal, remaining egg slices, then other half of veal, in layers. Pour rest of liquid over all. Press with a weight; chill until firm. Serve cold, sliced and garnished with parsley.

SUGGESTED MENU: Potato, celery and cucumber salad, hot, crusty rolls and assorted relishes with the veal loaf. For dessert, lemon ice cream.

VEAL CHOPS WITH PRUNES

6 Servings

1 ½ cups uncooked prunes
  1 can (6 oz.) mushroom crowns
  1 cup onions, coarsely chopped
  2 tablespoons fat or salad oil
  1 can (8 oz.) tomato sauce

4 large veal chops
  dash pepper
1 teaspoon salt
2 cups water

Cook prunes for 10 minutes in enough water to cover. Remove pits and cut into medium-size pieces. Drain mushrooms and cook with onions in hot fat or oil for 5 minutes. Add tomato sauce and cook 10 minutes longer. Add prunes, chops, salt, pepper and water. Cover and simmer for 1 hour. If desired, thicken sauce (page 195) before serving.

SUGGESTED MENU: With the chops serve fluffy rice, mashed butternut squash and green beans. For dessert, whipped coffee jelly with cream.

IDAHO VEAL DAUBE

4 to 5 lbs. veal rump or shoulder
    bacon fat
2 teaspoons salt
¼ teaspoon allspice
⅛ teaspoon mace
⅛ teaspoon pepper
⅛ teaspoon cloves
½ teaspoon thyme
2 bay leaves, crushed

¼ cup flour
3 to 4 tablespoons fat or salad oil
1 onion, chopped
4 carrots, sliced
1 turnip, cubed
½ cup celery, diced
1 cup boiling water
1 sweet red pepper, chopped

Rub veal with a little bacon fat. Combine seasonings with flour; rub mixture into meat, covering all sides. Brown meat in hot fat or oil. Add vegetables; sauté quickly to brown. Stir in boiling water. Cover and cook over low heat until tender, or about 2 hours. Thicken liquid in pan (page 195) for gravy.

SUGGESTED MENU: Simply add a salad of tossed greens to this hearty meal-in-a-dish. For dessert, fresh fruit in season.

STUFFED VEAL SHOULDER

1 shoulder of veal (about 7 lbs.)
3 teaspoons salt
¼ cup butter or margarine
¾ cup celery, finely chopped
1 can (9 oz.) crushed pineapple (undrained)

4 cups fine bread crumbs
1 cup canned whole cranberry sauce
½ teaspoon oregano
¼ teaspoon nutmeg
4 slices bacon

Have meat dealer bone and open the veal shoulder. Sprinkle cut side with part of salt (2 teaspoons). Heat butter or margarine in a small skillet. Add celery and cook covered over low heat until tender. Put celery into large bowl. Drain pineapple, reserving juice. Add pineapple to celery with the next 4 ingredients and remaining salt (1 teaspoon); mix well. Spread stuffing evenly over veal. Roll up like a jelly roll and fasten with twine. Set oven for moderate (325°). Place veal on rack in open roaster or shallow baking pan and garnish with bacon. Measure pineapple juice and, if necessary, add enough water to make ½ cup of liquid; pour over meat. Roast covered for 1 hour, then remove cover and continue roasting for 2 to 3 hours. Baste meat frequently with pan drippings. For easier carving, allow veal to become firm for about 10 minutes before slicing.

SUGGESTED MENU: Green lima beans, mashed butternut squash and endive salad round out the main course. For dessert, floating island.

VEAL CURRY

1 ½ lbs. veal stew meat, cubed
1 tablespoon fat or salad oil
½ cup onion, chopped
1 tart apple, chopped
1 ½ teaspoons salt
⅛ teaspoon pepper

1 tablespoon curry powder
1 teaspoon sugar
2 cups bouillon or water
¼ cup raisins
2 cups hot cooked rice
  flaked coconut or nuts, chopped (optional)

Brown cubed meat in hot fat or oil. Add onion, apple, seasonings and liquid. Cover and cook gently for 1 hour. Thicken gravy (page 195). Add raisins and cook 15 minutes longer. Serve over hot cooked rice. Sprinkle, if desired, with flaked coconut or chopped nuts.

SUGGESTED MENU: With the curry and rice serve fried eggplant, green peas and a tossed salad. For dessert, baked bananas topped with raspberry jam and flaked coconut.

VARIETY MEATS

The world of flavor remains only partially explored until you discover the so-called variety meats and exploit their infinite possibilities as menu brighteners.

Some are exceptionally rich in minerals and vitamins (particularly liver, heart and kidneys), all have important proteins and each type has a distinctive flavor all its own.

Prices of variety meats vary with demand. Calf's liver, veal kidneys, sweetbreads and tongue are more popular, while beef liver, beef kidneys, heart, brains, tripe and oxtails are lower in cost.

Buying Guide

Liver is rich in food value. The most popular liver—veal (or calf's)—is mild in flavor, tender and light in color.

Beef liver is less tender, darker in color and has a more pronounced flavor.

Kidney is highly nutritious. *Veal kidney* needs very little cooking. *Beef kidney* is stronger in flavor and most tastes require it to be well cooked.

Heart is too often neglected as a rich source of nutrients. Firm textured, both veal and beef heart require long, slow moist-heat cooking, although veal heart is more tender and has a more delicate flavor.

Tongue is sold fresh, smoked, corned, pickled and canned.

Sweetbreads, delicate and tender, are considered a great delicacy by gourmets everywhere.

Brains are both delicate in taste and perishable. They are interchangeable in recipes calling for sweetbreads.

Oxtails are mainly bone, but what meat there is has a fine, rich flavor. They are usually sold disjointed, and make a wonderful base for soup.

Tripe is available in three varieties: honeycomb, pocket and plain. Of these three, honeycomb tripe is preferred by most people. You can buy fresh-cooked tripe (which requires additional cooking), pickled tripe (thoroughly cooked, but must be soaked before use) and canned tripe (ready to heat and serve).

VARIETY MEATS

SAVORY LIVER

6 Servings

¼ cup onion, chopped
1 tablespoon parsley, chopped
2 tablespoons butter or margarine
2 tablespoons flour
¼ teaspoon salt

dash pepper
2 tablespoons vinegar
2 cups broth or stock
1½ lbs. beef liver, thinly sliced

Brown onion and parsley in butter or margarine. Stir in flour, seasonings and vinegar; simmer until mixture thickens. Add broth or stock; stir until smooth. Place liver slices in hot gravy and cook for 20 to 25 minutes.

SUGGESTED MENU: Buttered hominy grits, diced parslied carrots and sweet onion rings in seasoned vinegar accompany the meat. For dessert, bananas in cherry gelatin.

BEEF LIVER STACKS

4 Servings

3 slices bacon
2 tablespoons flour
½ teaspoon salt
¼ teaspoon pepper
¼ teaspoon sage

1 lb. beef liver, ½ in. thick
1 egg, slightly beaten
2 tablespoons milk
2 medium-size tomatoes
1 tablespoon butter or margarine

Cook bacon until crisp; remove from drippings. Drain and cut each slice in half. Mix together flour, salt, pepper and sage. Cut liver into 6 pieces; dip in seasoned flour, then in egg diluted with milk. Place in frying pan containing bacon drippings and sprinkle with any remaining flour. Brown liver slowly on both sides. Cut each tomato in 3 slices; cook slices in butter or margarine until each side is lightly browned and heated through. To serve, place a slice of tomato on each slice of liver and top with a half-slice of bacon.

SUGGESTED MENU: With the liver serve spinach soufflé and spaghetti with butter sauce. For dessert, baked applesauce and ginger cookies.

QUICK MUSHROOM-SMOTHERED LIVER

4 Servings

4 thin slices beef liver
  salt and pepper
  garlic salt

butter or margarine
1 can (4 oz.) button mushrooms, drained

Sprinkle liver with salt, pepper, and garlic salt. Dot with butter or margarine. Broil until done to taste. Remove liver to heated platter to keep warm. Add mushrooms to pan juices; heat through; pour over liver.

SUGGESTED MENU: Creamed potatoes and green beans Creole with the liver. Add an endive salad. For dessert, peppermint ice cream with chocolate sauce.

ARIZONA LIVER LOAF

6 to 8 Servings

1 ½ lbs. (3 cups) cooked ground beef liver
  1 cup fine bread crumbs
  3 fresh tomatoes, finely chopped
  1 medium-size onion, chopped

3 eggs
1 tablespoon butter or margarine, melted
1 can spaghetti sauce
  salt and pepper

Combine all ingredients; mix well. Turn into greased baking dish or casserole. Bake in moderate oven (350°) for 45 to 50 minutes.

SUGGESTED MENU: Kidney bean succotash and a mixed green salad round out the main course. For dessert, broiled sherried grapefruit.

SUPREME OF LIVER

4 Servings

  1 lb. calf's liver
½ teaspoon salt
¼ teaspoon pepper
¼ teaspoon sage

¼ cup corn meal
3 to 4 tablespoons fat or salad oil
  ½ cup heavy cream or sour cream
    salt and pepper

Slice liver thin. Roll in mixture of seasonings and corn meal and fry in hot fat or oil until browned on both sides. Remove to a warm platter. Drain all but about 1 tablespoonful of fat or oil from pan. Add cream or sour cream; season to taste. Bring to a boil quickly and pour over liver at once.

SUGGESTED MENU: Whipped potatoes, sautéed fresh mushrooms and grilled tomatoes accompany the meat. Add a water cress salad. For dessert, lemon chiffon pie.

LIVER AND RICE CASSEROLE

4 Servings

¾ lb. beef liver
½ cup celery, diced
¼ cup onions, diced
¼ cup green pepper, diced

¼ cup fat or salad oil
1 teaspoon salt
2 cups cooked rice
1 cup cooked tomatoes or juice

Simmer liver for 10 minutes in enough water to cover. Drain and grind or chop coarsely. Brown liver, celery, onions, and green pepper in hot fat or oil. Add salt. Mix in rice and tomatoes. Place in casserole, cover and bake in moderate oven (350°) for 30 minutes. Remove cover and brown lightly for 10 minutes.

SUGGESTED MENU: Buttered broccoli and Mexican-style corn accompany the casserole. Add a green salad. For dessert, chilled sliced pineapple and chocolate loaf cake.

LIVER CREOLE
4 to 6 Servings

1 lb. beef liver, sliced
  flour
3 tablespoons fat or salad oil

salt and pepper
2 tablespoons onion, chopped
1 No. 303 can (1 lb.) tomatoes

Dip liver slices in flour. Brown in hot fat or oil. Season to taste with salt and pepper. Add onion and tomatoes. Cover and cook slowly for 15 minutes. Uncover and cook 15 minutes longer, or until liver is tender and sauce has thickened.

SUGGESTED MENU: Baked potatoes and buttered mixed vegetables with the meat. Add a tossed green salad. For dessert, cream-topped squash pie.

CURRIED LIVER
5 to 6 Servings

1 lb. beef liver, sliced
  flour
1 large onion, thinly sliced
½ cup celery, chopped
3 tablespoons fat or salad oil

1 beef bouillon cube
1 cup water
2 teaspoons curry powder
2 teaspoons salt

Roll liver in flour. Pan-fry onion and celery in hot fat or oil; push to one side of pan. Brown liver on both sides. Spread onion and celery over the liver. Dissolve bouillon cube in water. Add seasonings and pour over liver and onions. Cover and cook slowly for 30 minutes.

SUGGESTED MENU: Mashed sweet potatoes, buttered broccoli and beet relish with the meat. For dessert, grapes in lime gelatin.

SAVORY LIVER AND BACON
6 Servings

½ cup flour
1 teaspoon salt
¼ teaspoon pepper
1 teaspoon Ac'cent

½ teaspoon sugar
6 slices beef liver
12 strips bacon
1 cup water

Combine first 5 ingredients. Dredge liver slices in this mixture; let stand. Fry bacon until crisp; drain. Brown liver slices on both sides in hot bacon fat; pour off any excess fat. Add water to pan, cover and simmer for 20 minutes, or until liver is tender and well-done. Put bacon strips on top of liver for last few minutes of baking time to reheat. Make gravy with pan drippings if desired (page 195).

SUGGESTED MENU: Creamed potatoes, chopped beet greens and carrots julienne with the meat. Add a cucumber salad. For dessert, rhubarb whip.

FRIED LIVER AND BACON

1 ½ lbs. calf's liver, ½ in. thick   salt and pepper
    flour   6 slices bacon

Cut liver in individual portions. Coat each piece with flour and sprinkle with salt and pepper. Place bacon in cold skillet; cook over low heat until crisp and brown. Pour off excess fat as it accumulates. Drain bacon on absorbent paper; keep hot.

Put liver into skillet with bacon fat left in the pan. Fry over medium heat for about 10 minutes, turning once. Most people prefer calf's liver slightly pink inside. Avoid overcooking, which toughens liver.

SUGGESTED MENU: Hashed-brown potatoes, sliced buttered beets and creamed spinach with the liver and bacon. Add lettuce wedges with Russian dressing. For dessert, pineapple sherbet.

LIVER TERRAPIN
4 to 5 Servings

1 lb. beef or calf's liver   1 can condensed cream of chicken soup
¼ cup flour $^1/_3$ cup cream
$^1/_3$ cup butter or margarine   4 hard-cooked eggs, chopped
1 ½ teaspoons salt   2 tablespoons parsley, chopped
⅛ teaspoon pepper

Cube liver and roll in flour. Brown in melted butter or margarine, stirring until liver is well browned. Season with salt and pepper. Add chicken soup mixed with cream. Cook slowly for about 5 minutes. Add eggs and parsley. Cover and cook slowly for 15 minutes.

SUGGESTED MENU: Serve the terrapin on hot, fluffy rice. Combine green beans and canned tomatoes as an accompaniment. Add raw carrot sticks. For dessert, coconut custard pie.

MOCK TURTLE ON TOAST
4 servings

3 slices bacon, halved   1 can condensed consommé
1 lb. calf's liver   2 teaspoons lemon juice
¼ lb. mushrooms, chopped   2 hard-cooked eggs, chopped
2 tablespoons flour $^1/_3$ cup stuffed olives, chopped
¼ teaspoon dry mustard   4 pieces toast
⅛ teaspoon pepper

Fry bacon until crisp; remove from pan. Dice liver; cook in bacon fat with mushrooms for 5 minutes, stirring constantly. Combine flour, mustard and pepper; add and blend well. Add consommé. Bring to a boil, then reduce heat and simmer for half an hour. Add remaining ingredients and crisp bacon. Serve on toast.

SUGGESTED MENU: For a Sunday night supper, add broccoli or asparagus and a tomato aspic salad. For dessert, chocolate angel food and ice cream.

CALF'S LIVER IN GRAVY

6 Servings

6 slices calf's liver, ½ in. thick
¼ cup flour
½ teaspoon salt

6 slices bacon
1 large onion, sliced
1 cup rich milk or light cream

Wipe liver slices to dry; dip in flour seasoned with salt until well coated. Fry bacon; remove to warm platter. Cook onion in bacon fat until soft; push to one side. Brown liver slices on both sides in bacon fat and top with onion. Pour milk or cream over all; simmer for a few minutes until gravy thickens. Place liver slices on platter with bacon; add hot gravy. Serve at once.

SUGGESTED MENU: Hot, fluffy rice, buttered asparagus and cucumber and radish salad complete the main course. For dessert, peach roly-poly.

BEEF KIDNEY STEW

4 Servings

1 beef kidney
  cold salted water
  fresh water (a little more than 3 cups)
1 medium-size onion, sliced
1 teaspoon dry mustard
1 teaspoon salt

⅛ teaspoon pepper
2 tablespoons flour
2 tablespoons butter or margarine
1 cup canned peas
1 cup celery, diced
1 tablespoon Worcestershire sauce

Split kidney; remove all fat and white tubes. Cut into ¼-inch slices. Soak for one hour in enough cold salted water to cover; drain. Pour in enough fresh water to cover. Bring to a boil; drain. Add more of the fresh water (3 cups) and bring to a boil. Skim, then add sliced onion, mustard, salt and pepper. Simmer for 1 hour, or until kidney is fork-tender. Brown flour in butter or margarine. Add peas, celery and Worcestershire sauce; stir into kidney broth. Simmer and stir for 10 minutes. Serve hot.

SUGGESTED MENU: Mashed potatoes, grilled tomatoes and wax beans vinaigrette with the stew. For dessert, apple crisp.

KIDNEY RAGOUT

4 to 6 Servings

2 beef kidneys
  cold salted water
3 tablespoons fat or salad oil
1 can condensed consommé
1 cup tomato juice
¼ cup flour
1 teaspoon salt

⅛ teaspoon pepper
1 cup carrots, sliced
1 cup onions, sliced
1 cup celery, sliced
2 teaspoons Worcestershire sauce
  dash Tabasco

Wash kidneys and remove skin and fat. Split lengthwise; remove core and membrane and cut into small cubes. Cover with cold salted water and let stand for 1 hour. Drain, then rinse under cold running water. Brown kidneys in hot fat or salad oil; remove from pan. Blend flour, salt and pepper into fat or oil. Add consommé and tomato juice; cook and stir over low heat until thickened. Return kidneys and simmer for 1 hour. Add vegetables and simmer for another hour, or until tender. Add Worcestershire sauce and Tabasco.

SUGGESTED MENU: Baked potatoes and a green salad complete the main course. For dessert, preserved figs with cream cheese.

KIDNEY IN SAVORY SAUCE   4 Servings

4 veal kidneys
1 medium-size onion, sliced
4 tablespoons butter or margarine
1 can condensed tomato soup

¼ teaspoon curry (optional)
½ teaspoon prepared mustard
2 cups hot cooked rice or 1 lb. cooked
   spaghetti

Prepare kidneys for cooking; cut into slices or small pieces. Cook with onion in butter or margarine. Stir and cook until kidneys are light brown in color. Add soup, curry and mustard. Heat and stir. Serve on rice or spaghetti.

SUGGESTED MENU: Add a salad bowl of raw vegetables and hot, crusty rolls. For dessert, chocolate layer cake.

DEVILED VEAL KIDNEYS   4 Servings

3 veal kidneys
½ cup mayonnaise

1 cup fine bread crumbs
½ cup butter or margarine, melted

Split veal kidneys lengthwise; cut away all fibrous parts. Rinse and pat dry. Spread kidney halves with mayonnaise; roll in bread crumbs. Let stand for a few minutes to dry slightly; dip in melted butter or margarine. Broil quickly. Serve hot.

SUGGESTED MENU: Broiled mushrooms, creamed green cabbage and French-fried potatoes with the meat. Add scallions and carrot sticks. For dessert, lime ice cream.

BAKED STUFFED HEART   6 to 8 Servings

2 slices salt pork
2 cups bread crumbs
½ cup onion, diced
2 teaspoons salt
1 beef heart or 2 veal hearts

3 tablespoons flour
3 tablespoons fat or salad oil
½ cup water
1 tablespoon Worcestershire sauce

Dice salt pork; fry until crisp. Combine with bread crumbs, onion, and half of salt (1 teaspoon) to make stuffing, Trim out white tubes from heart cavity and season with remaining salt (1 teaspoon). Fill heart with stuffing; fasten with skewers to hold in stuffing. Roll heart in flour. Brown in hot fat or oil in heavy kettle. Add water and Worcestershire sauce. Cover and simmer for 2 hours, or until heart is tender.

SUGGESTED MENU: Parslied potatoes, buttered Brussels sprouts and diced beets with the meat. Add a salad of lettuce chunks. For dessert, lemon-coconut layer cake.

GLAZED, STUFFED BEEF HEART   6 to 8 Servings

1 beef heart (about 5 lbs.)
  parsley dressing
1 cup onions, sliced
3 tablespoons fat or salad oil
6 cups boiling water
2 teaspoons salt
¼ teaspoon pepper

1 ½ teaspoons Ac'cent
1 teaspoon celery salt
1 teaspoon leaf marjoram
½ cup red-currant jelly
9 tablespoons water
2 teaspoons lemon juice
6 tablespoons flour

Remove fat, veins and arteries from beef heart. Stuff with parsley dressing. Cook onions in hot fat or oil in deep kettle or Dutch oven until lightly browned; push to one side. Brown beef heart on all sides. Add boiling water, salt, pepper, Ac'cent and celery salt. Simmer covered for 2½ to 3 hours or until meat is tender. Add marjoram about 15 minutes before end of cooking time. Remove beef heart from liquid. Break up currant jelly with fork and mix with 1 of the 9 tablespoons of water. Melt over low heat and brush over beef heart to glaze. Strain liquid; measure 3 cups back into kettle. Add lemon juice. Thicken with flour mixed to smooth paste with remaining water (8 tablespoons or ½ cup). Serve gravy separately.

PARSLEY DRESSING

4 cups soft bread crumbs
½ teaspoon salt
  dash pepper
¼ teaspoon Ac'cent

1 teaspoon poultry seasoning
1 tablespoon parsley, minced
¼ cup butter or margarine
¼ cup onion, minced

Combine first 6 ingredients. Melt butter or margarine, add onion and simmer until onion is soft, but not brown. Stir in crumb mixture; blend well.

SUGGESTED MENU: Mashed potatoes, asparagus au gratin, and a tossed salad with the meat. For dessert, raspberry gelatin whip with frozen raspberries.

BEEF HEART WITH RICE   6 to 8 Servings

1 beef heart
  cold water
  boiling water
1 onion, chopped
1 carrot, chopped
1 teaspoon salt

⅛ teaspoon pepper
2 tablespoons flour
2 tablespoons butter or margarine
1 tablespoon brown sugar
1 tablespoon vinegar
3 cups hot cooked rice or mashed potatoes

Wash heart; remove all tubes and veins. Dice and steep in enough cold water to cover for 15 minutes; drain. Add enough boiling water to cover. Add onion, carrot and seasonings; simmer for 3 hours or until very tender. Rub flour and butter or margarine together to make a paste. Blend meat liquid with flour mixture slowly. Cook, stirring until mixture begins to thicken. Add remaining ingredients. Serve meat and gravy in center of rice or mashed-potato border.

Suggested Menu: Buttered broccoli and marinated tomato wedges complete the main course. For dessert, deep-dish apple pie.

STEWED BEEF HEART

6 Servings

1 beef heart
 salted water
1 cup fine bread crumbs
3 slices salt pork, minced
1 small onion, chopped
1 teaspoon parsley, minced

½ teaspoon marjoram
 salt and pepper
1 to 2 tablespoons butter or margarine, melted
 boiling water
2 teaspoons lemon juice

Wash and clean heart; soak for 2 hours in enough salted water to cover. Combine crumbs, pork, onion, parsley and seasonings to make stuffing; moisten with butter or margarine. Stuff heart and sew up opening; tie firmly in a piece of clean cloth. Place in heavy kettle and cover with boiling water. Simmer for 3 hours. Remove heart; unwrap. Thicken 2 cups of the broth* (page 195); stir in lemon juice. Pour sauce over meat and serve sliced.

Suggested Menu: Scalloped potatoes, cauliflower and peas and an asparagus salad with the meat. Pineapple meringue pie for dessert.

SWEETBREADS SANTA BARBARA

4 to 6 Servings

1 lb. beef or veal sweetbreads
 salted water
1 egg
1 cup corn flakes, crushed
2 tablespoons butter or margarine

1 cup sour cream
1 cup orange juice
1 teaspoon salt
2 teaspoons sugar
2 teaspoons orange peel, grated

Simmer sweetbreads in salted water (2 teaspoons salt per quart of water). Simmer beef sweetbreads for 35 minutes, veal for 25 minutes. Remove from water; cool. Remove all loose membrane. Roll in beaten egg, then in corn flakes. Brown in butter or margarine. Place in baking dish. Combine sour cream, orange juice, salt and sugar; pour over sweetbreads. Sprinkle with orange peel. Bake in hot oven (400°) for 20 minutes.

Suggested Menu: French-fried potatoes, buttered asparagus and tomato slices in chive-French dressing with the sweetbreads. For dessert, charlotte russe.

*Save remaining broth for soup base.

SWEETBREADS EN BROCHETTE   4 Servings

1 lb. sweetbreads
  boiling salted water
2 tablespoons salad oil
2 tablespoons lemon juice

½ cup fine bread crumbs
1 teaspoon salt
4 slices bacon
8 pineapple chunks

Cover sweetbreads with boiling salted water; simmer for 25 minutes. Drain and cool. Remove thin membrane covering; divide into pieces about 1½ inches in diameter. Combine oil and lemon juice. Dip sweetbreads into this mixture, then into bread crumbs mixed with salt. Cut bacon into 2-inch pieces. Place on skewers alternating the bacon between the pineapple and sweetbreads. Broil on rack 3 inches from heat source. Turn to brown evenly.

SUGGESTED MENU: Mashed-potato cakes, green beans with celery and endive salad complete the main course. Strawberry sundaes for dessert.

SWEETBREADS DE LUXE   6 Servings

1½ lbs. sweetbreads
  boiling salted water
1½ lbs. beef chuck
  seasoned flour
3 tablespoons salad oil

1 onion, chopped
1 green pepper, chopped
  cold water
2 cans (8 oz. ea.) tomato sauce

Cover sweetbreads with boiling salted water; simmer for 15 minutes. Cube beef. Roll in seasoned flour and brown in hot oil. Add onion and pepper; simmer until onion is soft. Cool sweetbreads in enough cold water to cover. Peel off membrane; cut into chunks. Stir sweetbread chunks and tomato sauce into beef mixture in pan. Simmer until tender, or about 30 minutes.

SUGGESTED MENU: Fluffy, hot rice, buttered lima beans and a salad of mixed greens complete the main course. Custard pie for dessert.

SWEETBREADS SAVARIN   6 Servings

2 pairs sweetbreads
  cold salted water
1 bay leaf
1 sprig parsley
¼ teaspoon salt
  hot water

dash pepper
1 egg, slightly beaten
2 tablespoons milk
1 cup fine bread crumbs
  fat or salad oil (1½ to 2 in. deep)

Soak sweetbreads for 1 hour in enough cold salted water to cover; drain. Put in saucepan with bay leaf, parsley and salt. Add enough hot water to cover. Bring to a boil, then lower heat and simmer ½ hour. Cool in cooking water; drain. Remove connective tissue; cut sweetbreads in uniform chunks. Sprinkle with pepper. Combine egg and milk. Dip sweetbreads in egg mixture, then in bread crumbs, then in egg again. Fry in shallow fat or oil heated to 385° until golden brown. Drain on absorbent paper.

SUGGESTED MENU: With the sweetbreads serve whipped potatoes and buttered green peas. Add a salad of sliced beets and onion rings. For dessert, caramel custard.

SHERRIED SWEETBREADS   6 Servings

¼ cup butter or margarine
3 tablespoons flour
2 cups light cream
3 egg yolks
  salt and pepper

1 teaspoon lemon juice
¹/₃ cup dry sherry
4 cups diced, cooked sweetbreads
6 hot corn bread squares

Melt butter or margarine; blend in flour. Add cream. Cook and stir over medium heat until thickened. Beat egg yolks slightly; add salt, pepper, lemon juice and sherry. Add a little of the cream mixture to egg yolk mixture. Stir remaining cream mixture over low heat until smooth and blended. Add sweetbreads; heat thoroughly. Serve on squares of hot corn bread.

SUGGESTED MENU: Serve green peas and a salad of crisp mixed greens with the sweetbreads. For dessert, fruit cup and ladyfingers.

SWEET-SOUR TONGUE   6 Servings

1 fresh beef tongue
  salted water
2 tablespoons butter or margarine
2 tablespoons flour
½ teaspoon salt

¼ teaspoon pepper
1 cup broth from tongue
2 tablespoons sugar
2 tablespoons vinegar
¼ cup seedless raisins

Cook tongue in salted water to cover for 3 hours or until tender; reserve one cup broth for recipe. Skin tongue; cut in thin slices. Blend butter or margarine, flour, salt and pepper; stir in reserved broth. Cook and stir until thickened; add remaining ingredients. Heat well; pour over sliced tongue. Serve hot.

SUGGESTED MENU: Scalloped sweet potatoes and apples, buttered onions and a green salad complete the main course. For dessert, lemon sherbet with seeded, halved Tokay grapes.

BEEF TONGUE WITH RAISIN SAUCE 8 to 12 Servings

1 fresh or smoked beef tongue (3 to 5 lbs.)
  cold water
1 tablespoon salt
2 small onions

whole cloves
6 peppercorns
1 bay leaf
raisin sauce

When you buy tongue, allow 4 to 5 ounces of meat per person. Put tongue in a deep sauce pot; cover with cold water. Add salt along with one of the onions studded with cloves. Slice other onion and add with peppercorns and bay leaf. Bring to a boil, then reduce heat and simmer for 2½ to 3 hours, or until tender. Drain meat; cool slightly. Cut off bones and gristle at thick end; slit skin on underside from end to end. Peel off skin by pulling from thick end to tip. Slice diagonally. Serve topped with raisin sauce.

RAISIN SAUCE 6 Servings

  water (a little more than ½ cup)
½ cup sugar
½ cup raisins
 2 tablespoons butter or margarine
1 tablespoon vinegar

¼ teaspoon salt
¼ teaspoon cinnamon
½ cup currant jelly
 1 teaspoon cornstarch

Mix part of water (½ cup) with sugar in saucepan; heat to boiling. Stir until sugar dissolves and boil for 5 minutes. Add next 6 ingredients. Stir until jelly dissolves. Dissolve cornstarch in remaining cold water; add to sauce. Cook and stir over low heat until thickened.

SUGGESTED MENU: Mashed sweet potatoes, green peas and romaine salad with the meat. For dessert, Lady Baltimore cake.

BEEF TONGUE IN FRUIT SAUCE 6 Servings

1 beef tongue, cooked (3 to 5 lbs.)
3 tablespoons flour
2 teaspoons dry mustard
1 teaspoon salt
1 tablespoon chili powder
1 cup orange juice

½ cup pineapple juice
 3 tablespoons salad oil
 1 teaspoon Worcestershire sauce
 2 tablespoons lemon juice
½ cup golden seedless raisins
¼ cup sweet pickle relish

Cool tongue enough to handle; peel and trim off root end. Combine flour, mustard, salt and chili powder; blend in orange juice and pineapple juice. Add remaining ingredients. Cook and stir over medium heat until slightly thickened. Slice tongue. Pour some of the sauce over slices; serve remaining sauce separately.

SUGGESTED MENU: Serve seasoned, riced potatoes and buttered green beans with the tongue. Add a tossed salad. For dessert, coconut cream pie.

TONGUE SALAD

8 to 10 Servings

1 large beef tongue (4 to 5 lbs.)
  salt and pepper
1 teaspoon mixed pickling spices
1 cup celery, chopped
1 cup apple, chopped
1 cup sweet pickle, chopped

1 cup nutmeats, chopped
2 hard-cooked eggs, chopped
  juice of 1 lemon
  salad dressing
1 head lettuce

Boil tongue in water to cover with salt and pepper to taste and mixed spices; when tender, skin and cool. Chop or grind cooked tongue; combine with other ingredients, adding enough of your favorite salad dressing to moisten. Serve on lettuce.

SUGGESTED MENU: For a luncheon or supper, begin with chilled vichyssoise. Serve hot, buttered French bread with the salad. For dessert, honeydew melon.

BRAISED OXTAILS

4 Servings

2 lbs. disjointed oxtails
3 tablespoons fat or salad oil
1 large onion, chopped
  flour
2 teaspoons salt
¼ teaspoon pepper

1 tablespoon vinegar
2 cups water
3 carrots, sliced
1 cup celery, diced
1 green pepper, chopped
4 medium-size potatoes, halved

Wash oxtails in cold water; pat dry. Heat fat or oil in heavy skillet; add onion. Roll oxtails in flour; brown in hot fat with onion. Add salt, pepper, vinegar, and water. Cover tightly and simmer for 3 hours. (Add more water if necessary to prevent burning.) Add carrots, celery, green pepper and potatoes. Cover and simmer for 45 minutes. Place vegetables and meat on a hot platter. Thicken broth for gravy (page 195).

SUGGESTED MENU: Hot rolls and a tossed salad with the meat. For dessert, frosted chocolate chiffon cake.

TRIPE CASSEROLE

8 Servings

2 lbs. pickled honeycomb tripe
  cold salted water
2 medium-size onions, minced
¼ cup green pepper, minced
2 tablespoons butter or margarine

⅛ teaspoon pepper
2 tablespoons flour
2 cups hot water
½ teaspoon Worcestershire sauce

Cover tripe with cold salt water. Let stand for 15 minutes; drain. Cut in 2-inch strips. Cook onions and green pepper in butter or margarine until soft. Add tripe; cook for 5 minutes. Turn into casserole. Sprinkle with pepper and flour. Add hot water and Worcestershire sauce. Bake in slow oven (300°) for 1 ½ hours.

SUGGESTED MENU: Baked sweet potatoes, green peas and cucumber salad with the casserole. For dessert, crackers, guava jelly and cream cheese.

· **Variety Meats** · 155

SAVORY TRIPE   4 to 5 Servings

1 lb. cooked tripe
½ cup onion, sliced
2 tablespoons butter or margarine
1 tablespoon flour
1 sprig parsley, chopped
1 sprig thyme, chopped
½ sprig marjoram, chopped
1 bay leaf, chopped

½ cup carrots, diced
1 whole clove
¼ teaspoon peppercorns
1 teaspoon salt
1 tablespoon Worcestershire sauce
1 cup water
1 teaspoon vinegar (omit if pickled tripe is used)

Cut fully-cooked tripe into servings. Cook onion in butter or margarine until golden-brown. Add flour, herbs, carrots, and seasonings. Stir in water. Simmer for 25 minutes. Add vinegar (if using fresh tripe). Place tripe in pan; strain sauce over it. Cover and simmer for 15 minutes.

SUGGESTED MENU: Riced potatoes, summer squash Creole, raw carrot sticks and celery with the tripe. For dessert, custard raisin-bread pudding.

DRIED BEEF ELINOR   4 Servings

3 tablespoons butter or margarine
1 tablespoon flour
½ teaspoon paprika
⅛ teaspoon nutmeg
½ teaspoon Worcestershire sauce

1½ cups top milk
1½ cups dried beef, chopped
1 can (8 oz.) mushrooms, sliced
¼ cup ripe olives, sliced
4 pieces buttered toast

Melt butter or margarine in skillet. Stir in flour, paprika, nutmeg and Worcestershire sauce; add milk. Cook and stir until thickened. Stir in dried beef and drained mushrooms. Cook and stir until mushrooms and beef are heated thoroughly; add olives. Serve on buttered toast.

SUGGESTED MENU: Buttered broccoli and a tomato salad with the dried beef. For dessert, orange ice and vanilla ice cream.

DRIED BEEF SCRAMBLE   4 Servings

2 tablespoons butter or margarine
1 pkg. (4 oz.) dried beef

6 eggs
6 tablespoons milk

Melt butter or margarine in heavy skillet. Cut dried beef in 1-inch pieces (use scissors); fry for a few minutes in hot butter or margarine. Beat eggs slightly; stir in milk. Pour over beef. Stir gently while cooking.

SUGGESTED MENU: Begin with chilled tomato juice. Serve scalloped asparagus with the scramble. For dessert, fresh fruit cup and cookies.

QUICK-CREAMED DRIED BEEF

4 Servings

¾ cup milk
1 can condensed cream of mushroom soup
1 pkg. (4 oz.) dried beef
  boiling water

½ cup blanched almonds, slivered
2 tablespoons butter or margarine
4 pieces toast

Add milk to soup; cook slowly until smooth or about 2 minutes. Use scissors to cut beef into strips. Pour enough boiling water to cover over beef; drain. Add beef to soup mixture; heat thoroughly. Brown almonds in hot butter or margarine. Serve creamed dried beef on toast topped with almonds.

SUGGESTED MENU: Begin with chilled vegetable juice. Serve buttered broccoli with the dried beef. Add raw carrot sticks and cucumber sticks. For dessert, raspberry tapioca parfait.

CREAMED DRIED BEEF LISBON

4 Servings

2 tablespoons butter or margarine
1 pkg. (4 oz.) dried beef
2 tablespoons flour
1 cup milk

½ cup pimento olives, sliced
2 egg yolks, slightly beaten
⅛ teaspoon paprika
2 cups hot, fluffy rice

Melt butter or margarine in heavy skillet. Cut beef into 1-inch pieces (use scissors); fry in hot butter or margarine. Sprinkle flour over beef; stir. Add milk gradually, cooking and stirring until thickened. Add olives; remove from heat. Stir in egg yolks; add paprika. Serve over hot rice.

SUGGESTED MENU: Serve green peas and mushrooms with the dried beef. Add tomato-aspic salad. For dessert, grapes, Camembert cheese and potato wafers.

DRIED BEEF AND MACARONI CASSEROLE

4 Servings

2 cups hot water
1 pkg. (4 oz.) dried beef
1 can condensed cream of chicken soup
4 to 6 oz. elbow macaroni

boiling salted water
¼ cup shredded Parmesan cheese
paprika

Pour hot water over dried beef; drain. Cut with scissors into 1-inch pieces. Add to chicken soup; heat. Boil macaroni in a big kettle of salted water for about 10 minutes; drain well. Combine with dried beef and soup; pour into a 1½-quart casserole. Cover with cheese and sprinkle with paprika. Bake in moderate oven (350°) for about 30 minutes.

SUGGESTED MENU: Buttered green beans and marinated tomato wedges with the casserole. For dessert, spice layer cake.

SOUTHERN-STYLE DRIED BEEF   6 Servings

1 pkg. (4 oz.) dried beef
2 tablespoons fat or salad oil
4 tablespoons flour
2 cups cold milk

3 to 4 cooked sweet potatoes
$^1/_3$ cup butter or margarine
$^1/_2$ cup brown sugar

Lightly brown dried beef in hot fat or oil. Sprinkle with flour; mix. Add cold milk; stir constantly over low heat until mixture thickens. Halve sweet potatoes lengthwise; spread with butter or margarine and roll in brown sugar. Bake in hot oven (450°) for 20 minutes. Serve creamed beef in center of platter; circle with sweet potatoes.

SUGGESTED MENU: Buttered asparagus and a salad of raw vegetables round out the main course. Rhubarb pie for dessert.

CREAMED BEEF BACON*   4 Servings

$^1/_2$ lb. beef bacon, thinly sliced
    boiling water
1 $^1/_2$ tablespoons butter or margarine
1 $^1/_2$ tablespoons flour

$^1/_2$ cup light cream
1 cup milk
few drops Tabasco

Cover beef bacon with boiling water. Let stand for 10 minutes; drain. Meanwhile melt butter or margarine; blend in flour. Combine cream and milk; add with Tabasco. Cook and stir over low heat until smooth and thickened. Dice beef bacon; add. Cook 10 minutes longer.

SUGGESTED MENU: Baked potatoes with the creamed beef bacon. Add chopped beet greens and raw carrot sticks. For dessert, fruit compote.

---

*Beef bacon is cut from salted, smoked, beef plate.

COAST-TO-COAST BARBECUES

COAST-TO-COAST BARBECUES
"Light, stranger, and stake out your hoss"

According to Texans, the barbecue was born in Texas and spread to other states in the West and Southwest. Other authorities, however, say that the first people to barbecue meat were the pioneers, cowboys, hunters and early Spanish explorers, who of necessity cooked over an open fire. Whatever its origin, we know that at some point early in the history of the West it became a custom to give huge parties, featuring ox roasts, fireworks, games, races and square dancing.

No one knows exactly how the barbecue got its name. Dictionaries and encyclopedias are unable to furnish us with specific information on the subject. The Spaniards have borrowed the Americanism and call it "barbacoa." Possibly the first ox roast took place on a ranch with the brand —BQ.

Today the popularity of the barbecue has spread from coast to coast and from North to South, lending color and character to regional foods. "To barbecue" has come to mean to roast slowly on a pit or grill over coals, in a rotisserie or in an oven, basting from time to time with a highly-seasoned sauce. Let's take it from there.

How to Plan a Barbecue

A barbecue should be a carefree event. To make it so, spend a little time in planning so that supplies won't run out or too much food be wasted.

Keep the menu simple. Emphasize the barbecued food and have plenty of it. Keep the number of other courses at a minimum—a crisp salad or raw vegetable relishes and an easy-to-eat dessert. Make sure that there is lots of coffee or tea, hot or iced, according to the weather.

Write out a careful market order; check and recheck. Do as much preparation ahead of time as possible. Then let everyone help with on-the-spot jobs. Check equipment, both for barbecuing and serving. Sturdy, plastic-coated paper dishes and cups for hot or cold beverages make cleanup quick and easy. Don't forget large, sturdy paper napkins.

Barbecue Equipment

In addition to the barbecue unit itself you will find the following equipment helpful:

Gravel, for the bottom of the fire unit
Fire starter
Fire rake
Fire tongs
Asbestos gloves
Small shovel
Pail of water (for quenching briquets)
Long-handled fork
Long-handled broad spatula
Long-handled meat tongs
Sharp meat knives
Saucepans, kettle or Dutch oven
Wire hand grill.

If you are barbecuing on a spit you may want to use, in addition to the above:

Heavy-duty or broiler foil
Skewers
Heavy cord
Basting brush
Barbecue meat thermometer
Spit forks
Spit basket

How to Build the Fire

Charcoal imparts its own smoky, indescribably delicious flavor to grilled foods. Use charcoal briquets made from hard wood such as maple, birch, beech, oak or elm. Such briquets burn a long time, giving off an even, intense heat. Briquets made from soft wood, on the other hand, are uneven in size and sputter, smoke and spark, thus producing an uneven heat.

The first step in building a satisfactory fire is to cover the bottom of the firebox or fire bowl with gravel. This covering lets the fire "breathe" and distributes the heat evenly. Gravel also helps to eliminate flare-ups, which occur when fat drippings accumulate on the bottom of the firebox and as it retains heat, it saves fuel. After using it for several barbecues, you can wash the gravel in a pail of hot water and spread it in the sun to dry thoroughly before the next use. The gravel in a firebox should be ¾ to 1 inch deep. In a brazier bowl, use enough to make a bed level with the edge of the bowl.

Start the fire about 45 minutes before you begin to cook. Make a pyramid of briquets about 12 inches in diameter and 5 or 6 inches high. *Never* use gasoline, kerosene or alcohol. Use a safe liquid made especially for this purpose, a waxlike starter in a paper cup or an electric starter. Follow directions carefully for the type you choose.

When the initial fire has burned off the briquets, you will see gray spots which grow gradually. After about half an hour, spread the briquets with tongs so they are about

½ inch apart. Put an extra supply of briquets at the edge of the firebox, to warm slowly, and add them as needed.

As the surface of the charcoal burns, a deposit of fine gray ash is formed on the coals. Since the ash acts as an insulator, top it off gently with a fire rake or poker before beginning to cook.

Never add liquid fuels to briquets after the fire has been ignited.

Liquid smoke or smoke chips add distinctive flavor when used according to manufacturer's directions.

Foil drip pans are essential for spit barbecuing. They catch the fats and juices for making gravy or sauce and prevent fat from causing flare-ups by dripping on the fire.

To make a foil drip pan: Use 2 sheets of heavy-duty or broiler foil about 5 inches longer than the meat on the spit. Lay one sheet on top of the other. Fold in half lengthwise to make a 4-ply thickness. Fold up sides and ends all around, making them 1½ inches high. Make neat, mitered corners, folding them back against the sides. Place the drip pan in front of the briquets.

How Much Meat to Buy

Don't be skimpy! You can count on outdoor appetites, made even heartier by the aroma of charcoal cooking.

If you are buying meat with the bone in, such as a standing rib roast or porterhouse steak, allow ¾ of a pound to 1 pound per person. If you buy boned or boneless meat, ½ pound per person is usually enough.

Porterhouse, sirloin, club or rib steaks should be cut about 1½ inches thick. Never barbecue less than a 2-rib roast or a 4-pound rolled roast. Beef fillets weighing from 4 to 6 pounds are the smallest that can be barbecued satisfactorily.

Pioneer Pit Barbecue   Serves 200

If you are planning a barbecue for a large group of people, you will follow a somewhat different procedure.

The pit*

Dig a trench 3 to 3½ feet deep and no wider than 3 feet. The 3-foot length is needed for 100 pounds of boneless meat tied into rolls not less than 4 inches or more than 8 inches in diameter. Rolls should be as uniform as possible.

Good quality meat should be used, preferably the forequarter of a beef, as it contains the right amount of fat intermingled with lean to make it juicy. The hindquarter, however, breaks down into excellent boned cuts.

Season the meat with salt and pepper before wrapping in cheesecloth, muslin or

---

*If available, a large concrete pipe makes an excellent pit for barbecuing. Cover top with large metal disk or metal plate.

stockinet. First use a double layer of one of these materials, then a layer of clean burlap.

The coals

Any hardwood can be used to produce a heap of coals 15 to 18 inches deep. Hard, dry wood that measures 4 to 6 inches in diameter and no more than 3 feet long will burn down in 3 to 4 hours. Take care that all wood is burned thoroughly.

The sand

Use dry sand or fine gravel to cover the coals to a depth of 1 to 1 ½ inches, making sure no coals are left uncovered.

Wet the packaged meat to prevent burning before pit can be covered. Place it in the pit about 12 hours before time to be served. Don't worry about overcooking; the fire will have died down after 12 hours.

BARBECUE SAUCE

Have the following ingredients on hand:

> **12 bottles ketchup (148 oz.)**
> **6 bottles Worcestershire sauce (36 oz.)**
> **6 bottles prepared mustard**
> **4 cups prepared barbecue sauce**
> **2 cups vinegar**

SUGGESTED MENU:
>   100 lbs. meat
>   400 sliced buns
>   potatoes: 12 lbs. potato chips *or* 60 lbs. scalloped potatoes *or* 200 baked
>   potatoes
>   beans: 60 lbs. baked beans
>   salad: 60 lbs. potato salad *or* 40 lbs. coleslaw *or* 30 to 40 lbs. lettuce salad
>   pickles: 2 gallons
>   coffee: 14 to 16 gallons
>   dessert: 200 ice cream cups or fruit in season

The Sauce Is the Thing

Whether you are planning to serve a crowd or cooking the family dinner in your own back yard, the sauce is the thing that gives the barbecue that special touch. We learned an important secret about sauce from an old hand at barbecuing: *never* begin to baste until the last 10 minutes of cooking time, especially if you are using a sauce with a tomato base. The tomato will char unpleasantly if you begin too soon. If you marinate beef before barbecuing, no seasoning is needed. Steaks should be seasoned only with butter, salt and freshly-ground black pepper *after* they are taken off the grill. And *never* overpower the flavor of good beef with sauce. Use the sauce to enhance flavor, not to drown it. Again, don't begin too soon. Meat takes on the flavor of the sauce more readily when it's hot and the sauce keeps the meat moist during the end of the cooking period. If you baste from start to finish, you'll taste only the sauce—the meat flavor will be lost entirely.

Take the advice of this expert: use these sauce recipes with discretion and you will find barbecuing a more pleasurable experience.

CARIBBEAN BARBECUE SAUCE
Makes about ¾ cup

¼ cup light molasses
¼ cup prepared mustard
3 tablespoons vinegar
2 tablespoons Worcestershire sauce

½ teaspoon Tabasco
1 teaspoon ground ginger
2 tablespoons soy sauce

Blend molasses and mustard. Add remaining ingredients; mix well.

BACKWOODS BARBECUE SAUCE
Makes about 1½ cups

1 can (8 oz.) tomato sauce
1½ teaspoons seasoned meat tenderizer
1 tablespoon brown sugar

$^1/_3$ cup Burgundy wine
1 tablespoon prepared mustard
¼ teaspoon oregano

Combine ingredients; simmer for 5 minutes. Cool.

SPICY BASTING SAUCE
Makes about ¾ cup

¼ cup salad oil
¼ cup lime juice
¼ cup wine vinegar
1 garlic clove, minced
½ teaspoon salt

½ teaspoon ginger
1 teaspoon rosemary
1 teaspoon prepared horse-radish
½ teaspoon lime peel, grated

Combine all ingredients in large, screw-top jar. Close jar; shake to mix well. Chill. Shake before using.

BUCKAROO MARINADE

Makes about 3 ½ cups

1 ¼ cups salad oil
¾ cup soy sauce
¼ cup Worcestershire sauce
2 tablespoons dry mustard
2 ¼ teaspoons salt

1 tablespoon pepper
½ cup wine vinegar
1 ½ teaspoons dried parsley flakes
2 crushed garlic cloves (optional)
$^1/_3$ cup lemon juice

Combine all ingredients; mix well. You can drain marinade from steaks or chops and use it a second time. Store in the freezer indefinitely in a tightly-covered jar or in the refrigerator for one week.

SWEET-SOUR BASTING SAUCE

Makes about 1$^2/_3$ cups

½ cup flat beer
2 tablespoons vinegar
1 tablespoon Worcestershire sauce
1 tablespoon lemon juice

¾ cup chili sauce
2 tablespoons honey
$^1/_3$ cup brown sugar

Combine all ingredients in small saucepan. Cook and stir over medium heat until sugar dissolves. Keep sauce warm while basting meat.

TOMATO BASTING SAUCE

Makes about 1 ½ cups

2 tablespoons salad oil
1 small onion, minced
1 garlic clove, minced
1 teaspoon dry mustard
1 tablespoon Worcestershire sauce

½ cup vinegar
¼ cup brown sugar, firmly packed
1 can (6 oz.) tomato paste
½ cup water

Combine oil, onion and garlic in a saucepan. Simmer and stir for about 10 minutes to cook onion. Add remaining ingredients. Simmer 10 minutes longer, stirring occasionally. Brush meat frequently with sauce during last 10 to 15 minutes of barbecuing.

EASY BASTING SAUCE

Makes about 1 cup

$^1/_3$ cup wine vinegar
$^1/_3$ cup lemon juice
$^1/_3$ cup salad oil

½ teaspoon soy sauce
salt and pepper

Combine all ingredients, using salt and pepper to taste. Mix well.

TARRAGON MARINADE

Makes about 2 ¼ cups

1 large onion, peeled and chopped
1 cup salad oil
¼ cup tarragon vinegar
½ cup dry red wine
¼ cup lemon juice

1 teaspoon dry mustard
1 teaspoon salt
2 garlic cloves, minced
1 bay leaf
6 peppercorns

Combine all ingredients in a large screw-top jar. Cover jar; shake vigorously. Store in refrigerator. Shake well before using.

GOLDEN BARBECUE SAUCE

Makes about 1 quart

1 cup prepared yellow mustard
1 ½ cups light molasses
⅓ cup Worcestershire sauce
1 ½ cups vinegar

2 teaspoons Tabasco
¼ teaspoon marjoram
¼ teaspoon oregano

Blend mustard slowly into molasses. Stir in remaining ingredients. Store in tightly-covered jar in refrigerator and use as needed.

BARBECUE BEER SAUCE

Makes about 4 half-pints

1 ½ cups ketchup
½ cup chili sauce
2 tablespoons prepared mustard
½ cup brown sugar, firmly packed
2 teaspoons pepper
½ cup wine vinegar

⅓ cup lemon juice
¼ cup bottled steak sauce
   dash Tabasco
1 teaspoon soy sauce
2 teaspoons salad oil
½ cup flat beer

Combine all ingredients; mix well. Store in covered half-pint jars. If you like, you may add a crushed clove of garlic an hour before using sauce.

FESTIVAL STEAK SAUCE

Makes about 1 ½ cups

⅓ cup butter or margarine, melted
¾ cup onion, finely chopped
½ cup dry white wine

2 teaspoons salt
2 tablespoons parsley, chopped
1 tablespoon mint leaves, crushed

Cook onion in butter or margarine over low heat until soft, but not brown. Slowly stir in wine; add salt. Bring mixture to a boil, then reduce heat and simmer for 5 minutes. Remove from heat. Add parsley and mint; mix well.

SUPER BARBECUE SAUCE

Makes about 2 ½ cups

1 cup ketchup
1 cup water
1 small onion, chopped
1 tablespoon Worcestershire sauce
¼ cup vinegar
½ teaspoon seasoned meat tenderizer

1 tablespoon brown sugar
2 teaspoons dry mustard
1 teaspoon paprika
1 teaspoon chili powder
1 garlic clove, finely chopped

Combine ingredients; simmer slowly at side of grill in covered pan for about ½ hour before using. You may use this sauce 3 ways to flavor meats:

1. Let meat stand, or marinate, in sauce.
2. Dip meat into sauce before grilling.
3. Baste meat with sauce during cooking.

For hotter sauce: add a dash of cayenne pepper or more chili powder.
For lean meats: add 2 tablespoons butter, margarine or salad oil before sauce is simmered.

QUICK BARBECUE SAUCE

Makes about 2 cups

1 cup mayonnaise
1 can (6 oz.) tomato paste
¼ cup wine vinegar
3 tablespoons Worcestershire sauce

1 tablespoon chopped onion
2 teaspoons prepared horse-radish
1 ½ teaspoons salt
¼ teaspoon Tabasco

Combine all ingredients in small bowl; blend well. Use immediately or refrigerate in covered jar until needed.

BARBECUED FILLET OF BEEF

8 Servings

1 whole fillet or tenderloin of beef
   (about 4 lbs.)

3 garlic cloves, peeled and slivered

Cut several slits in the fillet; insert garlic slivers. Fillet may be marinated if desired. Put the meat on a spit; insert a barbecue thermometer in the thickest part of the fillet. Barbecue over hot coals for about 45 minutes; thermometer should register about 140°. The thick end of the fillet will be rare, the thinner end medium to well-done.

SUGGESTED MENU: Frozen French-fried potatoes and onion rings heated in foil packets, plus a big salad bowl complete the main course. For dessert, old-fashioned strawberry shortcake.

POOR MAN'S FILET MIGNON

4 Servings

2 lbs. top round steak
1 cup dry red wine

2 garlic cloves, minced
½ teaspoon pepper

One to 2 hours before cooking, use meat tenderizer according to directions on page 19.

Add wine, garlic and pepper; refrigerate until ready to cook. Then drain and grill or pan-fry until done to taste over quick fire, basting occasionally with marinade.

SUGGESTED MENU: Hot, crusty poppy seed rolls, green pepper and carrot coleslaw and roasted corn on the cob accompany the steak. For dessert, frosted orange chiffon cake.

BARBECUED JUMBOBURGERS   4 Servings

2 lbs. round steak, ground
2 teaspoons salt
  dash pepper

1 small onion, minced
1 cup bread stuffing

Mix meat with seasonings and onion. Divide into 8 portions; shape each portion into a large, thin patty. Mound ¼ cup stuffing in the centers of 4 patties. Top with remaining 4 patties; pinch edges of meat together to seal in filling. Put burgers in a hand grill. Barbecue about 3 inches from hot coals for 15 minutes, turning once.

SUGGESTED MENU: Toasted, buttered buns, a salad of cooked vegetables and a tray of assorted relishes accompany these giant burgers. For dessert, raspberry sundaes.

CATTLEMEN'S CHATEAUBRIAND   6 Servings

This is a snappy western version of the world's most elegant steak, traditionally made with the finest cut of tenderloin. Meat tenderizer makes it possible to use a thrifty cut with excellent results. The molasses barbecue sauce dates from days of the Texas longhorn.

3 lbs. of round bone chuck, about 1½ in.
  thick
4 slices bacon, chopped
½ cup green onions, chopped
1 garlic clove, minced
1 cup ketchup

1 cup water
¼ cup wine vinegar
¼ cup molasses
1 tablespoon Worcestershire sauce
2 teaspoons dry mustard
⅛ teaspoon Tabasco

Use meat tenderizer according to directions on page 19. Let stand at room temperature for one hour or cover loosely and refrigerate overnight.

To make sauce, cook bacon, green onions and garlic in skillet; drain off excess fat. Add remaining ingredients. Cover and simmer for 30 minutes. Keep handy near grill.

When you cook steak, brush with sauce and set over glowing charcoal on grill that is 4 to 6 inches from fire. Barbecue 6 to 8 minutes per side for rare, 8 to 10 minutes per side for medium. Be sure to follow these instructions, as the tenderizer cuts cooking time (and shrinkage) 25 per cent. Turn once; baste occasionally with sauce. Carve at an angle, going against the grain, in thick, generous slices.

SUGGESTED MENU: Serve with remaining molasses sauce, French-fried green pepper rings, hashed-brown potatoes and cabbage slaw with sour cream and blue cheese dressing. Deep-dish cherry pie for dessert.

BARBECUED INDIVIDUAL CHUCK STEAKS 4 Servings

4 individual chuck steaks, ½ to ¾ lb. ea. **½ cup salad oil or barbecue sauce**

Slash fat edges of steak to prevent curling. Use specially seasoned meat tenderizer according to directions on page 19. Do not add salt. Leave at room temperature for 1 hour or refrigerate a day ahead. Brush with salad oil or barbecue sauce. Set grill 4 inches from hot coals. Broil steaks as desired, about 8 to 10 minutes per side for rare, or 12 to 15 minutes per side for medium.

SUGGESTED MENU: Begin with fruit juice cocktail. With the barbecued steaks serve California long white potatoes baked in foil, combination salad and garlic bread. Watermelon for dessert.

SESAME STEAK BARBECUE 6 Servings

3 lbs. lean steak or sirloin tip
1 cup salad oil
¼ cup sugar
2 tablespoons soy sauce
4 tablespoons green onions (scallions), minced

2 garlic cloves, minced
½ teaspoon salt
½ teaspoon pepper
4 tablespoons sesame seeds
6 frankfurter rolls, toasted

Cut beef in long thin strips. Combine remaining ingredients; pour over beef. Let stand overnight in refrigerator. Before using, bring to room temperature and drain off excess sauce. Cook on narrow-mesh grill or thread on skewers. Baste with sauce as meat broils. Serve on toasted frankfurter rolls.

SUGGESTED MENU: Make a salad of potatoes, cucumber and celery to go with the steak rolls. Add red cabbage slaw. For dessert, apple turnovers and cheddar cheese cubes.

BARBECUED STEAK ROLLS 4 to 5 Servings

1 flank steak (about 2 lbs.)
¾ cup unsweetened pineapple juice
2 tablespoons lemon juice
2 tablespoons soy sauce
2 garlic cloves, minced
1 small bay leaf

⅛ teaspoon cloves, ground
$^1/_3$ cup fine bread crumbs
¼ cup apple, chopped
¼ cup onion, minced
1 tablespoon butter or margarine, melted

Lightly score both sides of steak in a crisscross pattern. Combine juices, soy sauce, garlic and seasonings; pour over steak. Marinate for 1 to 2 hours; drain. Save marinade. Combine remaining ingredients to make a stuffing; spread over steak. Starting at long side, roll steak up like jelly roll. Fasten edge with wooden picks inserted at 1-inch intervals. Cut steak between picks into diagonal slices 1 to 1½ inches thick; place slices in a hand grill. Barbecue over hot coals, turning often. Baste with marinade. Allow 10 minutes for rare, or 15 minutes for medium.

SUGGESTED MENU: Hot potato salad and sliced tomatoes and cucumbers in a sharp French dressing complete the main course. For dessert, Banbury tarts and cream cheese.

WINE-BARBECUED STEAK   8 Servings

½ cup salad oil
½ cup red table wine
2 tablespoons onion, grated
1 garlic clove, slashed
1 ½ teaspoons salt

1 teaspoon Ac'cent
few drops Tabasco
1 sirloin steak, 1 to 1 ¼ in. thick (about 3 lbs.)

Combine all ingredients except steak. Cover; chill several hours or overnight. At the cookout, heat the sauce. Use to brush steak as it broils, turning steak and brushing frequently.

SUGGESTED MENU: Foil-wrapped baked potatoes and roasted corn on the cob go well with the steak. Add a tomato and cucumber salad. For dessert, fresh peach ice cream and marble cake.

CHUCK-IN-A-BASKET BARBECUE   4 to 5 Servings

4 lbs. chuck steak 1 ½ in. thick
½ teaspoon rosemary
½ teaspoon tarragon

½ teaspoon thyme
½ cup salad oil
1 cup lemon juice or vinegar

Use top-quality beef; allow ⅓ to ½ pound per serving. Place meat in bowl. Combine remaining ingredients; pour over meat. Let stand several hours at room temperature; turn occasionally. Before cooking, drain steak, reserving marinade. Place steak in spit basket; fasten securely. Barbecue over hot coals, brushing often with marinade. Cook about 30 minutes for rare, or 45 minutes for medium. Serve steak sliced against the grain.

SUGGESTED MENU: Hot garlic bread, a salad of green peas, sliced celery, diced potato and assorted relishes with the steak. For dessert, seedless grapes, blue cheese and crackers.

GRILLED FILLET OF BEEF

1 fillet or tenderloin of beef   salad oil

Buy a whole fillet or tenderloin of beef. Allow ⅓ to ½ pound meat per serving. Rub grill with salad oil. Lay steak on grill; sear close to coals for 2 to 3 minutes. Moving meat about 3 inches from briquets, cook over medium heat until juices begin to rise on uncooked surface or about 15 minutes. Turn meat over at once; sear second side quickly, for 2 to 3 minutes. Return meat to medium-heat position. Continue to cook about 15 minutes more until done to taste.

SUGGESTED MENU: Serve potato chips and tomato coleslaw with the fillet. Hot, buttered French bread, too. For dessert, peaches and cream with marble loaf cake.

STEAKS WITH "STOCKADE" DIP
12 Servings

1 lb. butter or margarine
  juice of 3 lemons
½ cup Worcestershire sauce
1 garlic clove, minced
1 tablespoon pepper

1½ teaspoons dry mustard
¼ teaspoon Tabasco
2 sirloin steaks, 3 in. thick (total weight about 6 lbs.)

Combine butter or margarine, lemon juice and seasonings in saucepan. Heat; do not cook or boil. Broil steaks until done to taste; slice into ½-inch strips. Serve at once with hot dip.

SUGGESTED MENU: Hot garlic bread, raw vegetable relishes (such as spring onions or scallions, cucumber sticks, carrot sticks, radishes, olives and pickles) and potato salad. For dessert, orange chiffon cake à la mode.

GRILLED ROUND STEAK

boneless beef round steak, about 1 in. thick
salad oil

easy basting sauce (page 166)
salt and pepper

Allow about ½ pound of meat per person. Use meat tenderizer on steak (page 19). Arrange hot briquets for grill barbecuing. Rub grill with oil and brush steak with easy basting sauce (page 166). Place steak on grill; barbecue over medium heat about 3 inches from charcoal; brush often with sauce. Turn steak when juices begin to rise on uncooked surface. For steak 1 inch thick, allow about 12 minutes per side for rare, 16 minutes per side for medium and 20 minutes per side for well-done. Season to taste with salt and pepper.

SUGGESTED MENU: With the steak serve green peppers stuffed with Spanish rice, wrapped in foil and grilled and hot garlic rolls and tossed salad. For dessert, berries and cream.

GRILLED FLANK STEAK

1 flank steak, about ¾ in. thick
  salad oil

garlic cloves

Allow ½ pound per serving. If steak is to be marinated, prepare any favorite marinade (see Index) and pour it over steak several hours before barbecuing. Score steak lightly, crisscross fashion, on both sides with a knife or use tenderizer (page 19). Rub the grill with salad oil. Throw several garlic cloves on the fire. Grill steak over medium heat about 3 inches from briquets for about 5 minutes. Turn when the juices begin to rise on the uncooked surface. Continue to cook about 5 minutes longer, or until done as desired. To serve, cut in thin, diagonal slices.

SUGGESTED MENU: Hot, buttered French bread, stuffed celery, relishes and a mixed green salad with the steak. For dessert, cantaloupe halves filled with sugared strawberries.

LIVER AND BACON ROULADES
4 Servings

8 slices calf's liver, ¼ in. thick   16 slices bacon
1 cup packaged bread stuffing

Allow 2 slices liver per serving. Wipe liver with damp cloth. Prepare bread stuffing as directed on package. Lay liver slices flat; spread about 2 tablespoons of the stuffing mixture on each slice. Roll up liver from small end, like jelly roll. Hold roll firmly; wrap 2 slices bacon tightly around each roll; secure with wooden picks. Put meat rolls on grill over medium heat; barbecue until done as desired, or about 20 to 25 minutes. Turn often to cook and brown evenly. Avoid overcooking.

SUGGESTED MENU: Frozen potato patties grilled golden brown go well with the roulades, along with foil-wrapped grilled bananas. Add a salad of shredded lettuce. For dessert, watermelon slices.

BARBECUED BEEF RIBS
4 Servings

3 lbs. lean beef ribs, split   1 teaspoon salt
  boiling water   1½ cups favorite hot barbecue sauce

Place ribs in large kettle; add boiling water to cover. Add salt. Cover tightly and simmer for 45 minutes. Cool in broth. When ready to serve, drain ribs; dip in sauce. Arrange on broiler rack about 6 inches from heat. Broil, turning and basting several times with sauce until well browned and crisp or about 20 minutes. To barbecue out of doors, cook ribs as above; drain. When ready to serve, place on grill over hot coals and proceed as above.

SUGGESTED MENU: Potato salad, crisp raw relishes and toasted buns with the ribs. For dessert, strawberry shortcake.

STEAK WITH HERB BUTTER
4 Servings

2 medium-thick rib steaks (about 2 lbs.)   3 tablespoons parsley, minced
  salt and pepper   2 tablespoons chervil or tarragon, minced
3 tablespoons butter or margarine   2 shallots or 1 small onion, minced

Wipe steaks dry; salt and pepper both sides. Grill over hot coals until done to taste. Cream butter or margarine with herbs and shallots. When steaks are removed from grill, spread generously with butter (or margarine) mixture.

SUGGESTED MENU: Roasted corn on the cob and a salad of tomato wedges and sliced cucumbers with the steaks. For dessert, foil-wrapped baked bananas.

"OUT-OF-DOORS" OXTAIL STEW

6 Servings

1 oxtail, disjointed (about 2 lbs.)
  seasoned flour
⅛ teaspoon cloves, ground
¼ cup fat or salad oil
1 cup tomato juice
1 cup water
1 teaspoon salt

4 whole allspice berries
1 bay leaf
1 garlic clove, minced
1 cup onion, chopped
2 tablespoons vinegar
1 package (8 oz.) broad noodles
  boiling salted water

Roll pieces of oxtail in seasoned flour; sprinkle lightly with ground cloves. Heat fat or oil in Dutch oven over open fire and brown oxtail pieces. Add all remaining ingredients except vinegar and noodles; simmer until tender or about 3 hours, adding water as needed. Add vinegar. Cook noodles in boiling salted water according to package directions; drain. Remove all spice berries and bay leaf from stew; skim fat. Serve stew over noodles.

SUGGESTED MENU: Hot, crusty garlic bread and a salad of crisp raw vegetables complete the main course. For dessert, fresh fruits, assorted cheese and crackers.

BARBECUED BEEF ROLLS

4 Servings

8 thin cube steaks
1 cup bread stuffing

8 slices bacon

Spread steaks flat; place 2 tablespoons stuffing on each steak. Roll up like jelly roll; wrap in slice of bacon. Secure rolls with wooden picks or string. Place on grill about 3 inches from coals; turn frequently until done. Cook for about 20 minutes.

SUGGESTED MENU: Corn chips, kidney beans and a tossed salad with the steaks. For dessert, melon wedges.

BARBECUED RIB ROAST

8 to 10 Servings

  standing rib roast (about 6 to 8 lbs.)
¾ cup onion, minced
1/3 cup butter or margarine

½ cup dry white wine
2 teaspoons salt
2 tablespoons parsley, minced

Short ribs should be removed; roast bones should be about 7 inches long. Put meat on spit rod; insert barbecue thermometer, if desired. Cook onion in butter or margarine until soft; stir in remaining ingredients. Cook quickly for 5 minutes. As meat cooks over hot coals, baste with sauce. Allow 12 to 15 minutes per pound cooking time. The thermometer (if used) will register 140° for rare, 160° for medium, or 170° for well-done. When beef is done, lift out thermometer and remove meat from spit. Let stand for 10 minutes to become firm, then carve and serve with remaining sauce.

SUGGESTED MENU: Frozen potato patties browned in a hand grill, and a salad of raw vegetables with the roast. For dessert, peach ice cream and angel food cake.

SHORT RIBS CARIBBEAN   4 Servings

4 to 5 lbs. beef short ribs
  ½ cup rum
  ¼ cup soy sauce
  ¼ cup unsweetened pineapple juice
  2 tablespoons lemon juice

1 teaspoon dry mustard
1 tablespoon molasses
2 teaspoons ginger
1 garlic clove, crushed
½ teaspoon pepper

Have ribs cut in 2-inch squares. Combine all remaining ingredients; mix or shake to blend. Cover ribs with marinade; let stand 4 hours at room temperature. Turn several times. Drain ribs; reserve remaining marinade for basting. Place ribs on grill about 3 inches from hot coals; turn frequently until done. Cook for about 35 to 40 minutes. Baste with marinade while grilling.

SUGGESTED MENU: Potato chips or wafers, foil-baked bananas and grilled pineapple slices are good with this tropical dish. For dessert, lemon sherbet and coconut cookies.

CALIFORNIA STEAK   4 Servings

1 sirloin steak, 2 in. thick (about 2½ lbs.)
  olive or salad oil
  salt

garlic salt
pepper
fresh bay leaves

Brush steak on both sides with oil; sprinkle generously with seasonings. Grill as desired. Just before serving, quickly throw a handful of bay leaves on the coals. Turn steak so both sides are exposed to the aromatic smoke. Serve at once.

SUGGESTED MENU: Potatoes baked in foil and served with a bowl of sour cream and chives are delicious with this steak. So are black olives and gherkins. Add an avocado and grapefruit salad. For dessert, orange sherbet with crushed strawberry sauce.

BARBECUED BEEF KABOB   4 Servings

½ cup olive or salad oil
 1 teaspoon salt
½ teaspoon pepper
½ teaspoon rosemary or oregano

1 lb. tender lean beef, cut in 1½-in. cubes
2 large onions, cut in wedges
2 tomatoes, cut in wedges
8 ripe olives, pitted

Combine oil and seasonings. Add meat cubes and let stand for several hours. Using 4 skewers, place ¼ of meat cubes, vegetables and olives on each skewer. Broil over charcoal until brown, or about 12 minutes, turning to brown evenly.

SUGGESTED MENU: Have toasted frankfurter buns ready for the kabobs. Corn chips, olives, pickles, etc., as accompaniments. For dessert, strawberry sundaes.

LEFTOVER BEEF BARBECUE
4 Servings

6 to 8 slices leftover roast beef
  2 tablespoons butter or margarine
  1 small onion, chopped
    pinch garlic salt
  ½ teaspoon salt

¼ teaspoon pepper
2 tablespoons Worcestershire sauce
1 tablespoon vinegar
4 tablespoons chili sauce

Trim any excess fat from meat. Melt butter or margarine in hot skillet; simmer onion, garlic salt and meat until onion is soft. Mix remaining ingredients; add. Cover and cook over low heat for 15 minutes.

SUGGESTED MENU: With the beef serve instant mashed potatoes or mashed potato cakes, cucumber and onion slices in sweetened vinegar and assorted relishes. For dessert, fruit gelatin and chocolate cookies.

CUBAN-STYLE BARBECUED BEEF
4 Servings

2 tablespoons bacon fat
1 green pepper, chopped
1 onion, chopped
1 lb. flank steak, coarsely ground
1 No. 2½ can (3½ cups) tomatoes

1 cup uncooked rice
1 tablespoon salt
½ teaspoon pepper
½ teaspoon cumin
  pinch saffron

Heat fat in heavy kettle; add pepper, onion and meat. Stir until meat browns; add tomatoes, rice and seasonings. Cover tightly and cook over charcoal for 25 minutes, or until rice is tender.

SUGGESTED MENU: Hot garlic bread and a tossed salad with the beef. For dessert, ice cream and frosted cupcakes.

BARBECUED VEAL CHOPS
4 Servings

4 veal chops, ea. 1 in. thick
¼ cup salad oil
2 tablespoons lemon juice
½ teaspoon salt

¼ teaspoon pepper
1 garlic clove, mashed
2 tablespoons Worcestershire sauce
2 tablespoons ketchup

Place chops in bowl; combine remaining ingredients. Pour over chops; marinate for 1 hour. Drain, reserving marinade. Place chops in wire hand grill. Sear on both sides, close to coals, then place in a higher position. Turn often until tender. Cook for about 30 minutes, basting during last 10 minutes of cooking time.

SUGGESTED MENU: Chunks of buttered and seasoned summer crookneck squash cooked in foil packets, hot potato salad and relishes with the chops. For dessert, fruit cup and oatmeal cookies.

BARBECUED BEEF CAKES IN WINE   4 Servings

1 ½ lbs. lean ground beef   pepper
  2 cups dry red wine   salt
  ½ teaspoon garlic juice   3 tablespoons butter or margarine

Shape meat into 4 patties; cover with wine and garlic juice. Let stand at room temperature for 2 to 3 hours, then drain and reserve marinade. Pat cakes dry on paper towels
sprinkle with pepper and salt. Heat butter or margarine in heavy skillet; brown
meat cakes quickly on both sides. Add enough marinade to pan to make a generous
amount of sauce; simmer for 4 to 5 minutes. Serve meat cakes on toasted buns with
pan sauce poured over.

SUGGESTED MENU: Roasted ears of corn, tomato, cucumber and onion ring salad
with the beef. For dessert, lemon-filled gingerbread squares.

BARBECUED BEEF TARTARE   6 Servings

2 lbs. lean ground beef   1 tablespoon parsley, minced
1 garlic clove, mashed   2 Bermuda onions, sliced
1 tablespoon chives, minced   6 buns, toasted

Combine meat, garlic, chives and parsley; shape into 4-inch patties. Separate onions
into rings. Toast buns; keep warm. Heat greased griddle until very hot; sear meat
patties for 15 seconds only on each side. Serve at once on toasted buns with raw onion
rings.

SUGGESTED MENU: Potato and egg salad with the beef tartare, plus beet relish and a
tossed salad. For dessert, ice cream and brownies.

DELMONICO BARBECUE   10 Servings

  rolled sirloin roast (about 4 lbs.)   ½ cup dry red wine
½ cup salad oil   1 garlic clove, crushed
1 teaspoon salt   1 teaspoon chili powder
¼ teaspoon Mexican red pepper   1 can (8 oz.) tomato sauce

Have meat dealer roll meat with a thick layer of suet on the outside. Tie with heavy
cord. Combine all other ingredients to make a sauce; do not chill. Skewer the meat
on spit; barbecue over medium heat with foil drip pan below meat to catch fat. Cook
meat 18 minutes per pound for very rare, 30 minutes per pound for well-done. Baste
with sauce during last half hour. Remove from spit; serve hot with skimmed drip-pan
gravy and remaining basting sauce.

SUGGESTED MENU: Hashed-brown potatoes, cooked in a big skillet on the grill, and a
salad of raw vegetables accompany the roast. For dessert, deep-dish plum pie.

BARBECUED TOURNADOS
4 Servings

2 lbs. filet mignon
  salt and pepper
  barbecue sauce

1 tablespoon chopped chives
1 loaf French bread

Have filet mignon cut in rounds 1 inch thick; salt and pepper to taste. Dip each meat round in any favorite barbecue sauce (see Index); sprinkle with chives. Cook meat quickly on hot, greased griddle. Toast rounds of bread on griddle at same time. Serve meat on toast spread with butter or margarine. Add barbecue sauce, if desired.

SUGGESTED MENU: Macaroni, cucumber and celery salad, sliced tomatoes in French dressing and assorted relishes with the tórnados. For dessert, peach shortcake.

OPEN-FIRE BRAISED STEAK
4 Servings

3 lbs. top round, 1 in. thick
2 tablespoons fat or salad oil
1 onion, chopped

salt and pepper
1 teaspoon Worcestershire sauce
  boiling water

Use meat tenderizer on steak (page 19). Heat heavy skillet over open fire. Add fat or oil; drop in steak when fat or oil sizzles. Brown meat on one side, turn, then brown on other side. Add onion, seasonings and boiling water to cover bottom of pan. Cover and cook about 5 inches from coals until steak is tender.

SUGGESTED MENU: Instant mashed potatoes (easy to prepare at a barbecue), grilled tomatoes and a salad of iceberg lettuce chunks accompany the steak. For dessert, assorted fresh fruit, cream cheese and whole-wheat crackers.

YANKEE KABOB
4 Servings

1 ½ lbs. lean round steak
  ¼ lb. bacon
  4 celery stalks

1 large onion
4 frankfurter rolls
  mustard or ketchup

Cut steak in 1-inch cubes. Cut bacon strips crosswise in 1-inch pieces. Cut celery stalks crosswise in ½-inch pieces. Dice onion in ½-inch pieces. Use 8-inch skewers.

Skewer steak, bacon, celery and onion. Repeat until skewer is filled, beginning and ending with steak. Grill over charcoal, turning to cook on all sides. Slip off skewers into split, toasted frankfurter rolls. Serve with mustard or ketchup.

SUGGESTED MENU: Tomato and green pepper coleslaw and assorted relishes with the kabob. For dessert, doughnuts and cheese cubes.

GRILLED STUFFED HAMBURGER ROLL-UPS   8 Servings

1 ½ lbs. lean ground beef
   salt and pepper
   prepared mustard
1 dill pickle

¼-lb. package processed
   American cheese
8 frankfurter rolls

Season ground beef with salt and pepper; divide into 8 equal portions. Pat each portion into thin, oblong patty; spread with prepared mustard. Cut cheese into 8 sticks; cut pickle into 8 strips. Place 1 cheese stick and 1 pickle strip on each patty; roll up. Grill over hot charcoal until cheese melts. Serve in toasted frankfurter rolls.

SUGGESTED MENU: Potato chips and a salad of raw vegetables in a snappy French or Italian dressing with the roll-ups. For dessert, melon wedges.

TEXAS CHILI BARBECUE   12 to 14 Servings

2 to 3 tablespoons shortening
  ½ lb. suet, minced
  1 large onion, chopped
  2 garlic cloves, minced
  4 lbs. lean beef, chopped (not ground)

1 tablespoon chili powder
1 tablespoon salt
¼ teaspoon red pepper
1 ½ to 2 qts. water

Heat shortening and suet until brown in large, heavy kettle, deep pot or large stewpan —preferably over a charcoal fire. Brown onion and garlic. Have beef chopped, not ground, into coarse, uneven chunks. Add with seasonings to kettle; mix well. Cook for 15 minutes. Stir in water and simmer until meat is tender, or about 1 ½ hours.

SUGGESTED MENU: Serve the chili on tamales, accompanied with sliced Spanish onions, pickles, stuffed olives and a tossed salad. For dessert, lime sherbet and cookies.

CHARCOAL-BROILED STEAKS A LA ROQUEFORT   6 Servings

⅛ lb. Roquefort cheese
1 teaspoon Worcestershire sauce
1 tablespoon heavy cream

2 lbs. sirloin steak, 1 ½ in. thick
salt and pepper

Mash cheese; blend with Worcestershire sauce and cream. Broil steak over charcoal, or in preheated broiler until done to taste. Spread with cheese mixture. Broil quickly, close to heat, for 1 to 2 minutes. Sprinkle with salt and pepper. Serve at once.

SUGGESTED MENU: Macaroni salad garnished with tomato wedges, celery, olives and pickles with the steaks. For dessert, devil's food layer cake with coconut frosting.

BIG BARBECUE BURGERS   20 Servings

5 lbs. lean ground beef
  ⅔ cup salad oil
  ⅔ cup ketchup
  ¼ teaspoon Tabasco
  2 tablespoons Worcestershire sauce
  2 teaspoons salt
1 to 2 garlic cloves, minced

⅔ cup water
¼ cup liquid smoke
2 teaspoons sugar
2 teaspoons flour
  juice of 1 lemon
½ teaspoon pepper
20 toasted buns

Combine all ingredients except buns; mix well. Store in refrigerator for 24 hours. Shape patties; broil until done. Serve hot on toasted buns with the following barbecue sauce spooned over meat.

BARBECUE SAUCE

½ cup steak sauce
½ cup vinegar
½ cup ketchup
 3 large onions, minced
½ cup brown sugar

½ teaspoon celery seed
1½ teaspoons salt
½ teaspoon pepper
 1 teaspoon nutmeg
½ teaspoon cloves

Combine and simmer for half an hour. Serve hot.

SUGGESTED MENU: Frozen French-fried potatoes grilled in foil packets and a salad of cooked vegetables. Old-fashioned peach shortcake for dessert.

GRILLED SWEETBREADS   6 Servings

   3 pairs sweetbreads
2 to 3 tablespoons vinegar
   ¼ cup butter or margarine

1 tablespoon lemon juice
  salt and pepper
6 pieces toast

Parboil sweetbreads in water to cover and vinegar; drain. Remove membranes and tissues. Cut sweetbreads apart, then cut each in half lengthwise. Place on well-greased wire broiler and broil for 5 to 6 minutes, turning several times. Cream butter or margarine and lemon juice and season to taste with salt and pepper; spread on hot toast. Serve grilled sweetbreads on toast.

SUGGESTED MENU: Buttered frozen asparagus in foil packets, sliced tomato and chive salad and raw carrot sticks with the sweetbreads. For dessert, ice cream sandwiches.

BARBECUED CALF'S LIVER   4 Servings

1 lb. calf's liver, ½ in. thick
2 Spanish onions
  butter or margarine, melted

3 tomatoes
  salad oil

Wash liver; dry on paper towels. Peel and slice onions about ½ inch thick; brush with butter or margarine. Wash and quarter tomatoes; do not peel. When liver has reached room temperature, arrange hot briquets for grill barbecuing. Rub grill with oil; lay liver and onion slices on grill. Barbecue over medium heat for about 5 minutes. Turn meat and onions and put tomatoes on grill. Barbecue about 5 minutes longer. During the last few minutes, put onions on top of liver to blend flavors. Do not overcook liver.

SUGGESTED MENU: Serve frozen French-fried potatoes heated in foil packets with the liver. Add a tossed salad and French bread. For dessert, melon wedges, cookies or plain cake.

SKILLET-BARBECUED VEAL CUTLETS   4 Servings

2 lbs. veal cutlet, 1 in. thick   ¼ teaspoon pepper
1 garlic clove, mashed   ⅛ lb. salt pork
1 teaspoon salt   2 tablespoons dry sherry
1 teaspoon marjoram

Pound cutlet a little, then rub in mashed garlic. Sprinkle and rub with combined dry seasonings. Put salt pork in a heavy skillet; sear veal on both sides in pork fat. Add sherry. Cover and cook over charcoal until very tender, or about 45 minutes. Serve with any favorite barbecue sauce (see Index).

SUGGESTED MENU: Foil-wrapped baked potatoes, green peas and scallions in foil packets and a tossed salad with the veal. For dessert, jelly doughnuts.

SECOND-TIME SERVINGS

SECOND-TIME SERVINGS

There is no need for family rebellions against leftovers. If the cook has love in her heart and imagination in her head, leftovers can be transformed into enticing dishes that haven't the remotest resemblance to the original dish.

Try the recipes that follow and you'll see what we mean.

LEFTOVER TREAT
6 Servings

2 ½ cups cooked beef, diced
1 tablespoon onion, minced
1 tablespoon green pepper, minced
1 tablespoon fat or salad oil
1 cup leftover or canned beef gravy
1 teaspoon salt
⅛ teaspoon pepper

¼ teaspoon chili powder
1 tablespoon chili sauce
1 ½ cups cooked rice
3 tablespoons sharp cheddar cheese, grated
1 egg, slightly beaten
½ cup corn flakes, crushed

Cook meat, onion and green pepper in hot fat or oil until lightly browned. Add gravy, salt, pepper, chili powder and chili sauce. Combine rice, grated cheese and egg, mixing thoroughly. Alternate layers of rice and meat in a 1-quart greased baking dish. Sprinkle with corn flakes. Bake in a moderate oven (350°) for 30 minutes.

SUGGESTED MENU: Just add a green salad. For dessert, pineapple upside-down cake.

BAKED STUFFED FRENCH LOAF
6 Servings

1 small loaf French bread
5 tablespoons butter or margarine
3 tablespoons flour
½ teaspoon salt
1 ½ cups milk
½ teaspoon Worcestershire sauce

1 egg
2 cups American cheese, grated
1 cup ground or finely chopped cooked beef
1 cup ripe olives, chopped
1 garlic clove

Break open loaf of French bread along seam; remove soft center and crumble. Melt 3 of your 5 tablespoons of butter or margarine. Sift flour with salt and blend into hot butter or margarine. Add milk slowly, stirring and cooking until smooth and thick; remove from heat. Add Worcestershire sauce, egg, cheese, beef, olives and crumbled bread crumbs; mix well. Refill loaf and press edges together. Rub outside of loaf with garlic and brush with remaining 2 tablespoons of butter or margarine (melted). Bake in moderate oven (375°) for 25 to 30 minutes. Slice before serving.

SUGGESTED MENU: Serve creamy tomato soup as a beverage with the loaf. Add a tossed salad. For dessert, frosted squares of marble cake.

CHILI MEAT SAUCE ON RICE
4 Servings

1 ½ cups cooked meat, ground
  2 tablespoons onion, chopped
  ½ cup celery
  3 tablespoons fat or salad oil
  2 tablespoons flour

1 No. 303 can (1 lb.) tomatoes
1 tablespoon green pepper, chopped
¾ teaspoon chili powder
½ teaspoon salt
3 cups cooked rice

Brown meat, onion and celery in hot fat or oil. Stir in flour. Add tomatoes, green pepper and seasonings. Cover and cook slowly for 15 minutes. Serve on hot rice.

SUGGESTED MENU: Buttered lima beans and raw celery and carrot sticks with the meat dish. For dessert, lime ice cream.

JIFFY STEW
6 Servings

1 No. 303 can (1 lb.) carrots and peas
  (undrained)
1 No. 303 can (1 lb.) small white onions (undrained)

2 cups cooked beef, cubed
1 cup leftover or canned beef gravy
$^1/_3$ cup coffee
1 cup biscuit mix

Drain carrots and peas and onions; save liquid. Put vegetables and beef in casserole. Combine vegetable liquid, gravy and coffee; pour into casserole. Make biscuit dough according to directions on package. Cut out small biscuits; use as topping. Bake in hot oven (450°) for 20 minutes.

SUGGESTED MENU: Add a salad of sliced beets and onion rings. Bake additional biscuits for eating separately. For dessert, fruit cup and pound cake.

ROAST BEEF HASH
6 Servings

2 cups roast beef, chopped
3 cups cooked potatoes, diced
1 small onion, minced
1 egg, slightly beaten

1 tablespoon milk
  salt and pepper
2 tablespoons fat or salad oil

Combine meat, potatoes and onion. Then combine egg, milk, salt and pepper; add to meat mixture and mix well. Heat fat or oil in frying pan. Add hash; spread evenly. Cook over low heat until well browned on bottom. Fold over like an omelet. Turn out on hot platter.

SUGGESTED MENU: Buttered Swiss chard and raw carrot strips go well with the hash. For dessert, applesauce and hermit cookies.

REGAL HASH
6 Servings

1 large onion, finely chopped
¼ cup fat or salad oil
4 cups raw potatoes, cubed
4 cups cooked beef, cubed

1½ teaspoons salt
⅛ teaspoon pepper
½ teaspoon Worcestershire sauce
2 cups hot water

Cook onion in hot fat or oil until golden brown. Add remaining ingredients. Cover and cook until potatoes are tender. Thicken gravy (page 195). Heat thoroughly.

SUGGESTED MENU: With the hash serve broccoli au gratin and broiled tomatoes. Add a salad of green pepper rings and onion rings in sharp French dressing. For dessert, apricot upside-down cake.

RED-FLANNEL HASH
4 to 6 Servings

4 medium-size cooked beets, chopped
3 medium-size cooked potatoes, chopped
2 cups cooked corned beef, chopped
1 teaspoon salt

¼ teaspoon pepper
¼ cup butter or margarine
¼ cup onion, chopped
½ cup heavy cream

Combine chopped beets and potatoes, meat and seasonings. Melt butter or margarine in a heavy skillet or electric frying pan; sauté onions until golden brown. Stir in meat mixture; pour cream over top. Cook over moderate heat for 35 to 40 minutes, or until crusty and browned on bottom. Fold over and turn out on a hot platter to serve.

SUGGESTED MENU: Creamed cabbage and hot, crusty poppy seed rolls with the hash. For dessert, fresh fruit in season with any favorite cheese.

MOCK CHOW MEIN
4 Servings

½ cup onions, finely chopped
1 cup cooked beef, diced
3 tablespoons fat or salad oil
1½ cups celery, diced
11 tablespoons water
1 can mixed chop suey vegetables

3 tablespoons cornstarch
1 teaspoon brown sugar
½ teaspoon pepper
2 tablespoons soy sauce
2 cups cooked rice or 1 can chow mein
noodles

Brown onions and meat in hot fat or oil. Stir in celery and part of water (8 tablespoons or ½ cup). Cover and boil rapidly for about 4 to 5 minutes. Add chop suey vegetables. Combine cornstarch, brown sugar, pepper, soy sauce and remaining water (3 tablespoons); add. Stir over low heat until mixture thickens and clears. Serve hot with fluffy cooked rice or with crisp chow mein noodles.

SUGGESTED MENU: This dish is a complete meal for a light luncheon or supper. For dessert, preserved kumquats, cream cheese and crackers.

MEAT LOAF PIE

4 Servings

2 cups leftover meat loaf, cubed
1 pkg. (12 oz.) frozen mixed vegetables, cooked

1 can condensed tomato soup
2 cups mashed potatoes

Cut meat loaf into cubes; combine with vegetables and tomato soup. Spoon into casserole; top with hot mashed potatoes. Bake in hot oven (400°) for 25 minutes.

SUGGESTED MENU: Serve only a crisp salad and hot rolls with this one-dish meal. For dessert, banana floating island.

SHEPHERD'S BEEF PIE

6 to 8 Servings

4 cups cooked beef, cubed
2½ cups gravy, leftover or canned
2 to 3 cups cooked vegetables, leftover
2 teaspoons instant minced onion

2 tablespoons parsley flakes
salt and pepper
3 cups hot mashed potatoes
1 egg, well beaten

Combine meat, gravy, vegetables, onion, parsley flakes, salt and pepper. Heat to boiling, stirring often. Pour mixture into 2-quart casserole. Combine mashed potatoes and egg in a bowl; mix thoroughly. Make a border of mashed potatoes around edge of casserole or cover top completely. Bake in hot oven (425°) for 15 to 20 minutes, or until brown.

SUGGESTED MENU: Only a crisp salad is needed to complete the main course. For dessert, chocolate éclairs.

MOCK BEEF STROGANOFF

6 Servings

2 Bermuda or Spanish onions
¼ cup butter or margarine
½ lb. mushrooms, sliced, or 1 can (3 oz.) sliced mushrooms (undrained)
1 can condensed tomato soup
1 cup leftover gravy
1 small can tomato paste

1 cup sour cream
salt and pepper
½ teaspoon Ac'cent
leftover pot roast, thinly sliced (6 to 12 slices)
3 cups mashed potatoes

Put onions through food chopper, using coarse knife; drain, saving juice. Cook onions in butter or margarine over low heat for 20 minutes; push to one side. Brown mushrooms (if canned, drain first and reserve liquid). Combine soup, gravy, tomato paste, sour cream, salt, pepper, Ac'cent and onion juice (also mushroom liquid if canned mushrooms are used). Pour into pan with onions and mushrooms; blend. Add slices of pot roast; heat. Serve with border of hot mashed potatoes.

SUGGESTED MENU: Diced carrots and a green salad complete the main course. For dessert, lemon jelly roll.

VEAL AND RICE CUSTARD

4 Servings

4 eggs
1 can (14 ½ oz.) chicken broth
½ teaspoon salt
½ teaspoon oregano

⅛ teaspoon nutmeg
1 ½ cups cooked rice
2 cups cooked veal, diced
1 cup cooked green peas

Beat eggs slightly; add chicken broth, salt, oregano and nutmeg; blend well. Add rice, veal and peas. Bake in 1 ½-quart casserole in moderate oven (325°) for 45 minutes, or until set. Serve with mushroom sauce.

SUGGESTED MENU: Serve buttered sliced carrots and a green salad with the casserole. Top off with instant vanilla pudding with chocolate sauce and chopped walnuts.

JELLIED MEAT LOAF

6 Servings

1 envelope unflavored gelatin
¼ cup cold water
¾ cup boiling tomato juice or water
¼ cup vinegar
½ teaspoon salt
2 cups cooked beef, finely diced
¼ cup celery, diced

¼ cup pimento, chopped
¼ cup green pepper, chopped
¼ cup onion, minced
½ cup mayonnaise
2 hard-cooked eggs, sliced
lettuce, shredded

Soften gelatin in cold water; dissolve in hot liquid. Stir in vinegar and salt; chill until syrupy. Combine remaining ingredients, except eggs. Arrange egg slices along bottom and sides of loaf pan. Combine gelatin and meat mixtures; mix thoroughly. Turn into loaf pan and chill until firm. Serve cold on shredded lettuce.

SUGGESTED MENU: Begin with chilled grape juice. With the jellied meat loaf serve potato salad, coleslaw and hot French bread or rolls. For dessert, fruit tarts.

BEEF AND VEGETABLE SALAD

4 Servings

2 cups cooked beef, diced
1 cup cooked vegetable (potatoes, carrots, peas, etc.), diced
2 hard-cooked eggs, diced
1 onion, minced

½ cup sweet pickle, chopped
½ cup mayonnaise
salt and pepper
4 lettuce cups

Combine ingredients and season. Serve in lettuce cups.

SUGGESTED MENU: Begin with tomato soup. Hot rolls, muffins or biscuits with the salad. For dessert, raisin rice pudding with cream.

SPANISH HASH

4 Servings

1 cup cooked roast beef, chopped
4 cooked potatoes, diced
2 small onions, chopped
½ cup green pepper, chopped
1 cup canned tomatoes

dash Tabasco
1 egg
1 teaspoon salt
1 can (8 oz.) tomato sauce

Mix all ingredients; spoon mixture into greased individual ramekins or custard cups. Bake in moderate oven (350°) for 25 minutes. Serve in baking dishes with tomato sauce.

SUGGESTED MENU: With the hash serve broccoli with browned crumbs and cucumber salad. Top off with fruited tapioca cream.

BEEF HASH

4 to 6 Servings

2 cups cold roast beef, chopped
2 cups boiled potato, chopped

2 cups leftover or canned beef gravy
salt and pepper

Combine all ingredients in heavy skillet; heat. Stir occasionally to keep mixture from sticking. Serve very hot.

SUGGESTED MENU: Corn on the cob and green beans go well with the beef hash. Add a salad of sliced tomatoes. For dessert, melon wedges.

DUTCH MEAT SALAD

4 Servings

2 slices bacon
½ cup mayonnaise
1 tablespoon lemon juice
1 tablespoon vinegar

⅓ cup scallions and tops, finely chopped
1 small garlic clove, finely minced
2 cups julienne-style cooked beef or veal
salad greens

Cook bacon until crisp; break into small pieces. Combine mayonnaise, lemon juice, vinegar, onion and garlic. Add to strips of meat and toss lightly. Chill thoroughly and serve on salad greens. Sprinkle bacon on top.

SUGGESTED MENU: Begin with cold borscht. Serve dark pumpernickel bread with the salad. End with chilled red apples, Gruyere cheese and toasted crackers.

THURSDAY MEAT PIE

6 Servings

½ cup celery, diced
½ cup onion, chopped
½ cup green pepper, chopped
3 tablespoons fat or salad oil
2 cups cooked, leftover beef, cubed
1 cup cooked carrots, diced

1 cup cooked peas
1 cup cooked potatoes, diced
1½ cups leftover gravy
salt and pepper
3 slices bread, cubed

Brown celery, onion and green pepper in hot fat or oil. Add meat, vegetables and gravy. Season to taste with salt and pepper. Turn mixture into casserole; top with bread cubes. Bake in moderate oven (350°) for 35 minutes.

SUGGESTED MENU: With this one-dish meal only a salad is needed to complete the main course. For dessert, peach cobbler with cream.

COLD BEEF SALAD   2 Servings

1 cup leftover roast beef, diced
2 large pickles, diced
1 onion, chopped
½ green pepper, chopped

½ garlic clove, minced
French dressing
2 lettuce cups

Combine meat and vegetables. Toss lightly with French dressing to taste; serve in lettuce cups.

SUGGESTED MENU: Begin with cream of celery soup. Serve hot garlic bread with the salad. For dessert, burnt-sugar layer cake.

CHARTREUSE OF BEEF   6 Servings

2 cups cooked beef, ground
1 teaspoon salt
  dash pepper
1 teaspoon onion, grated
1 tablespoon parsley, chopped
½ cup soft bread crumbs

1 egg, beaten
  milk or tomato juice
4 cups cooked rice
  hot water
1 can (8 oz.) tomato sauce

Mix meat, salt, pepper, onion, parsley, bread crumbs and egg. Add enough milk or tomato juice to hold ingredients together. Line 6 greased custard cups with rice. Fill center with beef mixture; top with rice. Set cups in baking pan. Pour in hot water to a depth of 1 inch around cups. Bake in moderate oven (350°) for 45 minutes. Unmold; serve with tomato sauce.

SUGGESTED MENU: Serve buttered asparagus tips and mashed yellow turnips with the meat. Add a cucumber salad. For dessert, fruit gelatin.

TROPICAL VEAL SALAD   4 to 6 Servings

2 cups cooked veal, cubed
1 cup pineapple cubes
½ cup celery, diced
½ cup grapes, halved and seeded
⅓ cup pecans, chopped

3 tablespoons mayonnaise
2 tablespoons pineapple juice
  lettuce
  salad dressing

Combine all ingredients, except lettuce; toss lightly. Chill until ready to serve. Serve in lettuce cups or on shredded lettuce with extra dressing to taste.

SUGGESTED MENU: Begin with clear consommé. Serve hot rolls with the salad. For dessert, vanilla-fudge ice cream.

CORNED BEEF HASH RING

6 Servings

3 cups cooked corned beef, chopped
3 cups cooked potatoes, chopped
¼ cup onion, chopped
½ cup milk

salt and pepper
¼ cup fat or cooking oil
vegetable
1 can tomato sauce (optional)

Combine corned beef and next 3 ingredients. Season to taste with salt and pepper. Heat fat or oil in a skillet. Spread corned beef mixture evenly in skillet; heat and brown slowly, stirring often. Spoon mixture onto a heated platter, forming a ring. Fill center with any favorite vegetable. Serve with tomato sauce, if desired.

SUGGESTED MENU: Hot baking-powder biscuits, carrot sticks and celery complete the main course. For dessert, cottage pudding with chocolate sauce.

BEEF NOODLES

12 Servings

8 oz. noodles
2 teaspoons salt
  boiling water
1½ cups meat stock
2 cans condensed cream of mushroom soup

½ lb. American cheese, cubed
1 teaspoon Worcestershire sauce
3 hard-cooked eggs, sliced
4 cups cooked beef, chopped
½ cup potato chips, crushed

Cook noodles with salt in boiling water according to package directions; drain. Combine stock, soup, cheese and Worcestershire sauce; heat gently until cheese melts and blends. Stir in eggs, beef and noodles. Turn into large baking pan; top with crushed potato chips. Bake in moderate oven (350°) for 30 to 35 minutes.

SUGGESTED MENU: A salad of mixed cooked vegetables served with Russian dressing completes the main course nicely. For dessert, lemon chiffon pie.

MEAT AND POTATO CAKES

4 Servings

2 cups cooked veal, ground
2 cups mashed potatoes
2 eggs
2 tablespoons onion, minced
2 tablespoons celery, finely chopped

½ cup tomato juice
1 teaspoon salt
¼ teaspoon pepper
8 slices tomato, ½ in. thick
2 tablespoons butter or margarine, melted

Combine meat, mashed potatoes, eggs, onion, celery, tomato juice and seasonings. Mix well; shape into 8 patties. Place patties in greased baking pan; top each with tomato slice. Brush tomato slices with melted butter or margarine. Bake in moderate oven (350°) for 30 minutes.

SUGGESTED MENU: Serve kidney beans and carrot-raisin slaw with the meat cakes. For dessert, fruit gelatin whip.

VEAL CROQUETTES

2 cups cooked veal, ground
1 cup cooked peas, mashed
½ teaspoon salt
⅛ teaspoon pepper

1 teaspoon onion, grated
½ cup fine bread crumbs
1 egg, slightly beaten

Combine veal, peas, salt, pepper and onion. Shape into croquettes. Roll in bread crumbs, dip in egg and again in bread crumbs. Fry in deep fat heated to 360° for 1 ½ to 2 minutes or until brown; drain.

SUGGESTED MENU: Serve creamed potatoes and buttered carrots with the croquettes. Add a crisp salad. For dessert, lemon sponge pudding.

LADIES' AID SALAD

1 cup salted almonds
1 No. 303 can (1 lb.) pineapple chunks
4 cups cooked veal, diced
2 cups celery, diced

2 hard-cooked eggs, diced
mayonnaise
8 lettuce cups

Cut almonds lengthwise into quarters. Drain pineapple. Combine veal, pineapple, celery and eggs; chill thoroughly. Just before serving, add almonds and enough mayonnaise to hold ingredients together. Mix lightly; serve in lettuce cups.

SUGGESTED MENU: Begin with chilled tomato juice. Serve hot biscuits with the salad. For dessert, frozen cream puffs with butterscotch sauce.

RUSSIAN SALAD

2 cups cooked beef, diced
2 tart apples, peeled and diced
2 hard-cooked eggs, sliced
8 cold boiled potatoes, sliced
2 large pickled beets, diced
1 large onion, sliced

¼ cup small gherkins, chopped
salt and pepper
3 tablespoons salad oil
2 tablespoons vinegar
salad greens
capers (optional)

Combine all except last 2 ingredients; toss lightly to mix. Mound on salad greens; garnish with capers, if desired. Extra vinegar may be added for sharper flavor.

SUGGESTED MENU: Garlic bread or sesame seed rolls with the salad. For dessert, fresh pineapple chunks and chocolate wafers.

BEEF SANDWICH SPREAD

Fills 4 sandwiches

2 cups cooked beef, ground
¼ cup pickle relish, chopped
1 tablespoon onion, minced
2 tablespoons celery, chopped

½ cup mayonnaise or salad dressing
1 tablespoon prepared mustard
   salt and pepper (optional)
8 slices rye or whole-wheat bread, buttered

Combine all but last 2 ingredients; add seasonings, if desired. Spread between slices of buttered white, rye or whole-wheat bread.

SUGGESTED MENU: Serve any favorite hot soup with the sandwiches. For dessert, fresh cherries or other fruit in season, cream cheese and crackers.

RANCHER'S VEAL LOAF

8 Servings

1 envelope unflavored gelatin
½ cup cold water
2 cups seasoned veal stock
1 bay leaf
1 onion, diced

1 stalk celery, diced
½ cup pimento, diced
1 teaspoon parsley, minced
   juice of 1 lemon
2 cups cooked veal, chopped

Soften gelatin in cold water. Boil veal stock, bay leaf, onion and celery rapidly for 3 to 4 minutes; strain. Pour hot strained stock over gelatin; stir until dissolved. Cool; chill until slightly thickened. Stir in remaining ingredients. Pour into mold; chill until firm.

SUGGESTED MENU: Corn chips, a salad of mixed cooked vegetables and assorted relishes with the jellied veal loaf. For dessert, watermelon slices.

GRAVIES AND SAUCES

It's better to do without gravy altogether than to spoil good meat with lumpy gravy or wallpaper paste that has only a faint meat flavor. Whether you are making pan gravy or kettle gravy, thickening a stew or making a velvety-smooth sauce, there is a right way to do it.

Here are some tricks to remember. They apply to all sauces that start with a roux (fat and flour mixture), including white sauce:

1. Use the liquid *cold*.
2. Add it *all at once* and stir continuously over low heat until the sauce is thick and smooth.

If the liquid is hot, and if it is added gradually, lumping is almost inevitable.

Gravy for Pot Roast

1. Remove meat and vegetables, if any, from kettle. Keep hot.
2. Skim off fat; strain and measure broth.
3. Add water, if necessary, to make 2 cups liquid for every 3 pounds of pot roast.
4. Heat measured broth. Measure 4 tablespoons flour for every 2 cups broth. Blend with ½ cup cold water.
5. Stir flour mixture slowly into hot broth. Stir over low heat until thick and smooth. Simmer for 5 minutes. Season to taste.

Gravy for Roast Beef

1. Pour off clear fat, leaving brown flecks in the pan. Save fat.
2. Add 1 cup water to pan; bring to boil to loosen brown flecks.
3. Measure into a skillet 2 tablespoons reserved fat for each cup of gravy.
4. Blend in an equal amount of flour. Stir over low heat until lightly browned.
5. Stir in brown liquid in roaster.
6. Add 1 cup water, milk, vegetable cooking water, tomato juice or any desired combination of these for every 2 tablespoons flour used.
7. Stir over low heat until smooth and thick. Simmer for 5 minutes. Season to taste.

Gravy for Broiled Steak

Unthickened pan gravy is best.
1. Pour off excess fat, leaving brown drippings in broiler pan.
2. Add ¼ to ½ cup water to broiler pan; heat and stir. Season to taste.
If you prefer a thicker gravy, make it the same way as roast beef gravy.

Gravy for Braised Beef

If the meat has been dipped in flour before browning, the gravy will usually be thick enough. If more gravy is desired, remove meat and pour more liquid into the pan; bring to a boil.

To thicken, add ½ to 1 tablespoon flour blended with ¼ cup cold water for each cup of gravy.

Pan Gravy for Pan-Broiled or Pan-Fried Beef

Same as for roast beef.

Gravy for Stew

1. Remove meat and vegetables.
2. For each cup of broth blend 1 tablespoon flour with ¼ cup water.
3. Add flour mixture slowly to hot broth, stirring constantly.
4. Stir over low heat until thick.
5. Simmer for 5 minutes. Season to taste.
6. Return meat and vegetables to gravy.

TOMATO-HERB SAUCE   Makes 3 cups

½ cup onion, minced
2 tablespoons bacon drippings or fat
2 teaspoons sugar
1 cup water
1 can condensed tomato soup

⅛ teaspoon savory
⅛ teaspoon rosemary
 salt and pepper
1 tablespoon lemon juice

Brown onion in hot bacon drippings or fat. Add sugar, water and tomato soup; mix well. Add savory, rosemary, salt and pepper; simmer for 10 to 15 minutes. Add lemon juice.

USES: To lend zest to leftover roast beef or other cooked meats. As a flavorful partner for meat loaf or meat balls. As a sauce for spaghetti or noodles.

DEVIL SAUCE   Makes about 1¾ cups

¼ cup molasses
¼ cup prepared mustard
¼ cup brown sugar, firmly packed
¾ cup vinegar

½ cup canned pineapple juice
¼ cup Worcestershire sauce
½ teaspoon Tabasco

Combine molasses, mustard and brown sugar; mix well. Add vinegar, pineapple juice, Worcestershire sauce and Tabasco; mix well.

USES: Cut leftover roasts or pot roasts in thin slices and reheat in this flavorful sauce. Wonderful with oven-braised short ribs, too. Can also be used as a barbecue sauce.

TOMATO GRAVY

Makes about 1½ cups

¼ cup fat or drippings
¼ cup flour
½ teaspoon Ac'cent
  dash pepper
¼ to ½ cup leftover coffee

1 can (8 oz.) tomato sauce
  hot water
2 bouillon cubes
  salt

Melt fat or drippings; blend in flour, Ac'cent and pepper. Combine coffee and tomato sauce. Measure and add enough hot water to make 2 cups. Add bouillon cubes; dissolve. Add bouillon mixture to flour mixture; stir over low heat until thick. Salt to taste, if necessary.

USES: A delicious emergency gravy to serve with leftover beef, meat loaf or meat patties.

TANGY TOMATO SAUCE

Makes about 1 cup

1 can (6 oz.) tomato paste
1 teaspoon dry mustard
¼ cup brown sugar, firmly packed
1 teaspoon salt
  dash chili powder

1 tablespoon Worcestershire sauce
1 medium-size onion, minced
¼ cup wine vinegar
2 tablespoons water
2 teaspoons lemon juice

Combine all ingredients in saucepan. Heat to boiling, stirring occasionally. Remove from heat; let stand several hours at room temperature to blend flavors before serving.

USES: A fine sweet-sour sauce for sliced boiled beef, short ribs, leftover pot roast or roast beef. Good with meat loaf and hamburgers, too.

QUICK TOMATO SAUCE

Makes 1½ cups

1 can (6 oz.) tomato paste
1 garlic clove, crushed
1 teaspoon instant onion, minced
1 tablespoon brown sugar
1 cup water

½ teaspoon salt
  dash Tabasco
2 to 3 teaspoons chili powder
¼ cup lemon juice

Combine all ingredients; mix well. Cook over low heat, stirring often, for about 15 minutes.

USES: Excellent as an accompaniment for meat loaf or hamburgers. With tiny meat balls added, it's a fine sauce for spaghetti or noodles.

DE LUXE SPAGHETTI MEAT SAUCE

Makes about 6 cups

3 tablespoons fat or salad oil
1 medium-size onion, chopped
1 lb. lean ground beef
1 garlic clove, minced
1 No. 2½ can (3½ cups) tomatoes
1 can (6 oz.) tomato paste

1 teaspoon salt
¼ teaspoon pepper
1 teaspoon sugar
½ teaspoon chili powder
1 teaspoon Worcestershire sauce
½ to 1 cup ripe olives, sliced

Heat fat or oil in heavy, deep pan. Cook onion until light brown in color; push to one side. Add beef; sear thoroughly. Add garlic, tomatoes, tomato paste, salt, pepper and sugar. Cook covered over low heat for 45 minutes, stirring occasionally. Add chili powder and Worcestershire sauce and cook another 15 minutes. Add olives and a little water if sauce has become too thick. Add extra salt, if necessary. Serve over hot cooked spaghetti.

HORSE-RADISH SAUCE FOR BOILED BEEF

Makes 1 cup

¼ cup salad dressing
1½ tablespoons prepared horse-radish
½ teaspoon salt

dash Tabasco
1 teaspoon prepared mustard
$^1/_3$ cup heavy cream, whipped

Combine all ingredients except whipped cream in a bowl; stir to mix well. Gently fold in whipped cream. Chill until ready to use.

INDEX

INDEX

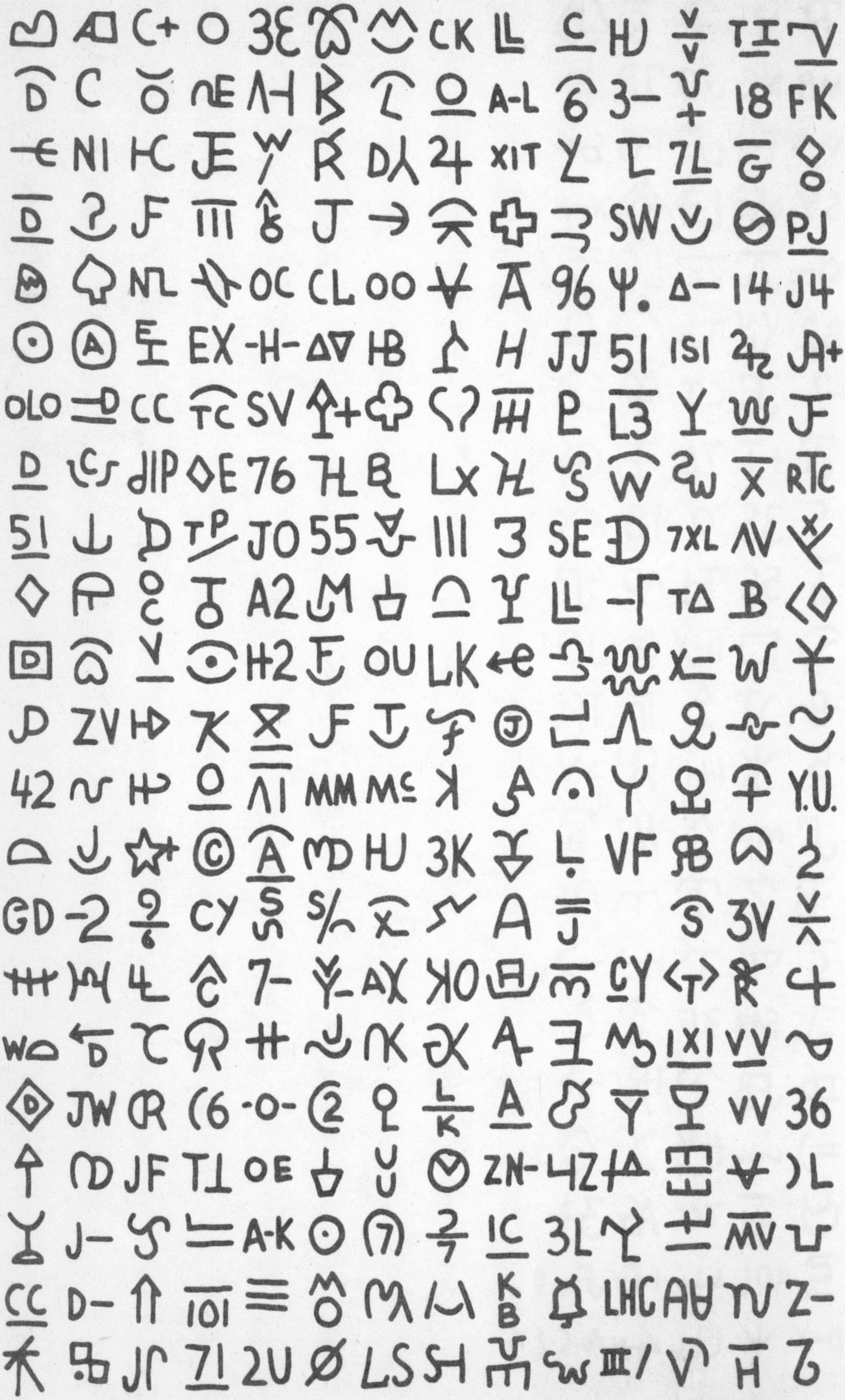